THE PSYCHOLOGY
OF LEARNING AND MOTIVATION

Advances in Research and Theory

VOLUME 28

THE PSYCHOLOGY
OF LEARNING AND MOTIVATION

Advances in Research and Theory

EDITED BY DOUGLAS L. MEDIN

DEPARTMENT OF PSYCHOLOGY
UNIVERSITY OF MICHIGAN, ANN ARBOR, MICHIGAN

Volume 28

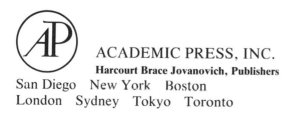

ACADEMIC PRESS, INC.
Harcourt Brace Jovanovich, Publishers
San Diego   New York   Boston
London   Sydney   Tokyo   Toronto

This book is printed on acid-free paper. ∞

Academic Press, Inc.
1250 Sixth Avenue, San Diego, California 92101-4311

United Kingdom Edition published by
Academic Press Limited
24–28 Oval Road, London NW1 7DX

Library of Congress Catalog Number: 66-30104

International Standard Book Number: 0-12-543328-X

PRINTED IN THE UNITED STATES OF AMERICA
92 93 94 95 96 97   QW   9 8 7 6 5 4 3 2 1

CONTENTS

CONDITIONED FOOD PREFERENCES

Elizabeth D. Capaldi

CLASSICAL CONDITIONING AS AN ADAPTIVE SPECIALIZATION: A COMPUTATIONAL MODEL

C. R. Gallistel

INVESTIGATIONS OF AN EXEMPLAR-BASED CONNECTIONIST MODEL OF CATEGORY LEARNING

Robert M. Nosofsky and John K. Kruschke

RECONSTRUCTING THE PAST: CATEGORY EFFECTS IN ESTIMATION

Janellen Huttenlocher and Larry V. Hedges

CONTRIBUTORS

Numbers in parentheses indicate the pages on which the authors' contributions begin.

Lorraine G. Allan (127), Department of Psychology, McMaster University, Hamilton, Ontario L8S 4K1, Canada

Elizabeth D. Capaldi (1), Department of Psychology, University of Florida, Gainesville, Florida 32611

C. R. Gallistel (35), Department of Psychology, University of California, Los Angeles, California 90024

Larry V. Hedges (251), Department of Education, University of Chicago, Chicago, Illinois 60637

Peter C. Holland (69), Department of Experimental Psychology, Duke University, Durham, North Carolina 27706

Janellen Huttenlocher (251), Department of Psychology, University of Chicago, Chicago, Illinois 60637

John K. Kruschke (207), Department of Psychology, Indiana University, Bloomington, Indiana 47405

Susan Mineka (161), Department of Psychology, Northwestern University, Evanston, Illinois 60208

Robert M. Nosofsky (207), Department of Psychology, Indiana University, Bloomington, Indiana 47405

Shepard Siegel (127), Department of Psychology, McMaster University, Hamilton, Ontario L8S 4K1, Canada

PREFACE

I was a graduate student when the first volume of *The Psychology of Learning and Motivation* appeared, and I well remember being tremendously impressed by the contributions. Amsel, Capaldi, Fowler, Bower, and Mandler provided not only integrative summaries of significant bodies of research but also models for how to think about learning and motivation. Volume 2 was no less exciting and, in my opinion, the series has had a remarkable history of contributions of high quality and scientific impact.

The entire field owes Gordon Bower a great debt for his 22 years and 25 volumes of editorship on *The Psychology of Learning and Motivation* series. In his own work Gordon has made several careers worth of research contributions in a variety of research domains. He embodies progress and innovation and he has been able to infuse the learning and motivation series with this same spirit. It is no wonder, then, that researchers in psychology have been heard to refer to these volumes simply as "the Bower series."

One secret to the success of the series is revealed in the preface to Volume 2, written by Gordon Bower and Janet Spence: "A serial publication such as this must be prepared to move where the research workers of a field take it. It must be responsive to the diverse trends of the current research scene, and not become committed to a particular tradition or viewpoint regarding what are 'important' scientific problems." The preceding volumes demonstrate Gordon Bower's outstanding success in achieving these ideals.

Therefore, it was with no little concern that I agreed to assume the role of editor of this series. Why take over something that can't get better? Fortunately, as you will see from the chapters in this volume, the field of learning and motivation, broadly defined, continues to experience vitality, excitement, and progress. The series continues to provide a unique outlet for integrative analyses in a format where researchers are given free rein to present their perspectives on important research problems. I thank this volume's contributors for continuing in this tradition.

A change in editors offers the opportunity for a series to shift its focus. However, given that the chartering prefaces laid out a mandate to avoid stagnation, I see no need to adopt different operating principles. Rather, my goal will be to identify leaders of the field who will write chapters that are informative, provocative, and of first-class quality.

Douglas L. Medin

CONDITIONED FOOD PREFERENCES

Elizabeth D. Capaldi

I. Introduction

Humans have receptors for four basic tastes: salt, sour, bitter, and sweet. Initial affective reactions to these four tastes appear to be genetically mediated. At birth human infants accept a nipple containing sweet solutions and reject sour and bitter tastes (Lipsitt & Behl, 1990). The infant is neutral to salt, but recent data suggest that neural responsiveness to salt is not completely developed at birth. Thus, the infant's neutrality seems a matter of lack of sensation rather than lack of preference. At about 5 to 6 months of age, when neural responsiveness to the taste of salt develops, a preference for salt is shown (Beauchamp, 1987). Adult taste preferences are thus built on a base of likes for sweet and salt, and dislikes for sour and bitter.

Although initial reaction to the four basic tastes appears to be genetically mediated, in omnivores such as rats and humans most food preferences are produced by experience. This may seem anti-intuitive because individuals seem to have strong preferences upon initial contact with food. In theory at least, many of these preferences can be accounted for in terms of differences in individual experiences with foods. Individuals differ widely in their experiences with foods, and laboratory research has shown that different experiences with foods can produce long-lasting conditioned food preferences.

By the age of 6 months, large individual differences in preference for sweet develop, and Beauchamp and Moran (1982) showed these differ-

1

ences can be traced to experience. Some infants are given sugar water as a pacifier, while others are not. When tested at 6 months of age, infants who have been given sugar water show a greater preference for sweet than those who have not had this experience. Differences in sweet preference between those given sweetened water and those not given sweetened water are still present when the children are 2 years old, even if sweetened water was discontinued (Beauchamp & Moran, 1984).

Exposure per se is one of the most potent influences on taste preferences. Up until about the age of 2 years, children willingly ingest almost anything, and their preferences increase for any foods they ingest. After they develop a repertoire of safe, familiar foods, children develop a dislike of novel foods. Leann Birch has found that two factors totally account for taste preferences of children between ages 2 and 3: sweetness and familiarity. Continued exposure to a novel food will ultimately produce a preference for it in a 3- or 4-year-old child, but a considerable amount of exposure is necessary. Birch and Marlin (1982) exposed children of this age to novel cheeses. Four different cheeses were used, and either 0, 5, 10, or 20 exposures to each were given. Initially children often rejected the cheese, but with continued exposure preference began to develop. However, preferences were not manifest until 10 exposures were given. Most parents do not give children 10 exposures to a food that is initially rejected. Instead, they assume that the child does not like the food if it is initially rejected, and that this dislike is not modifiable. Birch's work shows that the preference is modifiable, but considerable exposure is necessary.

Mere exposure has also been shown to produce preference in adult humans. Pliner (1982) showed that adult humans' preference for unfamiliar fruit juices increased with exposure. A juice ingested 20 times was preferred to one ingested only 10 times, which in turn was preferred to a juice ingested only 5 times. One way to increase preference for a novel food, then, is to ingest it repeatedly.

In addition to exposure per se, food preferences are affected by learning the consequences associated with ingestion of foods and by associations formed between foods that are experienced together.

The fact that an aversion can be established to flavors when nausea follows ingestion of a novel-flavored food is widely appreciated (see Domjan, 1980, for a review). Less widely appreciated is the fact that flavor preferences can be formed when flavors are followed by beneficial consequences. These flavor preferences are as robust as flavor aversions. The purpose of this paper is to review data from our laboratory showing increases in preference for flavors paired with beneficial consequences. Reviews of data from other laboratories can be found elsewhere (Booth, 1985, 1990; Sclafani, 1990).

Although it is popularly believed that negative effects are easier to demonstrate than positive (e.g., Rozin, 1976; Rozin & Kalat, 1971), the data reviewed here show that positive effects are easy to obtain, are possible with a long delay between flavor and nutritional consequence, and are highly resistant to extinction. There are good reasons why it can be difficult to demonstrate flavor preferences based on positive nutritional consequences at a delay, and those reasons are discussed later.

II. Learning and Food Preferences

There has been an explosion of research on learning of food preferences recently, beginning with the discovery of taste aversion learning, a particularly robust form of learning.

A. Taste Aversion Learning

If an animal becomes sick following ingestion of a food, an aversion will be produced for that food, a phenomenon termed *taste aversion learning*. This is a very robust form of learning that is rapid, highly resistant to extinction, and possible even if there is a long delay between ingestion of the food and subsequent illness. These apparently unusual features led to a huge volume of research in the past two decades on taste aversion learning, and there are at least two review papers considering whether unique learning processes are involved (Domjan, 1980; Logue, 1979).

In humans, taste aversions can be produced by chemotherapy. Even when subjects are aware that the chemotherapy is making them sick and not the food, aversions can be produced to foods ingested prior to the chemotherapy (Bernstein & Borson, 1986). Food aversions may also play a role in anorexia nervosa. Anorexics often show aversions to fat (Drewnowski, 1988), and fat seems to be a critical food element determining body weight. The most common aversions in the human population are to meat and meat products, and these can be produced by any experience that produces a disgust reaction to meat; it is not necessary to become ill following ingestion of meat. For example, Rozin (1986) reports a case of a person who formed an aversion to rare meat after cutting into it one day and seeing blood spurt out.

B. Conditioned Flavor Preferences

One way of forming food preferences based on positive consequences is directly related to flavor aversion learning. Preference increases for a flavor associated with recovery from illness, the *medicine effect*.

1. Medicine Effect

If two flavors are conditionally paired with one injection of apomorphine, the first flavor presented just prior to malaise and the second just before recuperation, preference for the first flavor will decrease and preference for the second will increase (Green & Garcia, 1971). The increased preference for the flavor associated with recuperation is an example of the medicine effect. As another example, if an animal is made thiamine deficient, a flavor that is associated with a diet that leads to recovery from the deficit will be preferred later (Zahorik & Maier, 1972). The medicine effect probably accounts for a very small proportion of human food preferences, because most preferred foods have not been associated with recovery from illness. Likewise, although robust and long lasting, taste aversions do not seem to account for a large proportion of human food preferences. Only 30% or so of people report taste aversions (Garb & Stunkard, 1974), so other processes must produce food likes and dislikes. A learning process that can produce either food likes or dislikes is *flavor–flavor learning*.

2. Flavor–Flavor Learning

A flavor that is associated with an already liked flavor will come to be liked, and a flavor that is associated with an already disliked flavor will be disliked. Holman (1975) showed that rats given cinnamon in solution with 0.15% saccharin and wintergreen in solution with 0.065% saccharin later showed an increased preference for cinnamon over wintergreen even when the flavors were no longer in differentially sweetened solutions. Because rats initially prefer 0.15% saccharin to 0.065% saccharin, pairing cinnamon with the preferred level of sweetness increases the preference for cinnamon. Fanselow and Birk (1982) showed that preference for a flavor given in solution with quinine declined. Quinine is initially disliked; thus preference for a flavor associated with quinine decreases.

In humans, this type of learning may be part of how some initially disliked flavors come to be liked, such as coffee. Most people first drink coffee with sugar and cream and only later come to like the bitter taste of black coffee. Pairing the bitter taste of coffee with the sweet taste of sugar will increase the preference for the taste of coffee (postingestive effects of sugar and cream will also increase preference, as is discussed below). Zellner, Rozin, Aron, and Kulish (1983) showed that humans given unfamiliar teas, some sweetened and some unsweetened, showed an increased preference for the tea they had sweetened, even if it was now unsweetened.

In these studies on flavor–flavor learning, the flavors were mixed in solution together. Flavor–flavor learning is also possible if there is a short delay between the two flavors. Lavin (1976) gave rats two distinct flavors to drink in succession and subsequently poisoned them for drinking the second flavor. A taste aversion was shown to the first flavor (as well as the second flavor), demonstrating that an association had been formed between the two flavors in the first phase. This association was formed only if the flavors were separated by 9 sec or less. No one has successfully demonstrated flavor–flavor learning at a delay longer than 9 sec. Flavor preferences can be formed with a delay between two foods, but there must be calories in the second food; thus we term this type of learning *flavor–nutrient learning*.

3. Flavor–Nutrient Learning

As early as 1955, LeMagnen suggested that the sensory properties of a food including its flavor can be associated with the postingestive consequences of that food (Le Magnen, 1955). He suggested that this process might increase the palatability of a food with positive consequences and might provide a basis for regulating meal size by means of a conditioned satiety process. Although this idea was suggested a long time ago, only recently have data been provided showing that this process does indeed occur. As we review in this section, associating a flavor with a food that contains nutrients will increase the preference for that flavor.

Flavor–nutrient learning can occur under the same conditions as flavor–flavor learning; thus special steps must be taken to distinguish the two types of learning. If, for example, one flavor is given in solution with 8% sucrose and a second flavor with 1% sucrose, preference for the first flavor will increase relative to the second on the basis of either flavor–flavor learning or flavor–nutrient learning, because sucrose contains calories. Flavor–flavor learning is demonstrated by Holman's study described above, where two distinctive flavors were differentially associated with two concentrations of saccharin. Preference increased for the flavor associated with the higher concentration of saccharin. This is flavor–flavor learning and not flavor–nutrient learning because no nutrients are involved when saccharin is used. Demonstrating flavor–nutrient learning independently of flavor–flavor learning is more difficult because most highly caloric substances also taste good and nutritious foods rarely taste really bad. There are three methods that have been used to show flavor–nutrient learning separately from flavor–flavor learning.

First, because flavor–flavor learning is not possible at a delay, showing conditioned flavor preferences with a delay between flavor and consequence illustrates flavor–nutrient learning as a process separate from flavor–flavor learning. Capaldi, Campbell, Sheffer, and Bradford (1987b) showed that rats preferred a flavor given in saccharin (cue) 30 min before lab chow (consequent) to a flavor in saccharin that preceded nothing. Capaldi et al. (1987b) also showed flavor preferences at a 30 min delay using dextrose or polycose (a form of hydrolyzed corn starch) or high-fat wet mash as reinforcing consequences.

Consistent with Lavin's (1976) and Holman's (1975) work, Capaldi et al. (1987b) found that flavor preference learning at a delay was not possible if the consequent did not contain calories. The conditioned preference shown at a delay was greater the greater the number of calories in the consequent solution and did not occur at all if there were no calories in the consequent. These experiments illustrate the basic phenomenon of flavor–nutrient preference conditioning. Preference increases for a flavor given prior in time to a nutrient. This is an important phenomenon, because in normal eating there is a delay between tasting the flavor of food and digesting the nutrients in the food. The phenomenon of flavor–nutrient learning shows that preference for the flavor of nutrient-loaded food can increase despite this built-in delay. Animals can thus learn to consume foods that contain nutrients.

A conditioned preference based on receiving calories at a delay also occurs if the cue solution contains calories (Capaldi et al., 1987b, Experiment 1). Most studies that have shown flavor–nutrient learning at a delay have delivered the cue flavors in noncaloric saccharin. Preference for a flavor given in saccharin that precedes food over a flavor given in saccharin alone could be attributed to an aversion to saccharin given without food. There is evidence that saccharin is less pleasant when given without food rather than with, perhaps due to unsatisfied digestive responses elicited by the sweet taste of saccharin (e.g., Powley, 1977; Tordoff & Friedman, 1989). Thus it is important to have shown that flavor–nutrient learning is possible at a delay even if the cue solution contains calories.

A second method has been used by Bolles and his colleagues to demonstrate flavor–nutrient learning independent of flavor–flavor learning. Mehiel and Bolles (1988) gave different flavors mixed with substances differing in taste but equal in calories, and then measured preference between the flavors. Preference for a flavor associated with ethanol (a caloric substance with a taste disliked by rats) was as large as preference for a flavor associated with corn oil or sucrose (caloric substances with tastes liked by rats) that were isocaloric with the ethanol. These findings suggest that flavor–nutrient learning occurs and that it is more powerful than flavor–flavor learning.

A third method to show flavor–nutrient learning independent of flavor–flavor learning is to bypass the oral cavity to deliver nutrients contingent on a flavor. Booth, Lovett, and McSherry (1972) showed that the normal preference for the sweeter of two solutions could be reversed by associating the less sweet solution with the postingestive consequences of 10% glucose. More recently, Sclafani (1990) has shown that intragastric infusion of nutrients contingent on rats' licking a tube containing a particular flavor increases preference for that flavor. Thus even if delivery of the consequent solution bypasses the oral cavity, the solution can produce a conditioned preference. There have been some failures to find a conditioned preference using this technique (e.g., Revusky, Smith, & Chalmers, 1971), and in some cases significant aversions have been produced with intragastric fat infusions (e.g., Deutsch, Molina, & Puerto, 1976). Under certain conditions, intragastric infusions can have aversive consequences that interfere with any reinforcing effects.

All these findings show that preference for a flavor increases if it associated with nutritional consequences. We have termed this flavor–nutrient learning because it seems that animals can discriminate between the postingestive effects of different macronutrients. For example, preference for a flavor previously paired with intragastric infusion of protein is suppressed by an intragastric protein load, but not by a carbohydrate load (Baker, Booth, Duggan, & Gibson, 1987). And intragastric loads of carbohydrate and fat are not equally effective in conditioning flavor preferences (Sclafani, 1990). For our purposes, however, the main point is that foods can condition flavor preferences, and that conditioning occurs with a delay between a cue flavor and a nutritional consequence only if the consequent contains calories.

Because flavor–flavor learning and flavor–nutrient learning can both occur when a flavor is mixed in a food or given a few seconds before, while only flavor–nutrient learning can occur with a delay, conditioned flavor preferences should be larger when a cue flavor is mixed in a food rather than given at a delay before the food. When the cue flavor is mixed in the food, two factors increase preference (flavor–nutrient learning and flavor–flavor learning), while when the cue flavor precedes the food, only flavor–nutrient learning occurs.

Sclafani (1990) reported that larger conditioned flavor preferences were produced by mixing flavors with solutions than by delayed conditioning of flavors. Boakes, Rossi-Arnaud, and Garcia-Hoz (1987) reported flavor preference conditioning reached asymptote after only two flavor–glucose pairings when the flavor was mixed with the glucose, while when the flavor preceded glucose, conditioning was much slower and preferences were smaller. Thus, following a flavor by a nutritional consequence produces a smaller flavor preference than mixing the flavor with the nutritional consequence.

Some investigators have had trouble demonstrating conditioned flavor preferences with a delay between the cue flavor and the reinforcer (e.g., Simbayi, Boakes, & Burton, 1986), which is why it is generally thought that conditioned flavor preferences are not easily produced. Yet there are good reasons why there may be trouble demonstrating these effects. First, the flavor of the reinforcer itself is more closely associated in time with its own postingestive effects (and any postingestive effects of the cue solution) than is the cue flavor. This factor is illustrated by the *dessert effect,* discussed next. Also, contrast effects and procedural factors can interfere with demonstrating conditioned flavor preferences, to be discussed later.

4.   Dessert Effect

If rats are given a meal, say of potatoes, followed by a dessert, say sucrose, an apparently paradoxical effect occurs. The preference for potatoes *decreases* as a result of being followed by sucrose (Capaldi, Campbell, Sheffer, & Bradford, 1987a). Figure 1 shows the preference for potatoes over rice when sucrose had followed potatoes and when sucrose had followed rice. As can be seen, the proportion of potatoes consumed in test is lower when sucrose followed potatoes than when sucrose followed rice. Why? Capaldi et al. (1987a) used an interval of 5 min between potatoes and sucrose, too long for flavor–flavor learning to occur. Yet sucrose does

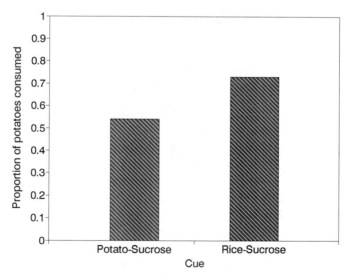

Fig. 1.   Proportion of potatoes consumed in a preference test between potatoes and rice for animals that experienced sucrose following potatoes (left bar) and for animals that experienced sucrose following rice (right bar).

contain calories. So on the basis of flavor–nutrient learning, the preference for potatoes should increase when potatoes are followed by sucrose, not decrease.

A closer analysis of flavor–nutrient learning suggests one possible reason for the dessert effect. Postingestive effects of consumption take some time. A flavor that follows a meal may be more closely associated in time with the postingestive consequences of the meal than is the flavor of the meal itself. Boakes and Lubart (1988) showed that a flavor of saccharin that followed ingestion of glucose was preferred to a flavor of saccharin that occurred alone. They suggested that what appears to be backward conditioning (glucose reinforcer precedes saccharin flavor cue) is really forward conditioning (saccharin flavor cue precedes reinforcer–postingestive consequences of glucose). Consistent with this hypothesis, they showed that a flavor of saccharin that followed glucose by 60 min was not preferred to a flavor of saccharin that occurred alone. After 60 min the postingestive effects of glucose will have dissipated.

Capaldi et al.'s (1987a) dessert effect may have occurred, then, because when sucrose followed potatoes, the flavor of sucrose was more closely associated with the postingestive consequences of potatoes than was the flavor of potatoes. For the group that received sucrose following potatoes and rice alone, the flavor of rice was associated with the postingestive consequences of rice while the flavor of potatoes was not associated with the postingestive consequences of potatoes. Therefore, rice was preferred to potatoes.

This analysis implies that our habit of eating dessert at the end of a meal will increase preference for the sweet taste of the dessert because the postingestive consequences of the meal are more closely associated with the flavor of the dessert than with the flavor of the meal.

In general, a flavor consumed later in the meal will be more strongly associated with the postingestive consequences of a meal than a flavor consumed earlier in the meal. To test this, one might give two flavors sequentially in a meal and later test preference between the two flavors. However, there is a complicating factor in comparing preference for a flavor given early in a meal with preference for a flavor given later in the meal. Hunger will decrease during a meal and hunger also affects food preferences, as is discussed later.

One way to avoid this problem is to use noncaloric saccharin as part of the meal. In an unpublished experiment, we repeatedly gave one group of rats a meal of chocolate milk preceding saccharin (C–S) while a second group always received saccharin preceding chocolate milk (S–C). The only calories involved are those in chocolate milk. If the postingestive effects of a meal are more strongly associated with the final flavor in a meal, Group S–C's preference for chocolate milk should be higher than Group C–S's, and Group C–S's preference for saccharin should be greater than Group S–C's. That is, preference for a food should increase as a result of being the final flavor in a meal. Because rats' preference for chocolate milk over saccharin is very strong, preference for chocolate milk over saccharin would not be a sensitive measure of conditioned flavor preferences. We used consumption over repeated trials as a measure of preference. Figure 2A shows the consumption of saccharin over days of training for Groups S–C and C–S, and Fig. 2B shows the consumption of chocolate milk over days of training for both groups. As can be seen, Group C–S consumed more saccharin as training proceeded than did Group S–C, and Group S–C consumed more chocolate milk than Group C–S. That is, over training, more was consumed of a substance if it was the second flavor in the meal rather than the first. This effect took some trials to develop, which is consistent with the hypothesis that a learned preference is developing.

In a flavor conditioning experiment where the cue flavor precedes a nutritional reinforcer, the flavor of the nutritional reinforcer is more closely associated in time with its own postingestive effects than is the cue flavor. This may be one reason why it is sometimes difficult to demonstrate conditioned flavor preferences based on positive postingestive effects with a delay between cue and reinforcer. The longer the delay between the cue and the reinforcer, the bigger the difference in time between the postingestive effects of the reinforcer and the cue, while the delay between the flavor of the reinforcer and its own postingestive effects does not change. This means that the longer the delay between the flavor and the reinforcer, the more likely that the flavor of the reinforcer is more strongly associated with its own postingestive consequences than is the cue flavor.

Elizalde and Sclafani (1988) showed that associations between the flavor of a nutritional reinforcer and its own postingestive effects can interfere with forming an association between a cue flavor and those postingestive effects. They used polycose as a reinforcer. One group was preexposed to polycose plus acarbose, a drug that blocks digestion of starch. The other group was not preexposed. Subsequently both groups were given flavor conditioning with polycose following a cue flavor at a delay. The group that had been preexposed to acarbose plus polycose formed a larger conditioned preference than the other group. Presumably, the preexposed group had learned in Phase 1 that the flavor of polycose was not associated with nutritional benefit; therefore in Phase 2 the flavor of polycose did not block learning about the flavor cue.

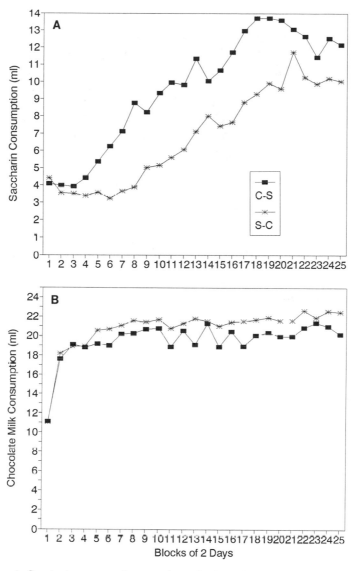

Fig. 2.   A, Saccharin consumption over days of training for a group given chocolate milk preceding saccharin each day (C–S) and for a group given saccharin preceding chocolate milk each day (S–C). B, Chocolate milk consumption over days of training for a group given chocolate milk preceding saccharin each day (C–S) and for a group given saccharin preceding chocolate milk each day (S–C).

5. *Summary*

These studies show that one problem in demonstrating conditioned preferences for a flavor that precedes a nutritional consequence is that
preference is increased most for the flavor that is most closely associated
with nutritional consequences, often not the flavor preference being measured. Preference for the flavor of the reinforcer or a flavor following it
may be increased, while preference for the preceding cue flavor is not
increased. Another factor that can interfere with measuring conditioned
flavor preferences based on positive consequences is *contrast effects*.

6. *Contrast Effects in Flavor Preference Learning*

The effectiveness of a reinforcer is reduced if it is closely accompanied by
a more preferred reinforcer, a phenomenon termed *negative contrast* (see
Mackintosh, 1974). Contrast effects have been demonstrated in consummatory behavior. Flaherty and Checke (1982) showed that consumption of
saccharin was reduced if saccharin was followed by sucrose. They termed
this *anticipatory negative contrast*. Consumption of saccharin is reduced
in anticipation of the following preferred sucrose. Note that the anticipatory contrast effect discovered by Flaherty is analogous to our dessert
effect, except we measured later preference for potatoes that preceded
sucrose while Flaherty and his colleagues measured current consumption
of saccharin that precedes sucrose. Perhaps preference for potatoes is
reduced by the following sucrose because sucrose is preferred to potatoes.
Contrast or comparison effects may account for the dessert effect.

If so, then following a food by a more preferred caloric food may
produce two opposing effects—the more preferred food may increase
preference for the first food (flavor–nutrient learning), and the more preferred food may reduce current consumption of the first food because of
contrast or comparison effects and may also reduce preference for that
food (dessert effect). Thus the final preference for a flavor may depend on
the algebraic sum of the increase in preference produced by flavor–
nutrient learning and the decrease in preference produced by contrast.

We first suggested that preference conditioning and negative anticipatory contrast may operate simultaneously and produce opposing effects on
intake to account for some paradoxical findings in preference learning
(Capaldi, Sheffer, & Pulley, 1989). For example, a higher concentration of
sucrose used as a reinforcer sometimes produces less of a conditioned
preference than a lower concentration. This may be because a higher
concentration of sucrose also results in a stronger negative contrast effect
that reduces the net conditioned preference.

In a subsequent series of experiments we measured both reinforcement and contrast simultaneously (Capaldi & Sheffer, 1992). In one experiment, rats received one flavor of saccharin preceding chocolate milk and a second flavor of saccharin alone. Consumption during training was measured, as well as subsequent preference between the two flavors of saccharin. Figure 3 shows consumption during training and flavor preference in a later test. As Fig. 3 demonstrates, rats that received saccharin preceding chocolate milk (Group S–C) suppressed consumption of saccharin compared to a control group that received only saccharin (anticipatory negative contrast). These same rats preferred the flavor of saccharin that preceded chocolate milk to the flavor that occurred alone in a later test of conditioned flavor preferences. Thus contrast (decreased consumption) and reinforcement (increased preference) can indeed occur simultaneously. An interesting aspect of the results is that, in training, consumption of the two different flavors of saccharin did not differ significantly, although the tendency was for rats to consume more of the flavor that preceded chocolate milk. Lucas and Timberlake (1992) also recently reported that rats consume more of a flavor of saccharin that precedes sucrose than of a flavor that occurs alone. Thus, when a within-subject comparison is made between two flavors, one of which precedes a rein-

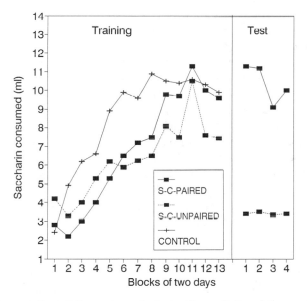

Fig. 3. Consumption of flavored saccharin by Group S–C and the control group in training, and for Group S–C in test. For Group S–C one flavor of saccharin preceded chocolate milk in training (paired); the other flavor occurred alone (unpaired). In test a choice was given between the two flavors.

forcer and one of which does not, the data are clear in showing preference for the flavor preceding the reinforcer (flavor–nutrient learning). This is so despite the fact that consumption of both flavors is suppressed compared to a control group that does not receive the preferred reward.

Summarizing, we have thus far discussed two reasons why it can be difficult to find evidence for flavor conditioning based on positive consequences: (1) A flavor that occurs closer in time to postingestive consequences will be more strongly associated with those consequences than an earlier occurring cue flavor. This includes the flavor of the reinforcer itself, and flavors that occur after the delivery of the reinforcer. (2) A comparison or contrast process can reduce the value of a cue flavor that precedes a more preferred reinforcer.

A third reason flavor preference learning over a delay can be difficult to demonstrate is use of *nonoptimal procedures*.

7. Procedural Factors

If a flavor is to be given prior in time to the reinforcer, animals must be induced to consume the flavor. Customarily, the to-be-conditioned cue flavor is given in a solution that rats will consume, but not a highly palatable one, often a low concentration of saccharin. Holman (1975), for example, gave his cue flavors in solution with 0.065% saccharin, a commonly used solution in studies since then. Cinnamon in 0.065% saccharin preceded a reinforcer at a delay, and wintergreen in 0.065% saccharin was given alone. Subsequently preference between cinnamon and wintergreen in 0.065% saccharin was measured. In test, rats are being asked to consume flavored 0.065% saccharin to show their preference; that is, flavors are given in a solution that the rats do not particularly like initially. In an unpublished experiment, we showed that use of a relatively unpalatable cue solution can prevent measuring a conditioned flavor preference. Half the rats were given their cue flavor (cinnamon or wintergreen) in 2% polycose; the other half received their cue flavor in 0.065% saccharin. For all rats, 20% polycose followed one flavor (cinnamon or wintergreen) and 2% polycose followed the other flavor, both at a 5-min delay. In test, rats were given a choice between cinnamon and wintergreen in the same solution they had received in training. Figure 4 shows the results. Rats given 2% polycose as a cue solution and test solution showed a conditioned flavor preference, while those given 0.065% saccharin did not. Thus the use of a relatively unpalatable cue solution can prevent demonstration of a conditioned flavor preference. Simbayi et al. (1986) used 0.065% saccharin as the cue solution when they failed to obtain conditioned flavor preferences at a delay. We have successfully obtained conditioned flavor prefer-

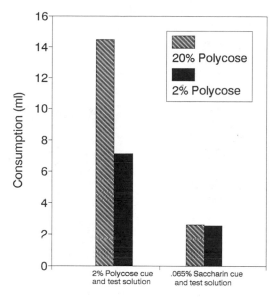

Fig. 4.   Both groups received one flavor of a cue solution preceding 20% polycose and the other flavor preceding 2% polycose. For one group the cue solution and test solution was 2% polycose, for the other group the cue and test solutions were 0.065% saccharin. Shown are milliliters consumed of each flavor in a two-bottle preference test between the two flavors.

ences at a delay using 0.065% saccharin as the cue solution but have had greater success when a more palatable 0.15% saccharin is used as the cue solution (Capaldi et al., 1987b).

Using 0.15% saccharin as the solution to deliver cue flavors, we have obtained preferences for a flavor associated with caloric consequences at intervals as long as 5 hr (Capaldi & Sheffer, 1992). Figure 5 shows preference for a flavor of saccharin (cinnamon or wintergreen) that preceded chocolate milk by five hours over a flavor of saccharin that occurred alone. To our knowledge, 5 hr is the longest delay yet used in a successful demonstration of conditioned flavor preferences based on positive consequences at a delay.

Finally, Elizalde and Sclafani (1988) showed that flavor preference learning at a delay is easier to obtain, the more salient the cue flavors. Most investigators, again following Holman, have used cinnamon and wintergreen as cue flavors. Elizalde and Sclafani (1988) showed that grape and cherry Kool-Aid™ as cue flavors produced larger conditioned flavor preferences at a delay than did cinnamon and wintergreen.

We have thus far considered two ways flavor preferences can be formed based on positive consequences: flavor–flavor learning and flavor–

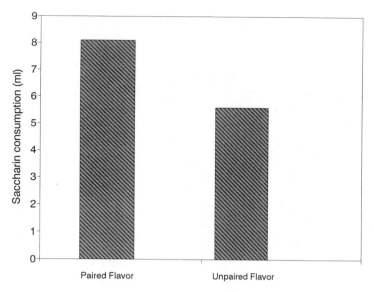

Fig. 5. Milliliters consumed in a two-bottle test of a flavor of saccharin that had preceded chocolate milk by 5 hr (paired flavor) vs. a flavor that had occurred alone (unpaired).

nutrient learning. A third major way in which preference for a flavor can be produced is by consuming a particular flavor when food deprived.

III. Hunger and Food Preferences

One way to induce an animal to eat is to deprive it of food. Consuming a food when deprived increases later preference for that food.

Revusky and Garcia (1970) and Revusky (1967) originally suggested that a food consumed when hungry would become preferred as a result of the taste of food being paired with the long-delayed consequences of consumption. Revusky (1967) showed that a flavor consumed under high deprivation was preferred later to a flavor consumed under low deprivation, even when the rats were tested under low deprivation. However, we showed in a series of studies (Capaldi & Myers, 1982; Capaldi, Myers, Campbell, & Sheffer, 1983) that Revusky's findings were due in part to his using a 24 hr deprivation schedule where the flavor given under high deprivation occurred immediately before the daily feeding and the flavor given under low deprivation occurred immediately after feeding. When this is done, the flavor given before feeding (high deprivation) can be associated with the following daily meal. (In Revusky's study the flavor given after feeding, under low deprivation, was probably not associated with the postingestive effects of the meal because it followed the meal by 1.5 hr). Thus Revusky's (1967) results may show that a flavor associated with a following meal is preferred to a flavor not associated with a meal (another example of flavor–nutrient learning), rather than having anything to do with the effects of deprivation level. It is important to give the flavors under different deprivation levels while not simultaneously associating the flavors differentially with the daily meal.

In a recent series of studies (Capaldi, Sheffer, & Owens, 1991), we showed that rats prefer a flavor that was experienced under high deprivation to one that was experienced under low deprivation if the flavors are given separately from feeding in unsweetened food. In the first experiment in this series, six different groups of rats were run in a factorial design combining amount of food used to deliver flavors (1 g or 16 g of wet mash) with three different combinations of high and low deprivation: 2 and 26 hr, 2 and 43 hr, and 24 and 43 hr. One flavor of wet mash was given under the higher deprivation and one under the lower. Subsequently, preference between the flavors was measured. Figure 6 shows the results of this experiment: There was a clear preference for the flavor of food given under high deprivation. This result occurred whether testing was given under high or low deprivation.

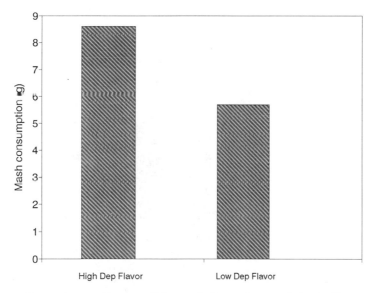

Fig. 6.   Grams consumed in a two-dish test of a flavor of wet mash that had been received under high deprivation vs. a flavor that had been received under low deprivation.

In previous work, we had found using the same procedures that if flavors are delivered in saccharin or sucrose solutions, preference is for the flavor received under the *lower* deprivation level (Capaldi & Myers, 1982; Capaldi et al., 1983). This cross-study comparison suggested to us that there might be something aversive about sweetness under high deprivation. Accordingly we ran an additional experiment using the same procedures, using sweetened or unsweetened food to deliver the flavors. In this experiment the low deprivation was 2 hr and the high deprivation was 43 hr. There were four groups in a factorial design combining amount of food used to deliver the flavor (1 vs. 20 g of wet mash) with whether or not the mash was sweetened. Figure 7 shows the results. Preference was for the flavor experienced under the higher deprivation when unsweetened food is used to deliver the flavors, but using sweetened food eliminated this preference.

Apparently there is something aversive or unpleasant about sweetness when food deprivation is high. This may explain why sweet foods are typically eaten at the end of the meal under low food deprivation rather than at the beginning of meals. Other anecdotal data also indicate that sweetness is not pleasant under very high food deprivation. When food deprivation is extreme, preference for food elements other than sweet

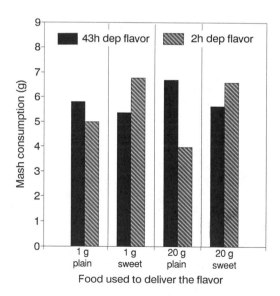

Fig. 7.   Grams consumed in a two-dish test of a flavor of wet mash that had been received under high deprivation vs. a flavor that had been received under low deprivation. Groups differed in the amount of wet mash received in training and in whether or not the mash was sweetened.

TABLE I

Conditioned Food Preferences: Major Findings

1. Mere Exposure: Preference increases for a food as a function of consuming the food.
2. Medicine Effect: Preference increases for a flavor associated with recovery from illness.
3. Flavor–Flavor Learning: Preference for a flavor mixed with an already preferred flavor increases, preference for a flavor mixed with an already disliked flavor decreases. Flavor–flavor learning will also occur with a short delay between the two flavors (no greater than 9 sec).
4. Flavor–Nutrient Learning: Preference for the flavor of a cue food that precedes a food (reinforcer) containing nutrients increases. This learning can occur with a delay between the cue and reinforcer (Capaldi et al. 1987b, delay 30 min; Capaldi & Sheffer, 1992, delay 5 hr).
5. Current consumption of a food can be decreased if a more preferred food follows. At the same time, later preference for the flavor of the first food can increase.
6. Preference increases for the second of two foods consumed in sequence, if satiation is not a factor.
7. Consuming an unsweetened food when food deprived increases preference for the food.
8. Consuming a sweetened food when food deprived either decreases preference for the food or has no effect on preference.
9. Consuming unsweetened food when food deprived will make that food reinforcing later under satiation.

study showing flavor–flavor learning. More recent studies have successfully used fewer pairings. Capaldi et al. (1983) used only 6 pairings (3 under high deprivation and 3 under low deprivation) and found a highly significant preference for the flavor given in a sweet solution under low deprivation. Mehiel and Bolles (1988) used only 4 pairings of sucrose with a flavor and showed a significant flavor preference. Boakes et al. (1987) found conditioning to be asymptotic following only two pairings in flavor–flavor learning, while learning was slower in flavor–nutrient learning at a delay.

The number of trials necessary to produce conditioned flavor preferences has not been systematically investigated in the different flavor conditioning paradigms. However, the data available suggest that certainly in flavor–flavor learning, conditioning is rapid. And in flavor–nutrient learning, enough studies have used small numbers of pairings (fewer than 10) to conclude that a large number of conditioning trials is not necessary to obtain effects.

B. Resistance to Extinction

Conditioned flavor preferences are surprisingly resistant to extinction. Figure 9 shows data from an experiment by Capaldi et al. (1983). In this

seems to increase. Lepkovsky (1977) reported that during World War II American soldiers in a German prison camp were subsisting on a ration 200 calories short of basal needs. They were ultimately saved by Red Cross food parcels. Trading of the food parcels produced a point value for each food that pretty much reflected the nutritional composition of the food. The two top items were powdered milk at 150 points and meat at 120 points. No points at all were listed for jam, sugar, or chocolate bars. Also in this connection, it is interesting to note that highly sweetened main dishes are uncommon in human cuisines.

These anecdotal data are consistent with our animal work showing that the reinforcing effect of food as measured by conditioned food preferences is increased by food deprivation only if unsweetened food is used.

While the reinforcing effect of sweet food does not increase with increasing deprivation, its palatability may increase. Cabanac (1971) reported that humans' ratings of the pleasantness of sweet solutions was higher immediately preceding a glucose load rather than following a glucose load. He postulated that the pleasantness of stimuli is related to their usefulness to the body, a phenomenon he termed *alliesthesia*. Cabanac's phenomenon may be related to the fact that the higher deprivation sweet solution was given prior to a glucose load and the low deprivation solution was given following the glucose load. Rats prefer flavors given shortly before a meal to those given after a meal (Capaldi & Myers, 1982; Revusky, 1967) but do not prefer flavors given in sweetened solutions under high deprivation to those given under low deprivation when the flavors are not associated with meals.

Yet there is other evidence that the palatability of sucrose may increase with a deprivation increase from zero to 48 hours. Berridge (1990) demonstrated that rats' orofacial responses showed an increase in appetitive aspects to sucrose when deprivation was increased from satiation to 48 hr deprivation. There was no significant increase at 24 hr. Orofacial responses have been taken as a measure of palatability. These data are not inconsistent with our findings that the reinforcing effectiveness of sweetness does not increase with deprivation, because palatability is only one aspect of reinforcing effectiveness. Our data show that the reinforcing effectiveness of sweet solutions or foods is not increased by deprivation increases from 2 to 48 hr. Accordingly, in addition to any presumed palatability increase, there must also be some aversive effects of consuming sweet solutions and food under high deprivation, effects that reduce the reinforcing effectiveness of sweetness.

We have seen thus far that preference for a flavor will increase as a result of being consumed when food deprived. A more dramatic demonstration that the reward or incentive value of the food is increased is provided by showing that the food will then function as a reinforcer for satiated rats. Capaldi, Davidson, and Myers (1981) showed that after rats had consumed food when food deprived, the pellets would serve as reinforcers when the rats were satiated. Rats (Group P) were given a total of forty Noyes pellets (0.045 g, portion of 4 once per day on Days 1 and 2, twice per day on Days 3–6). The animals were on a 13 g/day deprivation schedule for seven days prior to receiving the pellets and throughout the pellet experience. Following this experience, the rats were fed ad lib for 12 days until their weight reached their original ad lib weight or higher. They were then run in a differential conditioning problem while satiated, where the pellets were placed in one color alley (black or white) and no reinforcer was given in the other color alley. A control group (Group A) received the same deprivation experience as Group P but no pellets. They were also run on the differential conditioning problem when satiated to measure whether the pellets were inherently rewarding under satiation. As can be seen from the results shown in Fig. 8, Group P learned to run faster in the alley containing the pellets than in the other alley, while Group A did not. Note that this effect grew larger over the 20 days of satiated testing. Experiencing the Noyes pellets when hungry was sufficient to make them a reinforcer under satiation. Rats who had consumed the pellets when hungry in their home cage also continued to consume them when satiated (90% of the trials). The

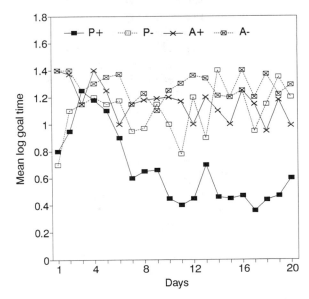

Fig. 8.   Mean log goal time in a differential conditioning problem. All rats were run satiated. Four pellets were placed in the ''+'' alley and no pellets in the ''−'' alley. Group P had received pellets previously when food deprived, Group A had not.

control group consumed the pellets on only 27% of the satiated test trials (and this was due to consumption by 2 of the 10 rats in this group).

This experiment shows that pellets become a conditioned reinforcer as a result of having been consumed under food deprivation. This can be viewed as an example of flavor–nutrient learning. The taste of pellets is paired with the postingestive effects of eating the pellets.

Capaldi and Myers (1978) showed that once rats had eaten pellets when hungry, they would continue to eat them when satiated. The strength of the eating response was dependent on the similarity of the cues present in training and test. Eating when satiated was more strongly elicited if the same reward magnitude was used in satiation than if a different one was used (Capaldi & Myers, 1978). Eating in satiated testing was also more strongly elicited following training with partial reward than following training with consistent reward. Perhaps the most interesting aspect of conditioned eating is that it is stimulus bound. An animal trained to eat pellets when hungry in a straight alley runway can be satiated on pellets in its home cage, and it will resume eating pellets when placed again in the runway. The conditioning situation is sufficient to re-elicit eating that has ceased from satiation (Capaldi & Myers, 1978). Weingarten reported the same phenomenon later (1983), using a specific punctate stimulus as a cue. Rats that had been given food every day following a specific conditioned stimulus resumed eating when satiated upon presentation of the stimulus.

Summarizing, another way to produce a learned food preference is to give the food to a hungry organism. This learned increase in preference transfers to the satiated state and is highly resistant to extinction.

Table I summarizes the major findings we have reviewed.

IV.   Characteristics of Food Preference Learning

As is well known, taste aversion learning occurs rapidly and is very resistant to extinction, and long delays between taste and sickness are possible. The data reviewed here show that flavor preferences based on positive systemic consequences are also possible. Less widely appreciated is the fact that these preferences are also established rapidly, are very resistant to extinction, and are possible with long delays between flavors and consequences.

A.   RAPIDITY OF LEARNING

In the earliest studies on flavor preference conditioning using positive consequences, a fairly large number of conditioning trials were used. Holman (1975), for example, used 20 pairings of flavors in his original

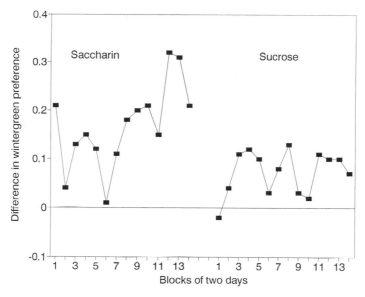

Fig. 9. Preference for wintergreen when it had been consumed under low deprivation in training minus preference for wintergreen when it had been consumed under high deprivation in training. Shown are data over 28 days of two-bottle testing (wintergreen vs. cinnamon) for rats trained with saccharin solution and rats trained with sucrose solution.

experiment rats received one flavored sweet solution under high deprivation and another under low deprivation. This conditioning produces a flavor preference for the flavor given under low deprivation. As Fig. 9 shows, this preference persisted over 28 days of testing with no sign of diminution.

Why are flavor preferences so persistent? Consider the data from the Capaldi et al. (1983) experiment shown in Fig. 9. In testing, rats are given both flavors side by side in a two-bottle test. In test the preferred flavor is consumed more than the nonpreferred. If anything, this behavior should increase preference for the already preferred flavor (preference increases with exposure). Thus test performance may produce an increase in the previously learned preference. Secondly, the initial difference in preferences is not explicitly counteracted by the experiences given in test. Both flavors in test are given under common test circumstances. In the Capaldi et al. (1983) experiment, one flavor had been experienced under high deprivation in training and the other under low deprivation. In test both flavors were experienced under both deprivation levels. The initial difference in affective value for the two flavors may be maintained under the common new experience. (The fact that conditioned flavor preferences are so persistent suggests that affective conditioning is involved, as is discussed below.)

Consistent with this idea, conditioned flavor preferences can be eliminated quickly by reversal training. Capaldi et al. (1983) reversed the contingencies experienced by the animals, thereby reversing affective conditioning, and this rapidly reversed the preference.

C. DELAY

Conditioned flavor preferences can be formed with a considerable delay between flavor and consequence. Capaldi et al. (1987b) used a 30 min delay between flavors and consequences and obtained significant flavor preferences; Capaldi and Sheffer (in press) found significant conditioned flavor preferences with a 5 hr delay between flavors and reinforcer. While not all investigators have obtained this result (see Simbayi et al., 1986), we discussed above a number of good reasons to expect difficulty in obtaining conditioned flavor preferences over a delay. The reinforcer for long-delay learning seems to be some aspect of postingestive consequences of consuming caloric food (recall that flavor–flavor learning is not possible over a delay). If a flavor precedes consumption of a caloric food at a delay, the flavor of the caloric food itself is more closely paired in time with the postingestive consequences of the food than is the cue flavor. Indeed, as discussed above, a flavor that occurs after a food may be more strongly associated with the postingestive consequences of the food than the flavor of the food itself.

Thus one reason flavor preference learning at a delay can be difficult to demonstrate is that the flavor of the reinforcing food can be associated with its own nutritional consequences, blocking conditioning of the flavor cue to those consequences.

There are also a number of procedural factors that can interfere with demonstrating conditioned flavor preferences at a delay. We discussed above the importance of palatability of cue solution and salience of cue flavor.

V.   Learning Processes Involved in Flavor Preference Learning

Theorists have most commonly considered flavor preference learning to be a case of classical conditioning. In taste aversion learning, the flavor is considered the conditioned stimulus (CS) and sickness the unconditioned stimulus (US). In flavor preferences based on positive consequences, the flavor is the CS and either another flavor (in flavor–flavor learning) or postingestive consequences (in flavor–nutrient learning) is considered the US. Flavor–flavor learning does not easily fit the CS–US framework, and there is also question whether this is the best way to view flavor–nutrient learning.

Flavor–flavor learning does not require a CS be paired with a US. Flavor–flavor learning also occurs when a flavor US is associated with a flavor US, that is, one of the flavors does not need to be neutral before conditioning. Rescorla and Cunningham (1978) showed flavor–flavor learning occurred when solutions were given of sucrose plus hydrochloric acid or quinine and sodium chloride plus hydrochloric acid or quinine. All these flavors can be used as USs. Flavor–flavor learning seems to occur whenever two flavors are given together, whether the flavors are neutral or not. Also, flavor–flavor learning is not possible with a delay longer than 9 sec between the two flavors and is optimum when the flavors are given in solution together. This is not characteristic of classical conditioning involving associating a CS and US, where it is optimum to have the CS precede the US.

Rescorla and Cunningham (1978) and Durlach and Rescorla (1980) have suggested that flavor–flavor learning involves formation of within-compound associations, a type of learning that can occur whenever two stimuli are presented in compound. This is a more neutral description that seems preferred to arbitrarily considering one flavor as a US and the other as a CS and the learning as involving an association between a CS and a US. Although flavor–flavor learning often involves a neutral flavor and a flavor that could be used as a US, neither flavor seems to be functioning as a US in flavor–flavor learning. Rather, both flavors becomes associated with each other as a result of being experienced together. It is true that no one seems to have investigated flavor–flavor learning when two neutral flavors are paired, but there is no reason to believe that flavor–flavor learning would not occur under these conditions, inasmuch as two neutral external stimuli become associated when experienced in compound.

The basic result of flavor–flavor learning is that any affective tone of one of the flavors transfers to the other flavor. This is so whether the affective tone of one of the flavors is inherent (as when sucrose or quinine are used), or if the affective tone of one of the flavors has been learned (as when one of the flavors has been paired with illness). Pairing a flavor with saccharin increases preference for the flavor (Holman, 1975); pairing a flavor with quinine or with a flavor that has been associated with illness decreases preference for the flavor (Fanselow & Birk, 1982; Lavin, 1976).

Flavor–nutrient learning, in contrast to flavor–flavor learning, requires that the consequent contain nutrients, that is, a US is necessary. A cue

flavor becomes associated with some aspect of the postingestive consequences of food containing calories. One hypothesis is that flavor–nutrient
learning is a form of operant conditioning. Eating can be viewed as an
operant response that is reinforced by the nutritional consequences of
eating. The flavor in conditioned flavor preference experiments can then
be viewed as a discriminative stimulus.

In most of the studies discussed above, consumption of food was used as
a measure of the increased preference for it. Data from these studies can
thus conceivably be interpreted in terms of operant conditioning of consumption. Capaldi et al.'s (1981) study of resistance to satiation used a
different measure of "preference"—reinforcement of a preceding instrumental response. This measure is a more powerful measure of conditioned
preference than is consumption because results cannot be interpreted in
terms of conditioning of consumption as an operant response. There is a
considerable amount of evidence that instrumental responses learned under high food deprivation are made more persistently and vigorously when
tested under low hunger than are responses learned under low hunger. For
example, rats trained to run a straight alley under high food deprivation
will run more rapidly in a low deprivation test than rats trained under low
deprivation, even if tested with no food present, so conditioned reinforcing
value of the food cannot be responsible for the effect (Capaldi & Hovancik,
1973). We have suggested that instrumental responses learned under high
deprivation are more strongly conditioned than those learned under low
deprivation. If this is so, learning to eat a particular food under high
deprivation may produce greater consumption of the food later because of
a stronger conditioned eating response (viewing consumption as an instrumental response).

Capaldi et al.'s (1981) experiment using pellets to reinforce a new response in test cannot be interpreted in this manner. In that experiment the
reinforcer previously consumed under high deprivation was used to reinforce a new response (running the alley) as a measure of reinforcing value
or preference. Since the running response was not made in high deprivation training, its greater strength for rats trained under high deprivation
cannot be attributed to stronger conditioning under high deprivation. This
experiment thus shows clearly that the reinforcing value of the pellets was
increased by their conditioning history. This experiment provides particularly strong evidence that the reinforcing effectiveness of food can be
changed by its conditioning history, and it provides evidence against the
hypothesis that learned consumption differences are responsible for the
effects.

Also arguing against learned consumption as a factor is the fact that in
many of the studies that measured consumption of flavors to show

preference, there were no consumption differences during training (e.g., Capaldi et al., 1983). Thus in these studies differences in test cannot be attributed to learned differences in consumption.

A reasonable question to ask is, Why were there no differences in consumption in training in these studies? One would expect that if one flavor predicts a nutritional consequence and the other does not, then consumption of flavors would differ in training—a learned increase in preference for a flavor should be manifest in training as it is in test. Two reasons can be suggested for why differences in consumption of flavors are more likely to occur in a two-bottle test than during training. One reason is that two-bottle preference tests have been shown to be more sensitive measures of preference than one-bottle acceptance tests (Sclafani, 1987). Secondly, in training, contrast effects can suppress consumption of the flavor preceding the reinforcer, as discussed above.

Because in many studies no difference in consumption of flavors occurred in training, while there were preference differences in test, results cannot be attributed to learned consumption differences. While operant conditioning of eating can occur in conditioned flavor preference experiments, this process does not seem to totally account for conditioned flavor preferences. Data from these experiments suggest instead that some aspect of the flavors has become more reinforcing and preferred as a result of being paired with nutritional consequences.

In flavor–nutrient conditioning, affect seems to transfer from the nutrient to the flavor, rather than a cognitive expectancy of receiving calories being conditioned to the flavors. If a cognitive expectancy of receiving nutrients were formed when a flavor is paired with nutrients, the conditioned flavor preference should extinguish when the nutrients no longer follow. Although conditioned flavor preferences of course do ultimately extinguish, they are highly resistant to extinction. This great resistance to extinction implies that the affect elicited by the flavor has changed as a result of the initial pairing.

Affect conditioning is a form of classical conditioning suggested by many theorists. For example, Konorski (1967) assumed that the animal's representation of any US includes both its sensory and affective components. The extent to which a CS elicits the different components of the US representation will determine what behavior will occur. Even external stimuli paired with different nutritional consequences appear to take on some affective properties. Delameter, LoLordo, and Berridge (1986) showed that an auditory CS that had been associated with sucrose would alter the animal's orofacial response to water that then followed the CS (it is not clear whether the CS was associated with the flavor of the sucrose or the postingestive consequences or both). Orofacial responses (Grill &

Norgren, 1978) have been used as a measure of palatability. Perhaps, then, flavor–nutrient learning is a form of classical conditioning. Food or a flavor cue is the CS; some aspect of postingestive consequences of the food is the US; and as a result of pairing the flavors with postingestive effects, positive affect accrues to the CS.

Garcia (1989) has suggested instead that conditioned flavor preferences and aversions differ in enough ways from ordinary classical conditioning involving external stimuli that a different form of learning is involved, a form that he calls *Darwinian learning*. In Darwinian learning, the association is between the US or reinforcer and its feedback (FB), or US–FB conditioning. Garcia suggests that a different form of learning is involved because of the following differences between CS–US conditioning and US–FB conditioning.

1. The CS–US interval must be a matter of seconds, but the US–FB interval can be a matter of hours.
2. The US must be presented to an alert subject, but FB (in taste aversion) is completely effective when delivered to the subject asleep under anesthesia (Bermudez-Rattoni, Forthman, Sanchez, Perez, & Garcia, 1988).
3. After CS–US training, the subject gains a precise appreciation of both stimuli and their association in time and space and modifies its behavior accordingly; but after taste aversion training as a specific case of US–FB learning, the hedonic value of the US is modified even in the absence of any memory of its association with the nauseous FB.
4. While many different CSs can be linked with a food US, there is a strong selective affinity of food FB for taste—odor potentiated by taste.

Garcia was discussing taste aversion learning, but these points also apply to some extent at least to conditioned flavor preferences. As discussed above, a conditioned flavor preference can be formed with a delay of hours between the flavor and the nutritional consequence (e.g., Capaldi & Sheffer, 1992). Although this result is not obtained as easily in conditioned flavor preferences as in taste aversion learning, we discussed reasons why this should be so above. We do not know if conditioned flavor preferences could be formed under anesthesia. We have already suggested that conditioned flavor preferences involve affect conditioning. And finally, selective associations have been demonstrated to some extent in conditioned flavor preferences. Lucas and Timberlake (1992) showed that conditioned flavor preferences were more likely to be formed by a nutritional reinforcer than was conditioned reinforcement to an external stimulus. Whether or not one agrees that these characteristics require postulation of a different form of learning, the notation suggested by Garcia is certainly useful. As we have seen, the US in flavor–nutrient learning is some aspect of the postingestive effects of consumption. Referring to these postingestive aspects as FB and food as the US clarifies the fact that an association can be made between food and its postingestive consequences as well as between other cues (CSs) and those postingestive consequences. This notation also clarifies the fact that in any situation using food as a reinforcer, US–FB conditioning will proceed along with any other associations that may be under study (CS–US, instrumental response–US). The data on conditioned flavor preferences are too limited at the present time to determine which is the most beneficial way to view conditioned flavor preference learning. Whether or not blocking and other classical conditioning phenomena occur in conditioned flavor preference learning is currently under investigation in our laboratory.

VI. Applications of Conditioned Food Preferences

The fact that individual differences in taste preferences can possibly be related to differences in experience with foods is of tremendous potential practical importance. Individual subjects differing in weight also differ in their taste preferences, particularly for fat. The obese show a greater preference for fat than normal weight subjects, while anorexics show less (Drewnowski, 1988). These differences in preferences may be produced by experience, and perhaps some of the methods that we know change food preferences could also be used to change an individual's preference for fat. Some work has been done on this in the case of salt.

Recall that mere familiarity is an important determinant of food preference. Exposure to particular intensities of flavors also affect preferences. People on a low salt diet ultimately show preferences for lower intensities of salt in soup and on crackers. This change in preference takes longer to occur than one might think: 2–4 months. The preference change is a sensory phenomenon. People given 10 g of extra sodium per day in the form of salt on their food show an increase in the level of salt preferred in soup on crackers; people given 10 g of extra sodium per day in the form of a salt tablet show no change in preference. It is tasting the salt that causes the preference changes, not ingesting the salt (Beauchamp, 1987). Would exposure to a low fat diet reduce the preferred level of fat, as exposure to a low salt diet reduces the preferred level of salt? If results with fat were similar to those with salt, we would expect that any change in preference would take months to develop. Knowledge that the taste of food will improve after months on a diet could motivate adherence to the diet.

Another way to reduce the preference for fat would be to pair it with already disliked tastes (flavor–flavor learning), a method that has not yet been tried.

ACKNOWLEDGMENT

This research was supported in part by National Institute of Mental Health Grant MH 39453 to Elizabeth D. Capaldi.

REFERENCES

Baker, B. J., Booth, D. A., Duggan, J. P., & Gibson, E. L. (1987). Protein appetite demonstrated: Learned specificity of protein-cue preference to protein need in adult rats. *Nutrition Research, 7*, 481–487.

Beauchamp, G. K. (1987). The human preference for excess salt. *American Scientist, 75*, 27–33.

Beauchamp, G. K., & Moran, M. (1982). Dietary experience and sweet taste preferences in human infants. *Appetite, 3*, 139–152.

Beauchamp, G. K., & Moran, M. (1984). Acceptance of sweet and salty tastes in 2-year old children. *Appetite, 5*, 291–305.

Bermudez-Rattoni, F., Forthman, D. L., Sanchez, M. A., Perez, J. L., & Garcia, J. (1988). Odor and taste aversions conditioned in anesthetized rats. *Behavioral Neuroscience, 102*, 726–732.

Bernstein, I. L., & Borson, S. (1986). Learned food aversion: A component of anorexia syndromes. *Psychological Review, 93*, 462–472.

Berridge, K. (1990, May). *Emotion & appetite: Facing neural substrates*. Paper presented at the meeting of the Midwestern Psychological Association, Chicago, IL.

Birch, L. L., & Marlin, D. W. (1982). I don't like it, I never tried it: Effects of exposure on two-year-old children's food preferences. *Appetite, 3*, 353–360.

Boakes, R. A., & Lubart, T. (1988). Enhanced preference for a flavour following reversed flavour–glucose pairing. *Quarterly Journal of Experimental Psychology, 40B*, 49–62.

Boakes, R. A., Rossi-Arnaud, C., & Garcia-Hoz, V. (1987). Early experience and reinforcer quality in delayed flavour–food learning in the rat. *Appetite, 9*, 191–206.

Booth, D. A. (1985). Food-conditioned eating preferences and aversions with interoceptive elements: Learned appetites and satieties. *Annals of the New York Academy of Sciences, 443*, 22–37.

Booth, D. (1990). Learned role of tastes in eating motivation. In E. D. Capaldi & T. L. Powley (Eds.), *Taste, experience and feeding* (pp. 179–194). Washington, DC: American Psychological Association.

Booth, D. A., Lovett, D., & McSherry, G. M. (1972). Postingestive modulation of the sweetness preference gradient. *Journal of Comparative and Physiological Psychology, 78*, 485–512.

Cabanac, M. (1971). Physiological role of pleasure. *Science, 173*, 1103–1107.

Capaldi, E. D., Campbell, D. H., Sheffer, J. D., & Bradford, J. P. (1987a). Non-reinforcing effects of giving "dessert" in rats. *Appetite, 9*, 99–112.

Capaldi, E. D., Campbell, D. H., Sheffer, J. D., & Bradford, J. P. (1987b). Conditioned flavor preferences based on delayed caloric consequences. *Journal of Experimental Psychology: Animal Behavior Processes, 13*, 150–155.

Capaldi, E. D., Davidson, T. L., & Myers, D. E. (1981). Resistance to satiation: Reinforcing effects of food and eating under satiation. *Learning and Motivation, 12,* 171–195.

Capaldi, E. D., & Hovancik, J. R. (1973). Effects of previous body weight level on rats' straight alley performance. *Journal of Experimental Psychology, 97,* 93–97.

Capaldi, E. D., & Myers, D. E. (1978). Resistance to satiation of consummatory and instrumental performance. *Learning and Motivation, 9,* 197–201.

Capaldi, E. D., & Myers, D. E. (1982). Taste preferences as a function of food deprivation during original taste exposure. *Animal Learning & Behavior, 10,* 211–219.

Capaldi, E. D., Myers, D. E., Campbell, D. H., & Sheffer, J. D. (1983). Conditioned flavor preferences based on hunger level during original flavor exposure. *Animal Learning & Behavior, 11,* 107–115.

Capaldi, E. D., & Sheffer, J. D. (1992). Contrast and reinforcement in consumption. *Learning and Motivation, 23,* 63–79.

Capaldi, E. D., Sheffer, J. D., & Owens, J. (1991). Food deprivation and conditioned flavor preferences based on sweetened and unsweetened foods. *Animal Learning & Behavior, 19,* 361–368.

Capaldi, E. D., Sheffer, J. D., & Pulley, R. J. (1989). Contrast effects in flavor preference learning. *Quarterly Journal of Experimental Psychology, 41B*(3), 307–323.

Delamater, A. R., LoLordo, V. M., & Berridge, K. C. (1986). Control of fluid palatability by exteroceptive Pavlovian signals. *Journal of Experimental Psychology: Animal Behavior Processes, 12,* 143–152.

Deutsch, J. A., Molina, F., & Puerto, A. (1976). Conditioned taste aversion caused by palatable nontoxic nutrients. *Behavioral Biology, 16,* 161–174.

Domjan, M. (1980). Ingestional aversion learning: Unique and general processes. In J. S. Rosenblatt, R. A. Hinde, C. Beer, & M. C. Busnel (Eds.), *Advances in the study of behavior* (Vol. 11, pp 275–336). New York: Academic Press.

Drewnowski, A. (1988). Obesity and taste preferences for sweetness and fat. In G. A. Bray, J. LeBlanc, S. Inoue, & M. Suzuki (Eds.), *Diet and obesity* (pp. 153–161). Tokyo: Japan Scientific Societies Press; Basel: S. Karger.

Durlach, P. J., & Rescorla, R. A. (1980). Potentiation rather than overshadowing in flavor-aversion learning: An analysis in terms of within-compound associations. *Journal of Experimental Psychology: Animal Behavior Processes, 6,* 175–187.

Elizalde, G., & Sclafani, A. (1988). Starch-based conditioned flavor preferences in rats: Influence of taste, calories and CS–US delay. *Appetite, 11,* 179–200.

Fanselow, M., & Birk, J. (1982). Flavor–flavor associations induce hedonic shifts in taste preference. *Animal Learning & Behavior, 10,* 223–228.

Flaherty, C. F., & Checke, S. (1982). Anticipation of incentive gain. *Animal Learning & Behavior, 10,* 177–182.

Garb, J. L., & Stunkard, A. J. (1974). Taste aversions in man. *American Journal of Psychiatry, 131,* 1204–1207.

Garcia, J. (1989). Food for Tolman: Cognition and cathexis in concert. In T. Archer & L.-G. Nilsson (Eds.), *Aversion, avoidance and anxiety: Perspectives on aversively motivated behavior* (pp. 45–85). Hillsdale, NJ: Erlbaum.

Green, K. F., & Garcia, J. (1971). Recuperation from illness: Flavor enhancement in rats. *Science, 193,* 749–759.

Grill, H. J., & Norgren, R. (1978). The taste reactivity test II. Mimetic response to gustatory stimuli in neurologically normal rats. *Brain Research, 143,* 263–279.

Holman, E. W. (1975). Immediate and delayed reinforcers for flavor preferences in rats. *Animal Learning & Behavior, 6,* 91–100.

Konorski, J. (1967). *Integrative activity of the brain.* Chicago: University of Chicago Press.

Lavin, M. J. (1976). The establishment of flavor–flavor associations using a sensory preconditioning training procedure. *Learning and Motivation, 7,* 173–183.

Le Magnen, J. (1955). La satiété induite par les stimuli sucres chez le rat blanc [Satiety induced by sugar stimuli in the white rat]. *Comptes Rendus des Séances de la Société de Biologie,* Paris, *149,* 1339–1342.

Lepkovsky, S. (1977). The role of the chemical senses in nutrition. In M. R. Kare & O. Maller (Eds.), *The Chemical Senses and Nutrition* (pp. 413–428). New York: Academic Press.

Lipsitt, L. P., & Behl, G. (1990). Taste-mediated differences in the sucking behavior of human newborns. In E. D. Capaldi & T. L. Powley (Eds.), *Taste, experience, and feeding* (pp. 75–93). Washington, DC: American Psychological Association.

Logue, A. W. (1979). Taste aversion and the generality of the laws of learning. *Psychological Bulletin, 86,* 276–296.

Lucas, G. A., & Timberlake, W. (1992). Negative anticipatory contrast and preference conditioning: Flavor cues support preference conditioning while environmental cues support contrast. *Journal of Experimental Psychology: Animal Behavior Processes, 18,* 34–40.

Mackintosh, N. J. (1974). *The psychology of animal learning.* New York: Academic Press.

Mehiel, R. & Bolles, R. C. (1988). Learned flavor preferences based on calories are independent of initial hedonic value. *Animal Learning & Behavior, 16,* 383–387.

Pliner, P. (1982). The effects of mere exposure on liking for edible substances. *Appetite, 3,* 283–290.

Powley, T. L. (1977). The ventromedial syndrome, satiety, and a cephalic phase hypothesis. *Psychological Review, 84,* 89–126.

Rescorla, R. A., & Cunningham, C. L. (1978). Within-compound flavor associations. *Journal of Experimental Psychology: Animal Behavior Processes, 4,* 267–275.

Revusky, S. H. (1967). Hunger level during food consumption: Effects on subsequent preference. *Psychonomic Science, 7,* 109–110.

Revusky, S., & Garcia, J. (1970). Learned associations over long delays. In G. H. Bower (Ed.), *The psychology of learning and motivation: Advances in research and theory,* (Vol. 4, pp. 1–84). New York: Academic Press.

Revusky, S. H., Smith, M. H., Jr., & Chalmers, D. V. (1971). Flavor preference: Effects of ingestion-contingent intravenous saline or glucose. *Physiology & Behavior, 6,* 341–343.

Rozin, P. (1976). The selection of food by rats, humans and other animals. In J. Rosenblatt, R. A. Hinde, C. Beer, & E. Shaw (Eds.), *Advances in the Study of Behavior* (Vol. 6, pp. 21–76). New York: Academic Press.

Rozin, P. (1986). One-trial acquired likes and dislikes in humans: Disgust as a US, food predominance, and negative learning predominance. *Learning and Motivation, 17,* 180–189.

Rozin, P., & Kalat, J. W. (1971). Specific hungers and poison avoidance as adaptive specializations of learning. *Psychological Review, 78,* 459–486.

Sclafani, A. (1987). Carbohydrate taste, appetite, and obesity: An overview. *Neuroscience & Biobehavioral Reviews, 11,* 131–153.

Sclafani, A. (1990). Nutritionally based learned flavor preferences in rats. In E. D. Capaldi & T. L. Powley (Eds.), *Taste, experience and feeding* (pp. 139–156). Washington, DC: American Psychological Association.

Simbayi, L. C., Boakes, R. A., & Burton, M. J. (1986). Can rats learn to associate a flavour with the delayed delivery of food? *Appetite, 7,* 41–53.

Tordoff, M. G., & Friedman, M. I. (1989). Drinking saccharin increases food intake and preference. IV. Cephalic phase and metabolic factors. *Appetite, 12,* 37–56.

Weingarten, H. (1983). Conditioned cues elicit eating in sated rats: A role for learning in meal initiation. *Science, 220,* 431–433.

Zahorik, D. M., & Maier, S. F. (1972). Appetitive conditioning with recovery from thaimine deficiency as the unconditional stimulus. In M. E. P. Seligman & J. L. Hager (Eds.), *Biological boundaries of learning.* New York: Appleton-Century-Crofts.

Zellner, D. A., Rozin, P., Aron, M., & Kulish, D. (1983). Conditioned enhancement of human's liking for flavors by pairing with sweetness. *Learning & Motivation, 14,* 338–350.

CLASSICAL CONDITIONING AS AN ADAPTIVE SPECIALIZATION: A COMPUTATIONAL MODEL

C. R. Gallistel

I. Introduction

An adaptive specialization of learning is a mechanism that has evolved to extract a particular kind of information from a restricted domain of the animal's experience. Imprinting (Lorenz, 1937), bait shyness (Garcia & Koelling, 1966; Rozin & Kalat, 1971), song learning in birds (Marler, 1991), the learning of the sun's azimuthal movement in bees (Gould, 1984), the learning of the center of rotation of the night sky in migratory birds (Emlen, 1969), and learning to localize sound sources relative to the optical axis in the maturing barn owl (Knudsen & Knudsen, 1990) are examples. As with adaptive specializations in other physiological domains, the design of the organ or process reflects the characteristics of the domain for which it is specialized. The correspondence between the structure of the organ or process and the peculiarities of the domain adapts it to its natural function, while rendering it ill adapted to any other function. The eye is an admirable optical instrument, but a poor ear.

Learning theorists took from the empiricist philosophy of mind the conviction that there is a basic learning process that is not adaptively specialized. Classical conditioning, an experimental procedure which pairs an initially neutral stimulus called the conditioned stimulus (CS) with a motivationally significant stimulus such as food or painful shock to the feet (called the unconditioned stimulus, US) and records the animal's increasing tendency to respond to the CS in a manner that anticipates the US, has been studied for close to a century in the conviction that this experimental paradigm will reveal the laws of association formation. The association forming process has long been regarded as the foundation of higher forms of learning (Gluck & Thompson, 1987; Hawkins & Kandel, 1984; Locke, 1690; Pavlov, 1928).

What is absent from discussions of associative learning is a specification of the domain for which the learning process is specialized. The marginal status that textbooks accord the learning that occurs in domains whose structure does not conform to the CS–US structure of the classical conditioning paradigm reflects the widespread conviction that this paradigm captures the prespecialization essence of learning. Recently, in a discussion of behavioral paradigms suitable for investigating the cellular basis of learning, a colleague of mine argued that spatial learning tasks were poorly understood because it was difficult to say what the CS was. His argument assumes that there is such a thing as an unspecialized learning process dependent on some kind of CS–US pairing. If, however, the learning that occurs in classical conditioning reflects the operation of a process specialized for a domain fundamentally different from the spatial domain, then his argument is analogous to the argument that hearing is a poorly understood perceptual process because it is difficult to say what the image is.

In classical conditioning, as in vision, one must begin by describing the properties of the domain within which the process operates. In vision, the domain is optics. The prepsychological aspect of the domain—what must be understood before one can undertake an investigation of the psychology of vision—is the physics of light. In classical conditioning, the domain is multivariate, nonstationary time series. The prepsychological aspect of the problem is the mathematics of time series analysis.

In a time series, the value of a variable is probabilistically related to its past values and/or to the present or past values of other variables. If the delivery of a pellet of food predicts another such delivery after some interval (as in a fixed interval schedule of reinforcement), we have an instance of a univariate time series—the times of past fluctuations in the value of a variable predict the times of future fluctuations in the same variable. If the probability that food will be delivered increases when a key is illuminated (as in autoshaping), we have an instance of a bivariate time series—fluctuations in one variable (the key light) predict fluctuations in another (food). If the experimental apparatus (the background) predicts a certain number of mildly painful shocks per minute and the presence of a transient tone predicts an additional number of shocks per minute, as in some conditions of Rescorla's (1968) background conditioning experiment, we have an instance of a multivariate time series—fluctuations in two or more variables predict fluctuations in a third variable. If the illumination of the key predicts food delivery during one phase of an experiment but ceases to do so in a subsequent phase (as in experimental extinction), we have an instance of a nonstationary bivariate time series—the predictive relation between two variables changes over time.

Optics is a complex and subtle domain, and the more one studies the eye and the neural processing of visual input, the more one is impressed with the complexity, subtlety, and particularity of the visual system's adaptation to the peculiarities of this domain. Peterhans and von der Heydt (1991, p. 117) write,

> It is important to note that the mechanisms present in visual cortex have evolved to a high degree of sophistication, incorporating a great deal of information about the environment, optical imaging and statistical correlations in images. This implicit knowledge makes the action of these mechanisms appear to be cognitive.

Multivariate, nonstationary time series also constitute a complex and subtle domain. Over the past quarter century, the experimental study of the classical conditioning process has revealed adaptations to the peculiarities of this domain that rival in their complexity and subtlety the adaptations we see in the visual system (Rescorla, 1988). Thus, the classical conditioning process, like the visual process, "appears to be cognitive." (The distinction between a process that merely appears to be cognitive and one that really is cognitive is perhaps best left to the metaphysicians.)

These same experiments—the experiments that make classical conditioning appear to be cognitive—have revealed deep and, I believe, intractable inadequacies in associative theory. Today, associative theories of learning are in the peculiar position of not being able to account for the results from the experimental paradigm that was conceived in order to reveal the laws of association formation. The shortcomings of the associative concept are many, obvious, and long recognized, but it lingers on for want of a more powerful explanatory framework. At the root of its shortcomings is the assumption of an unspecialized learning process whose design does not reflect the peculiar demands of a particular domain of function. The associative conceptual framework does not recognize the incorporation of implicit knowledge into the structure of the mechanisms that make associative learning possible.

In this article I analyze the results of some modern classical conditioning experiments from the perspective of a computational model based on the assumption that the underlying learning process is specifically adapted to the domain of multivariate, nonstationary time series. I focus particularly on the quantitative results from experiments on the effects of partial reinforcement on the rate of acquisition and extinction, because the other predictions of the model have been spelled out in some detail in Gallistel (1990), and because associative models are conspicuously unsuccessful at making quantitative predictions in this area. The model to be discussed is in the tradition of Hull (1952), Estes (1950), Bush and Mosteller (1951), and Rescorla and Wagner (1972), Pearce and Hall (1980), Gibbon and Balsam (1981), and Sutton and Barto (1981) in that it gives a mathematical characterization of the learning process from which one can derive the results of conditioning experiments. It is unlike these model in that it is not in the associative tradition. The model replaces the associative explanatory framework with a framework that treats the conditioning process as a computational mechanism adapted through evolution to the peculiarities of one domain—a mechanism that solves one and only one of the several fundamentally distinct learning problems that confront mobile, multicellular organisms.

II. Preliminaries

In most classical conditioning experiments, the US is brief, it does not vary in its magnitude or intensity from one presentation to the next, and it occurs in the presence of the CS (commonly at the moment of US termination). The model of the conditioning process to be presented here is only valid for experiments in which these conditions are satisfied, because the model assumes that the animal represents US occurrences as the result of Poisson rate processes. A Poisson rate process is a random process that generates point events (events of fixed magnitude and negligible duration) at an average number of events per unit of time, called the event rate. The process is random in that the probability that an event will occur in any short interval is independent of the time that has elapsed since the last event. The model assumes that what an animal learns in a classical conditioning experiment is the rate of US occurrence to be expected in the presence of a CS.

In the most common kind of conditioning experiment, the US occurs while the CS is present. For example, in an autoshaping experiment with pigeons (e.g., Gibbon, Baldock, Locurto, Gold, & Terrace, 1977), the key in the wall of the chamber is illuminated (CS onset) and some seconds thereafter the feeding hopper opens (US onset), with the illumination on the key extinguishing at the moment the hopper opens (CS offset). (This is called autoshaping because when the key light and the opening of the food hopper are paired in this manner, the pigeon learns to peck the key even when its pecking has no effect on food delivery.) By contrast, in so-called

also call α the liberalism/conservatism parameter, since its value determines how conservative the animal is in its willingness to act on an uncertain estimate. The lower α is, the less disposed the animal is to act in the face of uncertainty. The other parameter, s, which might be called the decisiveness parameter, determines how steeply confidence increases as p approaches the critical value α.

The value of α varies from experimental task to experimental task, reflecting the subjective payoff matrix for that task—the perceived costs and benefits of acting or not acting given that the CS does or does not affect the rate of US occurrence. If the benefit from responding to the CS given that it does affect the rate of US occurrence is perceived to be modest and the cost of not responding negligible, while the cost of responding given that the CS has no effect is perceived to be greater, then the animal will be conservative. The value of α will be low, so the animal will not respond to the CS until the null hypothesis has become very unlikely. The payoff matrix just described, which is shown in Fig. 1A, might arise in a food foraging situation, where the cost of traveling to a distant source of food was high. The animal would want the certainty that food was to be found more frequently there than in nearby regions to be high so as to offset the certain cost of the journey. The payoff matrix in Fig. 1A is said to be weighted against action.

In a payoff matrix weighted in favor of action, the costs of not responding when the CS did affect the US might be high, while the cost of responding when it did not were relatively much less. Such a matrix is shown in Fig. 1B. It is characteristic of tasks involving low-cost responses that ward off potentially very damaging threats. This state of affairs in-

	A			**B**	
	Act	Don't		Act	Don't
CS does affect US	+1	0		0	-10
CS does not affect US	-2	0		-1	0
TOTALS:	-2	-1	+0	+1	-11	-1	-10	0

Fig. 1. Pay-off matrices. A, A matrix weighted against action (because the total in the "Act" column minus the total in the "Don't [Act]" column is negative) that does not encourage decisiveness (because the difference between the totals on the diagonals, -2 and 1, is small). B, A matrix weighted in favor of action that promotes decisiveness. (-11 and 0 are the diagonal totals).

duces a high value of α, so the animal responds to the CS even when the probability that it has no effect on the rate of US occurrence is high. A high α is characteristic of an animal that we would call jumpy or rash.

The decisiveness parameter s determines how steeply the confidence function increases as p sinks toward and then below α. When s is high, confidence—hence the tendency to respond to the CS—remains low until p has sunk to very near the critical value, then it increases rapidly to near certainty as p sinks below α. Thus, the transition from not responding to the CS to responding vigorously is abrupt in an animal with a high s. When s is low, confidence increases more gradually as p drops toward and then below the critical value, so that the transition from not responding to responding is more gradual. The value of s will be high when the stakes are high, that is, when the consequences of either action or inaction or both are sizable. Under these conditions, the difference between the totals along the diagonals of the payoff matrix is large.

The model assumes that the shape of the normalized learning curve— the magnitude, probability, or rate of responding expressed as a fraction of the asymptotic magnitude, probability, or rate and plotted over successive conditioning trials—is determined by the confidence function. On the other hand, the height of the unnormalized learning curve, the difference between the animal's preconditioning responding to the CS and its asymptotic conditioned response, is determined by the magnitude of $\Delta\lambda$, the increment or decrement in the rate of US occurrence predicted by the onset of the CS. The magnitude of the change in US rate predicted by a CS determines the value of a scaling factor $k(\Delta\lambda)$ which specifies the asymptotic increment in the strength, probability, or frequency of the conditioned response. These three parameters—the liberalism/conservatism parameter α, the decisiveness parameter s, and the scaling factor $k(\Delta\lambda)$—are all characteristics of the decision or performance process rather than of the learning process. Their values may be estimated from the experimentally obtained learning curves, because the arguments p and $\Delta\lambda$ are objective parameters of the training protocols.

B.   The Absence of Parameters in the Learning Model

In the model to be presented, the values of the parameters of the decision or performance process, which translates what is learned into what is experimentally observed, are not confounded with the values of parameters of the learning process itself, because the learning process has no parameters. The absence of parameters in the model of the learning process contrasts with associative learning models, which commonly have many parameters. The values of parameters of the associative learning process are difficult to estimate because they are confounded with parameters of the performance process, which is not itself formalized. Also, in associative models, the values of learning parameters are themselves a function of the events. For example, the value of the associability parameter in the model of Rescorla and Wagner (1972), which determines how rapidly the associative bond between the CS and US grows when a US occurs or declines when a US fails to occur, is itself a function of whether the US occurs or not. The associability parameter is assumed to be higher when the US occurs than when it fails to occur. In other contemporary models, the value of the associability parameter is itself a function of the training experience (Mackintosh, 1975; Pearce & Hall, 1980). There has been little attempt to estimate the values of the many free parameters in these models, despite the fact that most of their predictions depend strongly on the values assumed for these parameters.

Their numerous parameters, with values that vary as functions of the events, make associative models computationally complex. Their predictions cannot in general be derived from closed form expressions (that is, the predictions cannot be derived algebraically); they must be derived from computer simulations using numerical (iterative) methods. The predictions of the model to be described here are derived algebraically. The model to be described has been implemented as an Excel™ spreadsheet. The implementation is described in detail in Gallistel (in press), so that it can be recreated on other spreadsheets that do matrix operations. The quantitative results in this paper were calculated using the spreadsheet implementation.

The spreadsheet, which may be obtained by writing to the author, permits those without training in algebra to derive from the model the results it predicts for novel training protocols—the predicted results of experiments not yet performed. It also allows scrutiny of the intermediate stages of computation, facilitating an understanding of why the model predicts what it predicts. Because the model is an analytic model, it does not have the opacity problems that arise with the most complex modern associative models—neural net models. These models are often opaque in the sense that when they succeed in predicting some result, it is not clear why or how they succeeded (McCloskey, 1991).

C.   Training Protocols

The model takes as input the experimental protocols, the times at which the conditioning events occur. An event is the onset or offset of a CS or the occurrence of a US. Since the US is treated as a point event, its onsets and offsets coincide. Onset–offset protocols are an unusual format in which to present conditioning experiments, although they are related to the commonly used schematic timelines format for showing graphically the temporal relations between CSs and USs. The more common format in which to present conditioning experiments is in terms of the types and sequence of trials the animal experiences. This form is natural for associative theories, which are built around the notion of a trial, but not for the current model, where the notion of a trial plays no role. The protocol form of presentation emphasizes the time-series nature of the data the animal is given. More importantly, it specifies the intervals that elapse between CS offsets and CS onsets (the intertrial intervals). These intervals are of no consequence in associative theories, but they are of fundamental importance in the current model. In associative models, when nothing happens the animal learns nothing; while in the present model, when nothing happens the animal learns that nothing has happened. This learning becomes relevant as soon as something does happen. If we focus on the trials—the intervals when something happens—we miss this essential aspect of the situation— the intervals when nothing happens.

The above comments on associative models do not apply to the model of Gibbon and Balsam (1981), which is like the present model in that their associations "spread in time" are really rate estimates. However, they are not treated as such, and the inferential statistics of rate estimation and stationarity testing play no role in the Gibbon and Balsam model. Their model still takes the trial as a basic unit of analysis, which is antithetical to the assumption that what is driving conditioning are the rates of US occurrences, not the probability of US occurrence.

III. The Model

In associative models of conditioning, it is assumed that the association-forming process is a learning primitive, on which foundation more elaborate forms of learning build. In the present model, the conditioning process is a higher-order learning process. It makes use of several more elementary learning capacities, namely, the capacity to learn the time at which an event occurs (see Gallistel, 1990, chap. 8 for a review of relevant experimental data), the capacity to measure or compute the duration of a stimulus (Church, 1984), the capacity to accumulate over successive occurrences of the stimulus the total amount of time it has been present (Roberts & Church, 1978), and the capacity to count the number of occurrences of a US (Gallistel, 1990, chap. 10; Meck, Church, & Gibbon, 1985). The recording of times of occurrence and the accumulation of temporal intervals go on whether USs occur or not. Thus, what the animal learns when nothing happens (that is, when no USs occur) are the times at which CSs came on and went off, their cumulative durations, and the cumulative durations of pairwise combinations of CSs. The values of these cumulative durations and counts enable it to estimate the conditional rates of US occurrence when USs do occur and to detect changes in the rate of US occurrence.

The experimental apparatus in which the animal is trained is treated as a CS, hereafter designated CS_1 or the background. When the animal is in the experimental box for half an hour, during which time a 12-sec tone sounds five times for a cumulative tone duration of 1 min, the animal accumulates three temporal totals—one proportionate to the 30 min the box (background) has been present, one proportionate to the 1 min the tone has been on, and one proportionate to the 1 min the tone and background have been jointly present. The animal also accumulates counts of the number of times the US has occurred in the presence of each CS. Thus, when a US occurs while the tone is on, this increments the counter for CS_2 (the tone) and the counter for CS_1 (the background), which is of course also present.

A. PRINCIPLES IMPLICIT IN THE COMPUTATION OF THE CONDITIONAL RATES

The computation of the rates of US occurrence to be ascribed to each CS (the rate of US occurrence conditional on the presence of a given CS) depends solely on the accumulated temporal and numerical totals. The computation is informed by three principles. These principles, which are implicit in the structure of the computation, are part of what adapts this learning mechanism to the domain in which it functions. They are like the lens of the eye; they only make sense in the context of a particular problem. One interest of this model is that it illustrates the concept of an implicit principle in a computational structure. The computations make no explicit reference to the principles that inform them. They are simply structured in such a way as to insure conformity to the principles. Similarly, the eye does not operate by explicit reference to the principles of optics, but those principles are everywhere implicit in its structure.

The first principle is *presumed or provisional additivity:* when CSs are present simultaneously, the rate of US occurrence is equal to the sum of the rates that would be observed in the presence of each CS alone. The second principle is *presumed or provisional stationarity:* the effect of a CS on the rate of US occurrence has been constant over the interval during which the temporal and numerical totals accumulated. The third principle is *predictor minimization:* when there is more than one way to ascribe rates to the various CSs consistent with the first two principles, the ascription that minimizes the number of predictors (the number of CSs with a non-zero effect on the rate of US occurrence) is preferable.

The implicit additivity and stationarity assumptions explain the blocking phenomenon. In blocking, one CS is paired with the US during an initial phase of conditioning, then, during a second phase, a second CS is presented along with the initial CS (and the US). No matter how many times the second CS and the US are thus paired, the presence of the first (previously conditioned) CS seemingly blocks the formation of an association between the second CS and the US (Kamin, 1967). The animal never learns to respond to the second CS as if it predicted the occurrence of the US. In the present model, the effect of the first CS on the rate of US occurrence is taken to be the same throughout the first and second phases (stationarity), and when the rate of US occurrence observed in the presence of the first CS alone is subtracted from the rate observed when both CSs are present, there are no supernumerary USs left for the second CS to account for (additivity). Hence, no effect on the rate of US occurrence is imputed to the second CS.

The implicit stationarity assumption is provisional in the sense that it is taken for granted in the computation of rate estimates, but when the rates have been computed, the system makes a retrospective computation that tests for stationarity. The system computes whether the number of USs observed since each remembered event in the series of training events is improbably discrepant from the number expected given the rate estimate based on the entire sequence of training experiences. Thus, for example, if the initial conditioning phase is followed by an extinction phase, the number of USs observed since the onset of extinction (0) will be much less than the number expected over that interval given a single rate estimate based on a lumping together of the data from the conditioning and extinction phases. If this computation shows that the data are not consistent with the stationarity assumption, then the time series is truncated at the time that the rate predicted by a given CS changed. (This time, for example the onset of extinction, is picked out by the stationarity computation.) The current estimate for the rate to be expected in the presence of a CS is then based only on the observations made after the point of truncation.

"Unique cue" or configural conditioning experiments demonstrate that rats and pigeons can learn nonadditive effects of CSs on rates of US occurrence. If, for example, the opening of the food hopper in a pigeon autoshaping experiment always follows the illumination of the upper half of the response key with a blue light and the opening also always follows the illumination of the lower half with diagonal stripes, but it never follows when the blue light on the upper half and the diagonal stripes on the lower half appear together, the pigeon eventually learns to peck at the key whenever either the blue light or the diagonal stripes are present, but not when they both are. The experiments of Rescorla (1972) and Rescorla, Grau, and Durlach (1985) indicate that these results are most readily explained by the assumption that the combination of the two CSs creates a third CS. The unique cue thus created—the cue that is present only when both of the other two CSs are present—can itself enter into conditioning, as if it were an ordinary CS. (The unique cue is present in addition to, not in lieu of, its constituents.) The model provides for nonadditivity in the manner suggested by the unique cue idea. It considers two CSs present together to be three concurrent CSs, one of which is the combination CS. If the data are consistent with an additive model for the effects of the elementary CSs, then the matrix computation of the rates of US occurrence to be ascribed to each CS ascribes a 0 rate to the unique or configural cue. But when the data are not consistent with an additive effects model, it ascribes an influence on rate to the unique cue, as well as to its constituents. In the above example, the unique cue is ascribed a negative (reductive) effect on the rate of US occurrence equal to the sum of the positive effects ascribed to the two elementary CSs.

The computational structures that test the stationarity of the time series and that treat the two CS configurations as a potential CS are another aspect of the knowledge of the world that is built into the structure of the learning mechanism, making it specifically adapted to a particular learning function. The time series with which animals are confronted in the natural world are often not stationary, and the effects of many variables often do not combine additively. Nonadditivity and nonstationarity are intrinsic to the domain in which the process involved in classical conditioning must operate.

Although the extinction of a conditioned response following repeated nonreinforcement has been an important phenomenon in classical conditioning since Pavlov's seminal work, associative models have difficulty dealing with it. Both Pavlov (1928, chaps. 19–22) and Hull (1943, chap. 16) grappled with the theoretical perplexities occasioned by this phenomenon. The problem is twofold: (1) Many associative models, including those of Hull and Pavlov, contain no computational structure that elaborates an expectation to which input is compared; hence, they have no straightforward way of explaining how the failure of a stimulus (the US) to occur can set a physiological process in motion (the weakening of an excitatory association or the strengthening of an inhibitory association). In common with modern neurophysiologically oriented theorists (Farley & Alkon,

1985; Gluck & Thompson, 1987; Hawkins & Kandel, 1984), Hull and Pavlov assumed that the association-forming process was triggered by the temporal pairing of stimulus-produced neural activities. But neural activity is initiated by stimulus energy acting on sensory receptors. How can the nonoccurrence of a stimulus give rise to neural activity? And if the nonoccurrence of a stimulus cannot give rise to neural activity, how can it set a learning process in motion (the weakening of an association or the formation of an inhibitory association)? (See Gleitman, Nachmias, & Neisser, 1954, for an analysis of the conceptual problems surrounding the Hullian explanation of extinction.) (2) In associative models, the system keeps no record of the sequence of events that generated the associations, so it cannot retrospectively compare data from portions of the sequence to expectations based on the entire sequence.

A given strength of association may be produced by a stable (stationary) pattern of CS–US pairing, or it may be a transitional value following a change in the training conditions. Compare, for example, the transitional associative strengths during extinction following continuous reinforcement to the more or less stable associative strengths generated by stationary partial reinforcement conditioning (Fig. 2). For the sake of illustration, assume that in the partial reinforcement condition the US occurs on aver-

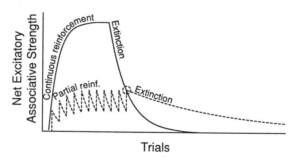

Trials

Fig. 2. The problem of distinguishing transitional from stable associative strengths. Continuous reinforcement produces stronger net excitatory associative strength than partial reinforcement does. At some point during extinction following continuous reinforcement, the net excitatory strength of the CS–US associations should equal that produced by continued partial reinforcement (circled point). If the partially reinforced association is no longer reinforced from this point on, the time course of this extinction does not coincide with the continued time course of the first extinction. Note that although the partial reinforcement training conditions are stationary from a statistical standpoint (until the onset of extinction), the net excitatory strength fluctuates, because, according to the associative analysis, the nonreinforced trials interpolated among the reinforced trials weaken net excitatory strength.

age on only one out of every ten occurrences of the CS. The net excitatory strength of the association(s) developed during continuously reinforced CS–US training is greater than the net excitatory strength of the association(s) that develop during partially reinforced conditioning, because, in the latter case, the numerous nonreinforced trials during conditioning weaken the excitatory association and/or increase the strength of a competing inhibitory association. During extinction following continuous reinforcement, the net excitatory strength declines toward zero. At some point in this decline, it must equal the net excitatory strength of the associations produced by continued partial reinforcement training. If we now begin the extinction of the partially reinforced CS–US association, the time course of that extinction should coincide with the continued time course of the extinction we are already tracing, because at this point the net excitatory strengths are the same. This principle is called pathway independence, because the path (training history) by which the associations came to have a given strength should have no effect on the course of subsequent learning. It is, however, well established that the time courses of the two extinction processes will not coincide. The partially reinforced association will take about 10 times as long to extinguish (Gibbon, Farrell, Locurto, Duncan, & Terrace, 1980).

B. THE TEMPORAL COEFFICIENT MATRIX

The assumptions that the rates of US occurrence predicted by different CSs are additive and that these conditional rates have been stationary over the period when the temporal and numerical totals accumulated makes the problem of computing the rates of US occurrence to be imputed to each CS an exercise in solving systems of simultaneous linear equations. Let λ_1 be the rate of US occurrence to be ascribed to the influence of CS_1, λ_2 the rate to be ascribed to the influence of CS_2, and so on. Algebraic analysis reveals that the coefficients of these unknown λ's in the equations that must be solved are simple, repetitive functions of the accumulated temporal totals. The coefficients are all of the form $T_{1,2}/T_1$, where $T_{1,2}$ is the accumulated time that CS_1 and CS_2 were on simultaneously and T_1 is the accumulated time that CS_1 was on.

The inhomogeneous terms in the equations (the terms on the right in the equations below) are the raw or uncorrected estimates of the rates of US occurrence. They are obtained by dividing the number of USs that occurred in the presence of a CS by the total time that CS was present. They are uncorrected estimates because they take no account of the simultaneous presence of other CSs. The corrected rate estimates are the λ's on the left (the unknowns). When 4 CSs are in play, the system of equations to be solved to obtain the corrected rate estimates is:

$$\lambda_1 + \frac{T_{1,2}}{T_1}\lambda_2 + \frac{T_{1,3}}{T_1}\lambda_3 + \frac{T_{1,4}}{T_1}\lambda_4 = \frac{N_1}{T_1},$$

$$\frac{T_{1,2}}{T_2}\lambda_1 + \lambda_2 + \frac{T_{2,3}}{T_2}\lambda_3 + \frac{T_{2,4}}{T_2}\lambda_4 = \frac{N_2}{T_2},$$

$$\frac{T_{1,3}}{T_3}\lambda_1 + \frac{T_{2,3}}{T_3}\lambda_2 + \lambda_3 + \frac{T_{3,4}}{T_3}\lambda_4 = \frac{N_3}{T_3},$$

$$\frac{T_{1,4}}{T_4}\lambda_1 + \frac{T_{2,4}}{T_4}\lambda_2 + \frac{T_{3,4}}{T_4}\lambda_3 + \lambda_4 = \frac{N_4}{T_4}.$$

In matrix algebra notation, the solution is $\boldsymbol{\lambda_c} = \boldsymbol{T}^{-1}\boldsymbol{\lambda_u}$, where $\boldsymbol{\lambda_c}$ is the vector of corrected rates (the set of values for the four unknowns, λ_1, λ_2, etc.), $\boldsymbol{\lambda_u}$ is the vector of uncorrected rates (the set of values on the right hand sides of the above equations, N_1/T_1, N_2/T_2, and so on), and $\boldsymbol{T}^{-1}$ is the inverse of the temporal coefficient matrix.

C.   Resolving Ambiguity

There are many experimental conditions in which the matrix computation does not yield a unique solution because it is inherently ambiguous whether the observed rates of US occurrence should be ascribed entirely to one CS, entirely to another, or apportioned between them. The simplest such situation is the overshadowing experiment in which two CSs, for example a tone and a light, are always presented together. It is inherently ambiguous whether the USs that occur in the presence of these two CSs do so entirely because of the tone, entirely because of the light, or partly because of the tone and partly because of the light. This ambiguity is immediately apparent in the matrix calculation because under these conditions the determinant of the matrix is zero, which means that the system of simultaneous equations has an infinite number of different solutions.

Ambiguity is a problem that a suitably adapted specialized processing system resolves by virtue of its innate structure. Visual input is often ambiguous, but the visual system resolves the ambiguities, because the rest of the brain wants answers, not agnostic shrugs. The systems that generate actions require an informational basis for those actions even when the data do not justify one answer rather than another. In a system that must act, a plausible answer about the state of the world is better than no answer. The learning process that deals with time series, like the visual system, has implicit principles that resolve ambiguities in favor of plausible answers. The learning model is so structured that it finds the solution that minimizes the number of CSs to which a nonzero effect on the rate of US occurrence is imputed.

The implicit principle underlying the computational structure that resolves inherently ambiguous time series is that minimizing the number of predictors minimizes the uncertainty associated with the estimates of the predicted rates. The uncertainty associated with an estimate of a Poisson rate is determined solely by the number of observations on which the estimate is based. The greater this n, the smaller the uncertainty. If an observed rate is apportioned among two predictors when it could be ascribed entirely to one or the other, then each of the two rate estimates is based on a smaller n (a prorated portion of the total number of US occurrences); hence, each estimate has a higher uncertainty associated with it. Thus, in minimizing the number of predictors, the system minimizes the uncertainty of the predictions.

At present, the model's principles for resolving ambiguity are incomplete in that it has no principled way of deciding which CS will overshadow which. This is known to be a function of several variables, including the intensities of the CSs (or more generally, if vaguely, their relative "salience") and the nature of the US.

D. Computing the Probability that the CS
   Has an Effect

The model assumes that in processing the training experience, the nervous system computes a value that plays the same role in the decision process leading to a conditioned response that the computed p value plays in the process of statistical hypothesis testing. From a statistical decision point of view, the problem confronting the animal is to decide whether the rate of US occurrence imputed to the combined effects of the always present background and another, transient CS is improbably greater than or less than the rate imputed to the background alone. The probability p that the difference between two independent estimates of rate λ_a and λ_b, based on observations of n_a and n_b occurrences during nonoverlapping intervals T_a and T_b, indicates a difference in the values of the underlying rate parameters is:

$$p\left\{F(2n_a, 2n_b) < \frac{n_a}{n_b}\frac{T_b}{T_a}\right\}.$$

When applied to the present situation, this formula becomes:

$$p \left\{ F(2n_{CS}, 2n_B) < \frac{\lambda_{CS} + \lambda_B}{\lambda_B} \right\},$$

where n_{CS} is the number of USs that occurred while the transient CS and the background were both present, n_B the number of USs that occurred when the background alone was present, λ_{CS} the estimated rate of US occurrence due to the influence of the transient CS, and λ_B the estimated rate of US occurrence due to the background.

In using this result in the model, one has to take into account that λ_{CS} may be negative; hence, the above formula for the value of the F statistic (the quotient at the extreme right within the braces) may yield an F that is negative or that is positive but significantly less than 1. Such eventualities cannot arise under more conventional circumstances where negative rates cannot exist. Thus, in applying this procedure one must add the absolute value of λ_{CS} to λ_B. The test is whether the estimated rate ascribed to the background (which is always positive) plus the absolute value of the rate ascribed to the CS is greater than the background rate alone—given the number of independent observations on which the two rate estimates are assumed to be based.

The degrees of freedom for the denominator and numerator are estimated by multiplying the rate estimates times the interval of observation on which they are based. The actual number of USs observed in this interval will often be different because other CSs will also have been present.

When no USs have been ascribed to the effects of the background alone, the model attributes one US to it, so that the rate of US occurrence due to the background alone is, in such cases, assumed to be 1/(total training time). This attribution reflects the implicit assumption that while no US has so far been observed that could be imputed to the background, one such will be observed in the next instant.[1] The assignment of one occurrence to the background sets the rate estimate for the background at the highest value consistent with the observations so far made, namely, that an interval equal to the duration of training has elapsed without the occurrence of a US imputable to the training apparatus.

---

[1] Without such an assumption, the rate estimate for the background alone is zero and the uncertainty of this estimate is undefined. One cannot therefore compute a likelihood for the hypothesis that a transient CS affects the rate of US occurrence.

E.   TESTING STATIONARITY

To test for stationarity, the model looks retrospectively at its record of the conditioning events. At each event time, it computes the number of USs one would have expected from the influence of that CS in the interval from the present back to the event. If the event occurred 20 min ago, and if during the past 20 min the transient CS has been present for 2 min, and if the rate of US occurrence attributed to the transient CS is 3/min, then the retrospectively accumulated expected number of USs for that CS at that event time is (3 USs/min)(2 min) = 6 USs. The model compares this expected number to the number of USs whose occurrence has in fact been ascribed to the CS since the event in question (the retrospectively accumulated number of ascribed USs).

The computation of the retrospectively accumulated ascribed USs is implemented in accord with the following principles: When a US occurs, credit for its occurrence must be prorated among the active, positive CSs in proportion to the relative rate estimates associated with them. An *active* CS is a CS that is present when the US occurs. A *positive* CS is one that has a positive effect on the rate of US occurrence. Similarly, when a US fails to occur due to the influence of one or more active, negative CSs, the failures to occur (the negative occurrences) must be prorated among the active, negative CSs. (*Negative* CS means a CS that is estimated to reduce the rate of US occurrence.)

Notice that the procedure for testing stationarity depends on the system's keeping a record of the training events—CS and US onset and offset times. It also depends on its computing expectations regarding how many USs should have been imputed to a given CS over a given subinterval of the time series. It is the absence of these features that make it difficult for associative models to explain what an animal learns when it experiences a nonstationarity, a change in the predictive relation between the CS and the US.

IV.   Derivations

A.   THE EFFECT OF THE DUTY CYCLE AND
PARTIAL REINFORCEMENT

1.   *Effect on Acquisition*

The rate at which the conditioned response develops during training and disappears during extinction is determined first by the animal's confidence that the CS does affect the rate of US occurrence and (in extinction) its confidence that the previously observed effect no longer obtains. Of secondary importance in most circumstances, but potentially important under some, is the absolute rate of US occurrence predicted by the CS. That is, within a broad range of rates of US occurrence, the animal will begin to respond to the CS as it reaches a certain level of confidence that the CS alters the rate of US occurrence. When, however, the rate of US occurrence strays outside these broad limits, the predicted rate itself may become an important determinant of whether the animal responds to the CS. The animal may be confident that the CS predicts a change in the rate of US occurrence, but the predicted rate may be so low that the animal has no interest in responding.

The rate estimate for the effect of a given CS and the animal's statistical confidence in the conclusion that the CS affects the rate of US occurrence are determined by the temporal and numerical totals that accumulate during training. In the case of simple conditioning, the CSs are the always present background (CS_1) and the transient CS (CS_2) hereafter often called simply *the* CS, in accord with common practice. In this case, the totals that determine the predictions of the model are T_1, the total time in the apparatus; T_2, the total time the CS has been on; N_1, the total number of USs that have occurred; and N_2, the number of USs that have occurred in the presence of the CS.

The temporal totals appear in the coefficients of the matrix that computes the corrected rate estimates. These coefficients are ratios of the form $T_{1,2}/T_1$. Hence, any manipulation that simply rescales the temporal totals (multiplies every total by a constant factor, the so-called scaling factor) leaves the temporal coefficient matrix unaltered, because the scaling factor appears in both the numerator and denominator of every coefficient.

The numerical totals appear in the uncorrected rate estimates, which are ratios of the form N_1/T_1. Any manipulation that increases the T's in the denominator by a constant factor without increasing the N's in the numerator reduces the corrected rate estimates by that same factor. Thus, scaling up all the temporal parameters in a conditioning protocol reduces all the rate estimates by the reciprocal of the temporal scaling factor.

Suppose an autoshaping experiment, such as the one conducted by Gibbon et al. (1977), in which the CS (the illumination of the key light) lasts 4 sec and the food occurs invariably at CS termination. The interval between CS onset and US onset is called either the CS–US interval or the interstimulus interval (ISI). Suppose further that there is a 24-sec intertrial interval (ITI)—the interval from the end of one trial (CS occurrence) to the beginning of the next. The duty cycle in this experiment is then:

$$(\text{ITI} + \text{ISI})/\text{ISI} = (24 + 4)/4 = 7.$$

Suppose now that we double the temporal parameters, making the CS 8 sec long and the ITI 48 sec long. At the end of any given number of trials, the temporal totals in the rescaled experiment will be twice what they were before, while the values of N will be the same as they were before. Thus, the rate of US occurrence ascribed to the influence of the key light will be half what it was. But so will the upper limit on the rate estimate for the background, which is $1/T_1$, the reciprocal of the total training time (total time in apparatus).

The confidence that the animal has that the CS affects the rate of US occurrence is determined by the value of the F statistic and by the total number of US occurrences attributed to the CS so far. The number of USs attributed to the CS is unaltered by the rescaling operation, because it is equal to the estimated rate of US occurrence, which is half its previous value, times the total duration of the CS, which is twice its previous value. The value of the F statistic is also unaltered, because it is a ratio of the rate estimates $(\lambda_{CS} + \lambda_B)/\lambda_B$; hence the scaling factor appears in both the numerator and the denominator. Therefore, insofar as the rate of US occurrence remains within that broad range for which the animal is willing to respond, scaling up the temporal parameters will have no effect on the rate of conditioning, assuming that the rate of conditioning is expressed in the conventional way as the increase in response strength per conditioning trial. This is the result that Gibbon et al. (1977) found in their study of the effect of trial and intertrial durations on autoshaping. Within broad limits, the rate of conditioning was the same regardless of the CS–US interval (ISI), so long as the ITI was scaled up or down along with the ISI, thereby keeping the duty cycle constant (Fig. 3).

Introducing a partial reinforcement schedule has the same effect as scaling up the temporal parameters. In the continuous reinforcement auto-shaping experiment used as an example above, at the end of 10 trials, the background has been present a total of 240 sec ($T_1 = 240$), the CS has been present a total of 40 sec ($T_2 = T_{1,2} = 40$ sec), and 10 USs have occurred, so that $N_1 = 10$ and $N_2 = 10$. Suppose that instead of continuous reinforcement, we used a $10:1$ partial reinforcement schedule—the US is paired with the CS on only a randomly chosen tenth of the trials. At the end of 100 trials, $T_1 = 2400$, $T_2 = T_{1,2} = 400$, $N_1 = 10$, and $N_2 = 10$, which is the same state of affairs that would obtain after 10 trials if we scaled up the temporal parameters by a factor of 10. It follows that the rate of conditioning during partial reinforcement should be constant provided we plot conditioning not as a function of the number of trials (CS occurrences) but rather as a function of the number of reinforcements (US occurrences). This is the result obtained by Gibbon et al. (1980) when they studied the effect of partial reinforcement schedules on the rate of autoshaping. If they

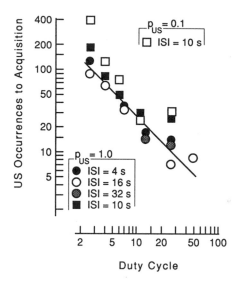

Fig. 3.   The median number of US occurrences prior to the pigeons' satisfying an acquisition criterion of at least 1 peck at the key on three out of four successive trials, as a function of the duty cycle. The circle data are from Gibbon et al. (1977, fig. 4). In their experiment, the ISI varied but there was always continuous reinforcement. The square data are from Gibbon et al. (1980, fig. 1). In their experiment, the ISI was always 10 sec, but the reinforcement schedule ranged from continuous (p_{US} = 1.0) to 1:10 (p_{US} = 0.1). The line has slope = −1.0, which is the slope predicted by the present model.

plotted trials (CS occurrences) to acquisition, partial reinforcement greatly retarded the development of the conditioned response, but if they plotted reinforcements (US occurrences) to acquisition, partial reinforcement had only a small and inconsistent effect on the rate of conditioning (Fig. 3).

The obverse of the above argument is that a manipulation of the temporal parameters that does not alter them all by the same multiplicative factor must affect the rate of conditioning when that rate is expressed in the conventional way as a function of trials (CS occurrences). More particularly, the larger the duty cycle, the more rapidly conditioning should proceed. Halving the CS–US interval (the ISI) without changing the ITI doubles the rate of US occurrence ascribed to the CS. Doubling the ITI without changing the ISI halves the upper limit on the rate attributable to the background after a given number of trials, without changing the rate ascribed to the CS. After either manipulation, a given F ratio is reached in half as many trials (US occurrences). The fewer the US occurrences required to reach a given F ratio, the lower the degrees of freedom for the numerator of the F ratio. However, the degrees of freedom for the numerator have negligible effect on the p value associated with a given F when they are more than 10. Thus, the model predicts that the number of trials to reach a fixed criterion of conditioning will be inversely proportionate to the duty cycle.

Another way of expressing this same conclusion is that the amount of training time required to reach a given level of conditioning is proportionate to the CS–US interval and independent of the duty cycle. Doubling the duty cycle by lengthening the intertrial interval halves the number of trials (cycles) to criterion; hence, training time to criterion does not vary as a function of the intertrial interval.

Figure 3 plots the median number of US occurrences prior to pigeons' satisfying an acquisition criterion, as a function of the duty cycle, on log–log coordinates. The data are from the experiments of Gibbon et al. (1977) and Gibbon et al. (1980). They cover a wide range of values for both the CS–US interval (ISI) and the reinforcement schedule in an autoshaping paradigm. As just noted, the present model predicts that it is the number of US occurrences (not trials, i.e., CS occurrences) and the duty cycle that determine the rate of conditioning. It further predicts that trials to acquisition should vary inversely with the duty cycle. Thus, it predicts a slope of -1.0 for the log of US occurrences (to criterion) versus the log of the duty cycle. As is apparent in Fig. 3, the predictions of the model regarding the effects of partial reinforcement and the duty cycle on the rate of conditioning are in reasonable quantitative agreement with the experimentally obtained results, at least for autoshaping in the pigeon, which is the conditioning paradigm from which we have the best data on the effects of these variables.

The agreement between theory and data seen in Fig. 3 is perhaps somewhat more remarkable in that these quantitative predictions do not depend on the values of any free parameters. The prediction that the number of US occurrences required to produce a given level of conditioning should vary inversely with the duty cycle is inherent in the basic premises of the model.

2. Effect on Extinction

In the model, the animal brain is assumed to look back continually over the events of its training experience. For each event, it computes the number of US occurrences that would have been expected from the influence of a given CS over the interval between the present and the time of the past event. It compares this to the number of US occurrences imputed to the influence of the CS over the same interval. During extinction, when US occurrences cease, the peak discrepancy between the expected and imputed number of USs grows as the time in extinction increases. This peak discrepancy always coincides with the time at which extinction commenced. To estimate how likely the discrepancies are, the brain is assumed to divide each discrepancy by the total number of USs imputed to the CS over the entire training interval. This quotient is the normalized discrepancy. The normalized discrepancy, also called the Kolmogorov-Smirnov statistic, together with its denominator n, determines the likelihood of having observed a discrepancy that great or greater if the CS–US relation were stationary throughout training.

In the Gibbon et al. (1980) experiment on the acquisition and extinction of autoshaped key pecking in pigeons as a function of the duty cycle and the schedule of reinforcement, each acquisition session lasted until the bird had received 25 reinforcements (CS–US pairings) and each extinction session lasted until the bird had missed 25 reinforcements (25 scheduled USs had been omitted). Thus, for birds on a duty cycle of 26 with a reinforcement schedule of 10 : 1 (10 CS occurrences on average for each US occurrence), a session lasted more than 100 times longer than a session for birds on a duty cycle of 2.5 with a 1 : 1 reinforcement schedule. The birds were trained for 15 sessions after the session in which they met the acquisition criterion (pecking on three out of four successive trials) and then exposed to 10 sessions of extinction. The birds on a 2.5 duty cycle with a 1 : 1 reinforcement schedule took a median of somewhat more than 175 trials to meet the acquisition criterion. Thus, after 15 more sessions (375 trials), such a bird would have been exposed to about 575 trials (and 575 US occurrences) at the beginning of extinction. Figure 4 plots the normalized discrepancy function for these birds at the end of the first extinction session (dashed line) and at the end of the second session (solid line). It also indicates the levels that the peak of this function would have to

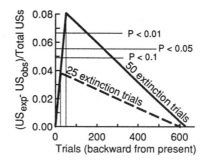

Fig. 4. The normalized discrepancy function at end of the first (dashed line) and second (solid line) sessions of extinction for a bird in which extinction began after 575 continuously reinforced autoshaping trials. The abscissa is the cumulative number of trials (CS occurrences) looking backward from the most recent trial. The vertical hairlines indicate the trials on which the functions peak. The horizontal lines give critical values of the Kolmogorov-Smirnov statistic.

attain for the associated likelihood to exceed the standard critical values for rejecting the null hypothesis.

At the end of the first extinction session, the peak of the normalized discrepancy function occurs 25 trials ago, but it does not approach a statistically improbable value. Therefore, one would not expect much decline in the strength of the conditioned response during this session and indeed, Gibbon et al. (1980) observed that the median rate of pecking the key during this first session was slightly greater than normal (Fig. 5, top panel, top filled circle). By the end of the second session, however, the peak of the normalized discrepancy function, which now occurs 50 trials before the most recent trial, substantially exceeds the critical value for $p < .01$, meaning that the odds are better than 100 : 1 against the hypothesis that the discrepancies now observed have arisen by chance. Therefore

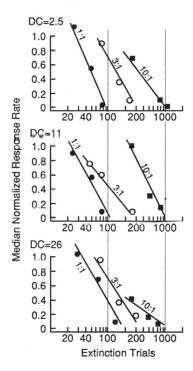

Fig. 5. Median normalized response rate (response rate in a session divided by the mean of the last three conditioning sessions) as a function of the number of extinction trials for birds on different duty cycles (panels) and reinforcement schedules (regression lines within panels). Data are from Gibbon et al. (1980, fig. 4), showing in each case the results from the first three extinction sessions (= first 75 omitted USs). The regression lines were computed by Gibbon et al. for the data from the first four sessions.

one would expect a substantial decline in the rate of responding during the second session, which is what Gibbon et al. found (middle filled circle in top panel of Fig. 5). Also, one would expect very little responding in the third and subsequent sessions, which is again in accord with the results.

The duty cycle, which has a profound effect on the number of trials to reach an acquisition criterion, should have no effect on the number of trials to an extinction criterion. The course of extinction is determined by the peak normalized discrepancy between observed and expected US occurrences, and the duty cycle has no effect on this quantity. Thus, the result in the top panel of Fig. 5, which was obtained with a duty cycle of 2.5, should also be obtained at much greater duty cycles, as in fact it was (middle and bottom panels of Fig. 5).

Partial reinforcement, on the other hand, should have the same effect on the rate of extinction as it does on the rate of acquisition. Extinction—expressed as a function of the number of trials (CS occurrences)—should be prolonged in proportion to the thinning of the reinforcement schedule. Extinction after a 10:1 training schedule should take 10 times as many trials as after a 1:1 training schedule, because it takes 10 times as many trials to reach the same value for the peak normalized discrepancy. Put another way, if extinction is plotted as a function of the number of expected reinforcers omitted rather than as a function of trials, the rate of extinction should be the same for different schedules of reinforcement. This was approximately what Gibbon et al. (1980) found. As already noted, their session lengths were determined not by the number of trials but by the number of expected reinforcers. As can be seen in Fig. 5, roughly the same session-by-session pattern of extinction was seen in the birds trained on the 3:1 and 10:1 partial reinforcement schedules as in the birds given continuous reinforcement. This means, of course, that when extinction is plotted as a function of trials, it takes much longer following partial reinforcement. Instead of the 100 trials required for the extinction of key pecking following continuous reinforcement, it takes 1000 trials following a schedule in which only every 10th CS occurrence is, on average, paired with a US occurrence.

These predictions regarding the rate of extinction following various schedules of reinforcement do not depend on the values of free parameters in the model. The prediction regarding the number of USs that must be omitted before the conditioned response extinguishes do depend somewhat on what one assumes the birds' criteria for statistical improbability to be, but as Fig. 4 shows, the session-by-session pattern observed by Gibbon et al. (1980) would be predicted over a very wide range of assumed values for this parameter (from $p \gg .1$ to $p \ll .01$).

The above discussion has been couched in terms of trials because that is how experiments in classical conditioning are traditionally conceptualized. It must be emphasized, however, that the notion of a trial plays no role in the current model, whereas it plays a fundamental role in associative models. At the conclusion of their paper on the effects of partial reinforcement, Gibbon et al. (1980) write, "Evidently, subjects and experimenters are not always in agreement as to what constitutes a trial in the partial reinforcement experiment." This uncertainty about how to define a trial—which is also a serious if often ignored problem in the associative analysis of background conditioning—poses no problems for the current model, because the notion of a trial plays no role in its analysis of conditioning.

B. BACKGROUND CONDITIONING, BLOCKING,
OVERSHADOWING, OVERPREDICTION, AND
INHIBITORY CONDITIONING

A fundamental result of modern experiments on classical conditioning is that what the animal learns or has learned about one CS alters what it learns about other CSs. In consequence, the effect of pairing a CS and a US cannot be predicted in the absence of knowledge of what the animal has learned about other CSs that are also present. If the rate of US occurrence in the presence of the background alone (the training apparatus) is as great as in the presence of a transient CS, such as a tone, then pairing the transient CS and the US does not induce a conditioned response to the transient CS (Rescorla, 1968). Similarly, if one CS, say a tone, has already been paired with the US, and then a second CS, say a light, is presented together with the tone and the US, the second CS does not become conditioned to the US (Kamin, 1967). In both cases, the development of a conditioned response to one CS is said to be blocked by the other CS. Overshadowing occurs when the two CSs, say a tone and a light, are presented together from the outset, but the development of a conditioned response to one, say the tone, blocks the development of a conditioned response to the other.

There have been two general sorts of hypotheses about these blocking phenomena. One class of models treats them as consequences of attentional processes that select which CSs will be gain entry to the association-forming process (Mackintosh, 1975; Pearce & Hall, 1980). As the likelihood of a CS's gaining entry to the association-forming process is reduced, its effectiveness as a CS (its associability) is said to be reduced. Other models treat these phenomena as manifestations of properties of the association-forming process. For example, in the model of Rescorla and Wagner (1972), the process that increments or decrements the strength of one CS–US association following a trial on which the US either occurred or failed to occur looks at the difference between the maximum possible strength of that CS–US association and the sum of the strengths of the associations of the US to all the other CSs present on that trial. The change in associative strength is proportionate to this difference. When the sum of the associative strengths for the other CSs is as strong as the maximum possible association between, say, the tone and the US, then this difference is zero and no conditioning of the tone occurs. One way of thinking about this kind of model is to say that the US loses its effectiveness (its capacity to promote association formation) to the extent it is predicted by the active CSs (Pearce & Hall, 1980).

In the present model, there is no sense in which either a CS or a US loses effectiveness in the course of conditioning. The model predicts the above-mentioned blocking effects without parametric assumptions of any kind, but these predictions follow directly from the solving of the system of simultaneous equations to obtain the corrected rate estimates. The same is true for the model's account of the "overprediction" findings and for its explanations of inhibitory conditioning in general. Overprediction occurs when the US has first been conditioned to two independently occurring CSs, then these two CSs are presented together with a third, newly introduced CS and one US. By the additivity assumption, the cooccurrence of the first two CSs should predict two USs, but only one US in fact occurs. The unique solution to the resulting system of simultaneous equations is the one that ascribes to the third CS an effect on the rate of US occurrence equal in magnitude but opposite in sign to the effect of each of the first two CSs. In other words, a negative effect on the rate of US occurrence is imputed to the third CS. When this experiment is run, the animal in fact reacts to the third CS as though it predicted a reduction in the rate of US occurrence (Kremer, 1978), despite the fact that this CS was paired with a US on every one of its occurrences.

Similarly, in an explicitly unpaired training protocol, where the US occurs when a transient CS is not present but never when it is, the unique solution to the resulting system of equations is one that ascribes to the CS a negative effect on the rate of US occurrence. In short, the phenomena of inhibitory conditioning are explained by the present model in the same manner as are the phenomena of excitatory conditioning. They do not require the postulation of a mechanism that generates an expectation. The only role for the expectation-generating algorithm in the present model is in the analysis of stationarity.

V. What Does Change over Trials?

Modern associative models postulate trial-by-trial changes in the effectiveness (associability) of the US and/or the CSs. As has just been emphasized, there is no such postulate in the present model. There is no notion of diminished CS or US effectiveness. Further, the solutions—the corrected rate estimates—do not change over successive trials. The rate estimate for a given CS is constant from the first trial on which that CS is introduced, provided the protocol for the relation between the CS and the US is stationary. What does change over trials are statistical ambiguities inherent in the data from the first trial or two on which a new CS is presented.

The experimental evidence cited in favor of associative models that postulate the progressive attenuation of CS effectiveness (loss of associability) comes from studies of the conditioning that occurs on the first trial or two after a new CS is introduced, often in conjunction with a change in the number of USs given per trial (Dickinson, Hall, & Mackintosh, 1976; Mackintosh, Bygrave, & Picton, 1977). For example, Mackintosh et al. (1977) gave six groups of rats four trials on which a light CS was paired with a shock US. On the fifth trial, a tone came on with the light. For half the six groups, there were also two shocks rather than one on this fifth trial. Four of the groups then received a sixth trial. On this trial, there were also two shocks for some groups and one for others, so allocated that between the four groups one had all possible permutations of two versus one shock on the fifth trial and two versus one on the sixth. All groups were then tested for the strength of their conditioned emotional response to the tone alone. From the pattern of similarities and differences between groups, Mackintosh et al. (1977) and also Pearce and Hall (1980) conclude that the associability of the CS changes rapidly in the first few trials.

The present model does not offer the rigorous account of these "first few trials" effects that it does of the various forms of blocking and inhibitory conditioning, but it does offer a new conceptual basis for thinking about them. On the fifth trial of the just described experiment, when the tone CS first makes its appearance and when, for some groups, there is also a change in the number of USs, the various ambiguities inherent in a time series analysis of limited data are all present to a strong degree. It is, for example, highly uncertain whether the net rate of US occurrence (due to all CSs) has been stationary. The rats cannot know whether from the outset of training the process chosen by the experimenter to generate USs was such that one could expect one US on some trials, two on others, and none on still others. If the experimenter relied on a Poisson process to generate USs in the presence of the transient CSs (as did Rescorla, 1968), then the experiences of these rats over the first five trials are what one would very likely observe without any change in the process that generates US occurrences. Thus, the two USs on Trial 5 do not begin to justify from a statistical standpoint the inference that there has been a change in the underlying process for generating USs. When, however, both the tone and the double USs occur again on the sixth trial, the statistical justification for concluding in favor of nonstationarity increases fairly dramatically. Thus, there are purely statistical reasons why the experiences from the fifth and sixth trials together should be grounds for a reaction that would not be justified given only the experience on the fifth trial alone.

The ambiguity about whether there has been any change in the net rate of US occurrence is only one of several statistical ambiguities in the Mackintosh et al. (1977) experiment and in others like it. It is also ambiguous whether there has been a change in the rate of tone occurrence (the "blocked" CS). Perhaps the tone has been slated from the outset to accompany the light on only one trial in five. Or perhaps, the co-occurrence of tone and light is pure coincidence. Also, stipulating for the moment that the average net rate of US occurrence did in fact increase on Trial 5, it is ambiguous whether this was due to a change in the rate of US occurrence predicted by the light, or to the influence of the newly appeared tone, or to a change in the rate predicted by the background, and so on.

The ambiguities inherent in the animal's experience of the first few trials are emphasized here because a fundamental pretheoretical intuition underlying the present model is that in conditioning experiments the occurrence of conditioned responses to CSs is largely determined by the complex strategies animals bring to bear in deciding how to react to new events in the face of statistically ambiguous past experiences. The experiments that focus on the reactions after one or two experiences with a CS (or US) maximize the role of an animal's sensitivity to statistical ambiguity in the determination of conditioned behavior. The explanation of these results is therefore likely to be found not in rapid trial-to-trial changes in the animals' attention to the CSs but rather in their reactions to the rapidly changing statistical evidence provided by their training experiences.

This sort of intuition about the appropriate kind of theoretical analysis for conditioning data is strongly dependent on whether one believes that the conditioning process does or does not manifest the same degree of problem-specific adaptive specialization that we expect to find in the visual system. If we expect sophisticated adaptive specialization, then this kind of analysis may seem plausible. If we do not, if we think that the conditioning process is a primitive unspecialized process, then this sort of analysis seems utterly implausible. It is therefore of no small consequence to consider the justification for the implicit assumption that, unlike any other biological process, the basic learning process in classical conditioning has not been subject to adaptive specialization through evolution by natural selection.

ACKNOWLEDGMENTS

I am grateful to Tom Wickens for discussions that led to the algorithm for testing stationarity. The costs of preparing this manuscript were partially covered by NSF Grant BNS89-96246.

REFERENCES

Bush, R. R., & Mosteller, F. (1951). A mathematical model for simple learning. *Psychological Review, 58*, 313–323.

Church, R. M. (1984). Properties of the internal clock. In J. Gibbon & L. Allan (Eds.), *Timing and time perception* (pp. 567–582). New York: New York Academy of Sciences.

Dickinson, A., Hall, G., & Mackintosh, N. J. (1976). Surprise and the attenuation of blocking. *Journal of Experimental Psychology: Animal Behavior Processes, 2*, 213–222.

Emlen, S. T. (1969). The development of migratory orientation in young indigo buntings. *Living Bird, 8*, 113–126.

Estes, W. K. (1950). Toward a statistical theory of learning. *Psychological Review, 57*, 467–517.

Farley, J., & Alkon, D. L. (1985). Cellular mechanisms of learning, memory, and information storage. *Annual Review of Psychology, 36*, 419–494.

Gallistel, C. R. (in press). Classical conditioning as a non-stationary, multivariate time series analysis. A spreadsheet model. *Behavioral Research Methods, Instruments, and Computers*.

Gallistel, C. R. (1990). *The Organization of Learning*. Cambridge, MA: Bradford Books/MIT Press.

Garcia, J., & Koelling, R. A. (1966). The relation of cue to consequence in avoidance learning. *Psychonomic Science, 4*, 123–124.

Gibbon, J., Baldock, M. D., Locurto, C. M., Gold, L., & Terrace, H. S. (1977). Trial and intertrial durations in autoshaping. *Journal of Experimental Psychology: Animal Behavior Processes, 3*, 264–284.

Gibbon, J., & Balsam, P. (1981). Spreading associations in time. In C. M. Locurto, H. S. Terrace, & J. Gibbon (Eds.), *Autoshaping and conditioning theory* (pp. 219–253). New York: Academic Press.

Gibbon, J., Farrell, L., Locurto, C. M., Duncan, H. J., & Terrace, H. S. (1980). Partial reinforcement in autoshaping with pigeons. *Animal Learning and Behavior, 8*, 45–59.

Gleitman, H., Nachmias, J., & Neisser, U. (1954). The S–R reinforcement theory of extinction. *Psychological Review, 61*(1), 23–33.

Gluck, M. A., & Thompson, R. F. (1987). Modeling the neural substrates of associative learning and memory: A computational approach. *Psychological Review, 94*(2), 176–191.

Gould, J. L. (1984). Processing of sun-azimuth information by bees. *Animal Behaviour, 32*, 149–152.

Hawkins, R. D., & Kandel, E. R. (1984). Is there a cell-biological alphabet for simple forms of learning? *Psychological Review, 91*, 375–391.

Hull, C. L. (1943). *Principles of behavior.* New York: Appleton-Century-Crofts.

Hull, C. L. (1952). *A behavior system.* New Haven: Yale University Press.

Kamin, L. J. (1967). "Attention-like" processes in classical conditioning. In M. R. Jones (Ed.), *Miami symposium on the prediction of behavior: Aversive stimulation.* Miami: University of Miami Press.

Kaplan, P. (1984). Importance of relative temporal parameters in trace autoshaping: From excitation to inhibition. *Journal of Experimental Psychology: Animal Behavior Processes, 10,* 113–126.

Knudsen, E. I., & Knudsen, P. F. (1990). Sensitive and critical periods for visual calibration of sound localization by barn owls. *Journal of Neuroscience, 10*(1), 222–232.

Kremer, E. F. (1978). The Rescorla-Wagner model: Losses in associative strength in compound conditioned stimuli. *Journal of Experimental Psychology: Animal Behavior Processes, 4,* 22–36.

Locke, J. (1690). *An essay concerning human understanding.*

Lorenz, K. (1937). Imprinting. *Auk, 54,* 245–273.

Mackintosh, N. J. (1975). A theory of attention. *Psychological Review, 82,* 276–298.

Mackintosh, N. J., Bygrave, D. J., & Picton, B. M. B. (1977). Locus of the effect of a surprising reinforcer in the attenuation of blocking. *Quarterly Journal of Experimental Psychology, 29,* 327–336.

Marler, P. (1991). The instinct to learn. In S. Carey, & R. Gelman (Eds.), *The epigenesis of mind* (pp. 37–66). Hillsdale, NJ: Erlbaum.

McCloskey, M. (1991). Networks and theories: The place of connectionism in cognitive science. *Psychological Science, 2,* 387–395.

Meck, W. H., Church, R. M., & Gibbon, J. (1985). Temporal integration in duration and number discrimination. *Journal of Experimental Psychology: Animal Behavior Processes, 11,* 591–597.

Pavlov, I. V. (1928). *Lectures on conditioned reflexes: The higher nervous activity of animals* (W. H. Gantt, Trans.). London: Lawrence & Wishart.

Pearce, J. M., & Hall, G. (1980). A model for Pavlovian learning: Variation in the effectiveness of conditioned but not of unconditioned stimuli. *Psychological Review, 87,* 532–552.

Peterhans, E., & von der Heydt, R. (1991). Subjective contours—bridging between psychophysics and physiology. *Trends in Neurosciences, 14,* 112–119.

Rescorla, R. A. (1968). Probability of shock in the presence and absence of CS in fear conditioning. *Journal of Comparative and Physiological Psychology, 66*(1), 1–5.

Rescorla, R. A. (1972). "Configural" conditioning in discrete-trial bar pressing. *Journal of Comparative and Physiological Psychology, 79,* 307–317.

Rescorla, R. A. (1988). Pavlovian conditioning: It's not what you think it is. *American Psychologist, 43,* 151–160.

Rescorla, R. A., Grau, J. W., & Durlach, P. J. (1985). Analysis of the unique cue in configural discriminations. *Journal of Experimental Psychology: Animal Behavior Processes, 11,* 356–366.

Rescorla, R. A., & Wagner, A. R. (1972). A theory of Pavlovian conditioning: Variations in the effectiveness of reinforcement and nonreinforcement. In A. H. Black, & W. F. Prokasy (Eds.), *Classical conditioning II* (pp. 64–99). New York: Appleton-Century-Crofts.

Roberts, S., & Church, R. M. (1978). Control of an internal clock. *Journal of Experimental Psychology: Animal Behavior Processes, 4,* 318–337.

Rozin, P., & Kalat, J. W. (1971). Specific hungers and poison avoidance as adaptive specializations of learning. *Psychological Review, 78,* 459–486.

Sutton, R. S., & Barto, A. G. (1981). Toward a modern theory of adaptive networks: Expectation and prediction. *Psychological Review, 88,* 135–170.

Wagner, A. R. (1981). SOP: A model of automatic memory processing in animal behavior. In N. E. Spear, & R. R. Miller (Eds.), *Information processing in animals: Memory mechanisms* (pp. 5–47). Hillsdale, NJ: Erlbaum.

OCCASION SETTING IN PAVLOVIAN CONDITIONING

Peter C. Holland

I. Introduction

Pavlovian conditioning is often simply described as the transfer of control of reflexes (unconditioned responses, URs) from stimuli that elicit them unconditionally (USs) to other stimuli that normally are incapable of eliciting them (conditioned stimuli, CSs). Although auditory cues seldom elicit substantial salivation spontaneously, a tone can come to provoke that response if it consistently predicts food delivery. This new-found control of salivation by the tone is typically attributed to the acquisition of some association or potentiated connection between the CS and US pathways: by virtue of that association, the CS becomes a substitute elicitor of activity along some portion of the US–UR pathway. This is often described as the CS's "activating a representation of the US" (Fig. 1A).

Another behavioral control function occasionally ascribed to Pavlovian CSs is modulation. Rather than acquiring its own ability to elicit behavior usually controlled by another reflex system, a Pavlovian CS may influence the efficacy of the normal elicitor of a response. For example, the ability of an auditory cue to elicit a startle response is potentiated by the presence of a visual cue previously paired with a shock US (e.g., Davis, 1984). The visual CS does not itself elicit the startle response, but rather enhances the ability of the tone to do so (Fig. 1B). Analogies abound in the literatures of behavioral neuroscience, such as the distinction between primer and re-

69

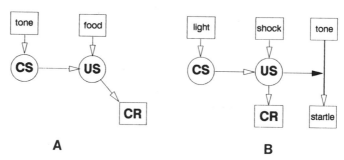

A   **B**

Fig. 1. Diagrams of associations in Pavlovian conditioning. In panel A, the tone CS controls a CR that is normally elicited by the US. In panel B, the light CS modulates a startle response that is normally elicited unconditionally by the tone. In this and all subsequent figures, rectangles signify external events and responses, circles represent internal representations of events, open arrows represent excitatory associations, and the closed arrow reflects an excitatory modulatory action.

leaser effects of pheromones, and that between neurotransmitters, whose release directly produces excitatory or inhibitory postsynaptic potentials, and neuromodulators, which have little direct excitatory or inhibitory effect on the postsynaptic membrane but modulate the effectiveness of regular neurotransmitter mechanisms.

This review is concerned with a particular modulatory function of CSs in rats' solutions of elementary conditional discriminations, in which one CS modifies the efficacy of Pavlovian associations between other cues and the US. This function, which I call *occasion setting,* can often be readily distinguished from elicitation both conceptually and empirically, and perhaps anatomically as well. Furthermore, this occasion-setting function may involve a hierarchical, multilayered organization of representations of events and relations and thus may aid the expansion of the domain of Pavlovian accounts of behavior.

In this chapter, I discuss three broad issues. First, what operations and outcomes distinguish occasion setting from elicitation? Second, what circumstances favor the establishment of occasion setting, rather than elicitation? And finally, what associative structures underlie occasion setting? Although my studies of these three issues are intertwined both conceptually and historically, I consider the issues sequentially here.

II. Distinguishing Conditioning from Occasion Setting

Although informed by earlier studies (e.g., Moore, Newman, & Glasgow, 1969), the study of occasion setting in my laboratory grew from initial work with Robert Ross and Jennifer Lamarre on the nature of feature-positive and feature-negative discriminations, in which a compound stimulus and one of its elements are arranged to have different consequences for reinforcement. In those discriminations, one cue, the target A, is sometimes followed by the US and sometimes not, depending on the presence or absence of another cue, the feature X. In a feature-positive (FP) discrimination, when A is accompanied by X, the US is presented, but when A is presented alone, no reinforcement is delivered ($XA+/A-$). Conversely, in a feature-negative (FN) discrimination, A is reinforced when presented alone, but not when A is accompanied by X ($A+/XA-$). According to most popular theories of learning (e.g., Pearce & Hall, 1980; Rescorla & Wagner, 1972), these procedures should result in the formation of excitatory associations between X and the US in FP discriminations and inhibitory associations between X and the US in FN discriminations.

We believed, however, that under some circumstances, X could acquire the ability to depress or enhance the expression of an association between A and the US. Casually speaking, instead of signaling that the US would or would not occur, X might indicate when A was to be reinforced or nonreinforced, setting the occasion for reinforcement or nonreinforcement of A. Our attempts to distinguish between these eliciting and occasion-setting functions of X were guided by working hypotheses about both the conditions under which occasion setting would occur and the nature of the resulting learning: First, that X was more likely to acquire occasion-setting powers when the stimulus elements within the compounds were presented serially ($X \rightarrow A$) rather than simultaneously (XA), and second, that occasion setting involves X's modulation of a representation of an A–US association or unit (Fig. 2). Although later work was to modify these views somewhat, they served well early on by generating at least three sets of criteria for distinguishing eliciting and occasion-setting functions: response form, extinction and counterconditioning effects, and transfer effects.

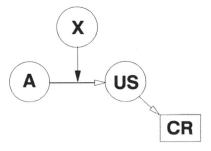

Fig. 2.   Diagram of associations and occasion setting in an FP discrimination.

A. Response Form

The simple conditioning and occasion setting accounts for the solution of
$XA+/A-$ FP discriminations differ most obviously in their specification of
the stimulus that is thought to instigate behavior when the XA compound is
present. The conditioning account assumes that responding to the compound is the consequence of X–US associations, whereas our working
hypothesis about occasion setting claimed that responding to the compound is the consequence of A–US associations, which are gated or
enabled by the presence of the occasion setter X.

Robert Ross and I (Ross and Holland, 1981) exploited an appetitive
conditioning preparation previously studied in my laboratory (Holland,
1977, 1984b) to determine whether responding controlled by the XA compound in FP discriminations reflected X–US associations or A–US associations. In this preparation, food-deprived rats receive food pellets delivered to a food cup after brief (5–30 sec) presentations of auditory or
visual stimuli. Interestingly, the form of the conditioned response (CR) is
determined not only by the US, but also by the nature of the CS. For
example, with the visual cues we use, rats rear on their hind legs at the
onset of the stimuli and then stand quietly with their heads in the food cup;
but with the auditory cues, they exhibit a startle response to stimulus
onset, followed by short, rapid head movements (head jerk), usually in the
vicinity of the food cup. These behaviors are clearly differentiable, do not
simply reflect performance effects, and occur as the consequence of the
Pavlovian CS–US contingencies (see Holland, 1984b, for a review).

For the present purposes the important feature of this preparation is that
the form of conditioned responding during a light + tone compound paired
with food reveals its associative origin. That is, if the CR comprises rearing
and quiet food cup behaviors, then it is the consequence of light–food
associations, but if the CR to the compound comprises startle and head
jerk behavior, it is the consequence of tone–food associations.

Ross and I observed the responding of rats in simultaneous ($XA+/A-$)
and serial ($X \rightarrow A+/A-$) FP discriminations. With simultaneous compounds, the form of the CR acquired to the XA compound was characteristic of the predictive X feature. When a 10 sec light + tone compound was
reinforced and the 10 sec tone alone was nonreinforced, the tone alone
elicited no behavior and the compound evoked rear and food cup behavior
(right bars of Fig. 3). When the light feature was presented separately in a
test session, it also elicited only rear and food cup behaviors. Similarly, if
the light + tone compound was reinforced and the light alone was nonreinforced, the light alone elicited no behavior, and the compound evoked
startle and head jerk behavior (as did the tone alone). Thus, responding in

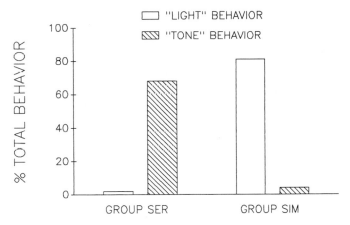

Fig. 3. Frequency of "tone" (head jerk) and "light" (rear and quiet food cup) behaviors during a light + tone (LT) compound stimulus, after LT+/T− training. In Group Sim (right bars), the light and tone were coterminous, but in Group Ser (left bars) the light preceded the tone (only responding during the tone is shown). "Percentage (%) total behavior" is an absolute frequency measure, obtained by dividing the number of observations of a particular behavior by the total number of observations made during the CS. Observations were made at 1.25 sec intervals during the CSs. Data shown are from Ross and Holland (1981).

our simultaneous FP discrimination procedures was entirely the consequence of feature–US associations, as anticipated by most conditioning theories.

However, we observed quite a different pattern of behavior when the X feature preceded the A target on compound trials during training. When a 5 sec light → 5 sec empty interval → 5 sec tone serial compound was reinforced and separate presentations of the tone were nonreinforced, the rats exhibited substantial head jerk behavior (characteristic of auditory CSs) during the tone on compound trials (left bars of Fig. 3), but not on tone-alone trials, as well as rear behavior during the light. Similarly, when a tone → empty interval → light compound was reinforced and the light alone was nonreinforced, the rats acquired both head jerk and startle during the tone feature and rear behavior during the light, but only on compound trials. Thus, in addition to behavior occurring as the consequence of feature–US associations, the target cues also controlled behavior characteristic of target–US associations. Because responding to the target occurred only on serial compound trials, we suggested that the feature set the occasion for the occurrence of responding based on target–US associations.

Rescorla (1985) presented similar data from pigeon autoshaping experiments. Although pigeons come to peck localized key light signals for food delivery, no such pecking occurs in the presence of auditory or diffuse visual cues paired with food. Nevertheless, Rescorla (1985) found that if a diffuse cue signaled when a key light was to be reinforced in FP discriminations, it acquired the ability to set the occasion for pecking the lighted key on compound trials. Thus, consideration of response form under various training conditions supports a distinction between occasion setting and simple excitatory conditioning.

B.   EXTINCTION AND COUNTERCONDITIONING

To the extent that responding during a compound CS in FP discrimination procedures is the consequence of simple conditioning of X, repeated presentations of X alone after training should extinguish that conditioning and hence abolish any responding to the compound that reflected X–US associations. Indeed, we found that nonreinforced presentations of X substantially reduced responding to an XA compound after simultaneous $XA+/A-$ FP training, in three different conditioning procedures (Fig. 4A): the appetitive conditioning procedure just described (Holland, 1989b), conditioned suppression of lever-pressing anticipatory to electric shock (Holland & Petrick, unpublished data), and a discrete-trial operant procedure (Holland, 1991a, see section III,A,3) in which food was delivered during the XA compound in training only if a lever-press occurred.

The effects of X extinction after serial FP training were more complex (Fig. 4b). Although responding controlled directly by X (e.g., rearing elicited by a visual X in a light → tone $X → A$ compound) was significantly reduced, X's ability to modulate behavior controlled by the A target was unaffected (again, in all three preparations, Holland, 1989b, 1991a; Holland & Petrick, unpublished data). Further, Rescorla (1986a) found identical results in pigeon autoshaping procedures.

A similar effect was seen when nonreinforced X presentations were *intermixed* with $X → A+$ and $A-$ trials. Ross and Holland (1981, 1982) and Holland (1989a) found no deleterious effects on occasion setting of adding nonreinforced X trials, even when there were three times as many X-alone trials as $X → A+$ trials. At the same time, those nonreinforced X trials significantly reduced responding attributable to X–reinforcer associations. This immunity of X's occasion-setting powers to simple nonreinforcement is consistent with our working hypothesis that whereas simple conditioning involves only X–US associations, occasion setting also involves X's modulation of an A–US association. Simple presentation of X alone may be sufficient to weaken or counteract X–US associations while at the same time have little effect on X's links to the A–US unit.

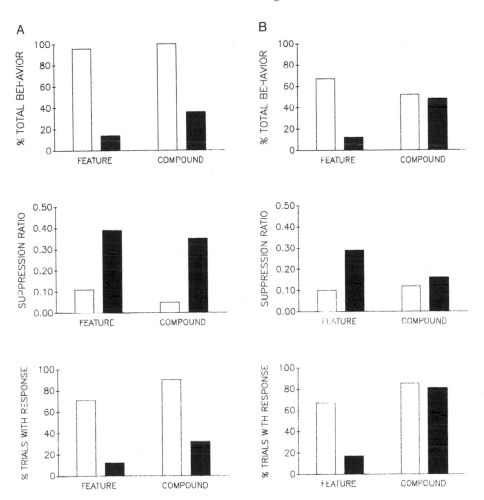

Fig. 4. Test responding of rats trained with either (A) simultaneous $XA+/A-$ or (B) serial $X \rightarrow A+/A-$ FP procedures, after either nonreinforced presentations of the feature alone (solid bars) or no such treatment (open bars). The left graphs show data from Holland (1989b, 1989c), the center graphs show previously unpublished data of Holland and Petrick, and the right graphs show data from Holland (1991a).

We found analogous effects with feature-*negative* discrimination learning, both within our appetitive conditioning preparation (Holland, 1989d) and in a conditioned suppression procedure with shock USs (Holland, 1984a). Rats received either serial $A+/X \rightarrow A-$ or simultaneous $A+/XA-$ training, followed by *reinforced* presentations of X. We anticipated that simultaneous training would establish inhibitory associations between X and the US, but that serial training would endow X with the ability to modulate the effectiveness of the A–US association. Not surprisingly, with simultaneous training, counterconditioning of X abolished its ability to inhibit responding to A on XA trials. Indeed, the excitation acquired to X on counterconditioning trials summed with that originally established to A: responding was greater on XA trials than on either X or A trials alone (top panels of Fig. 5).

However, after serial FN learning, establishment of excitation to X had relatively little effect on its ability to inhibit responding to A (bottom panels of Fig. 5). Even though responding to both X and A was substantial when they were presented separately, responding was reduced when they were presented together (recall that after simultaneous training, the compound elicited *greater* responding than the individual elements). As with the effects of extinction on occasion setting in FP discriminations, this immunity of occasion setting to counterconditioning is consistent with our working hypothesis that occasion setting involves X's modulation of an A–US association: X's excitatory links with a US representation

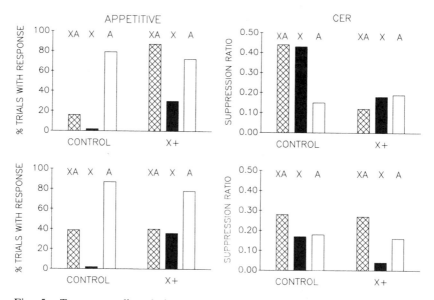

Fig. 5. Test responding during XA compound, X-alone, and A-alone trials after counterconditioning of the X feature (bars labeled $X+$) or no such treatment (bars labeled control). The top panels show responding on simultaneous compound trials after simultaneous feature negative training $(A+/XA-)$, and the bottom panels show responding during A on serial $X \rightarrow A$ compound trials after $A+/X \rightarrow A-$ training. The data in the left panels are from Holland (1989d), and those in the right panels are from Holland (1984a).

might well be independent of its inhibitory links with the A–US association (Fig. 6).

Recently, Rescorla (1991) presented what is perhaps the most dramatic example of the independence of a feature's occasion-setting and simple associative powers. In several experiments with a pigeon autoshaping procedure, he examined the effects of reinforcement of the feature cue concurrent with serial FN discrimination learning. Under circumstances in which the feature's excitation did not directly compete with the display of negative occasion setting, Rescorla found that occasion setting was *enhanced* by concurrent reinforcement of the feature. Responding to the target cue was suppressed more by the reinforced feature than by a concurrently *non*reinforced feature or by a feature that had not previously been presented outside the serial compound. After ruling out a number of relatively uninteresting sources for this effect, he attributed it to an enhancement of attention to the feature engendered by its conditioning. Regardless of the exact mechanisms by which the reinforced feature's suppressive powers were enhanced, these data showed convincingly the independence of X's simple conditioning and occasion-setting powers.

C. TRANSFER EFFECTS

The assumption that a cue's simple excitatory or inhibitory associative strength combines arithmetically with the strength of other cues paired with the same reinforcer is basic to most learning theories. For example, suppose that we establish some cue X as an excitor within a simultaneous FP discrimination procedure $XA+/A-$, in which, asymptotically, X's associative strength should be high and A's low or nonexistent. X's excitatory associative strength should be revealed whether X is presented in com-

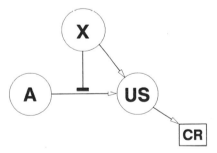

Fig. 6. Diagram of the representation of serial $A+/X \rightarrow A-$ FN learning after $X+$ counterconditioning. The arrows represent excitatory associations and the bar represents an inhibitory modulatory influence (negative occasion setting).

pound with A, alone, or in compound with some other cue, say, B. Indeed, if B's strength is also excitatory, we would anticipate the XB compound to control more responding than X alone; furthermore, if B's excitation is greater than the residual strength of A in the original discrimination, then responding during an XB compound should exceed that to the original XA compound.

Similarly, if X was established as an inhibitor within a FN discrimination procedure, $A+/XA-$, X should reduce responding normally controlled by another excitor B, if X is presented together with that cue. In fact, the occurrence of such decremental effects in the latter case is a part of the standard definition of conditioned inhibition (Rescorla, 1969).

These summation effects follow from the view that simple excitation and inhibition derive from associations with a representation of the US. Consequently, the strengths of any cues with associations with that US should sum (Fig. 7A,B). Conversely, if the occasion-setting power of a cue is not dependent on the simple association of that cue with the US, but rather involves the modulation of another, target–US, association, then an occa-

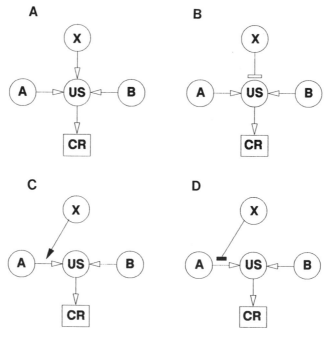

Fig. 7.   Diagram showing A–US and B–US excitatory associations and either (A) excitatory X–US or (B) inhibitory X–US associations; and either (C) positive or (D) negative modulatory influence of X on the A–US association.

sion setter in an FP or FN discrimination should only modulate responding to its original target cue, apart from any stimulus generalization between the original and test targets (Fig. 7C,D).

Several experiments (e.g., Holland, 1986b, 1989a, 1989d; Lamarre & Holland, 1987), using a variety of conditioning preparations, showed that whereas cues trained as features in simultaneous FP and FN discriminations controlled responding when presented in compound with cues other than their original targets, the effects of cues trained as features in serial discriminations were much more constrained by their targets. For example, Fig. 8A shows the results of transfer tests after either simultaneous or

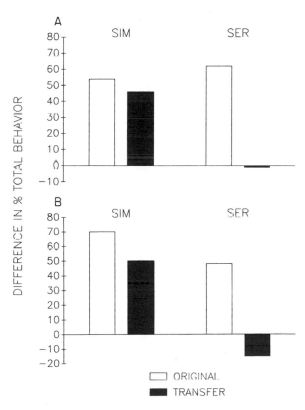

Fig. 8. Differential responding during compounds of the feature and either the original target or a separately trained transfer target, after either simultaneous or serial FP (top panel) or FN (bottom panel) discrimination training. The ordinate measure indicates the difference between responding on compound trials and on target-alone trials (compound minus target in the top panel and target minus compound in the bottom panel). The data shown in the top panel are from Holland (1986a), and those in the bottom panel are from Holland (1989d).

serial FP discrimination training. The features were presented in compound with either their original targets O, or with a transfer target T that had been conditioned and then extinguished to a low level of responding (Holland, 1986a). Transfer was nearly complete after simultaneous training but nearly nonexistent after serial training. Similarly, Fig. 8B shows the results of transfer tests after either simultaneous or serial FN discrimination training. The features were presented in compound with either their O or with a T that had been separately trained (Holland, 1989d). Again, there was substantial transfer after simultaneous training, but no evidence of transfer after serial training.

All in all, the failure of serially trained features' occasion-setting power to transfer to new targets both supported the distinction between CSs and occasion setters, and substantiated the claim that occasion setters act on particular target–US associations.

In summary, then, three kinds of early evidence supported a functional distinction between simple conditioning, obtained in simultaneous FP and FN discriminations, and occasion setting, observed after serial discrimination training. First, the form of the conditioned behavior indicated that responding observed in simultaneous FP discriminations was the consequence of feature–US associations, but a major portion of responding observed in serial FP discriminations was generated by target–US associations, apparently gated by the occasion-setting feature. Second, although the simple associative strengths of features in simultaneous discriminations were altered dramatically by extinction and counterconditioning manipulations, the occasion-setting powers of serially trained features were little affected. Finally, in transfer tests, whereas the simple associative strengths of simultaneously trained features were evident regardless of whether they were combined with their original targets or other cues, the occasion-setting powers of serially trained cues were quite specific to their original targets.

D.   LEARNING/PERFORMANCE FACTORS

Other data indicated that the temporal arrangement of the elements of the compound affected the *acquisition* of different response tendencies rather than only the *performance*. For example, Holland (1986a) showed that after serial $X \rightarrow A + /A -$ training, responding of a form characteristic to A was seen even on simultaneous XA compound test trials, whereas serial testing of simultaneously trained cues showed no evidence for responding characteristic of the target cue. Similarly, serially trained X's maintained their inhibitory powers after X–reinforcer counterconditioning when subjects were tested with simultaneous XA compounds (Holland, 1984a,

1989d). Finally, the lack of transfer observed after serial FP and FN training was observed even when the elements in the test compound were presented simultaneously.

It is important to note that this list of operations is not an exhaustive one. As our work proceeded we identified several other empirical distinctions between occasion setting and simple conditioning, some of which are described later, in the service of answering other questions about the genesis and nature of occasion setting. However, the three techniques just discussed provided the basis for operationally distinguishing occasion setting from simple conditioning in most of our subsequent work.

III. Conditions for the Acquisition of Occasion Setting

The previous data show clearly that the serial and simultaneous training procedures generate different learning, and that the serial procedure favors the acquisition of occasion setting. In this section, I first consider the critical temporal features of serial discriminations that encourage the acquisition of occasion setting and then consider other, nontemporal factors that also affect its acquisition.

Although to a large extent this research comprised systematic investigation of procedural variables that differentiated the serial and simultaneous procedures that we used, it was guided by four hypotheses about the conditions that favor the establishment of occasion setting. Our first notion was a fairly vague gestalt hypothesis, that occasion setting was induced whenever there was a "perceptual discontinuity" (Holland, 1983) between the feature and other elements in the stream of events experienced by the animal: serial presentation of feature and reinforced target, for example, might encourage subjects to parse the sequence as feature → (target → US).

A second casual hypothesis was that occasion setting occurred when there were conflicts between the relative contiguity and validity relations of the elements of the compound. In a serial FP procedure, for example, although the target cue is a relatively poor predictor of *whether* the US will occur, it is highly predictive of *when* the US will occur (by virtue of its close contiguity with the US on reinforced trials). Conversely, although the feature is highly predictive of reinforcement, it is relatively noncontiguous with it. If, because of the feature's delay to the reinforcer, the rate of conditioning to the feature was lower than the rate of conditioning to the target, and if occasion setting could operate over longer interstimulus intervals than simple conditioning, then the most efficient strategy of anticipating the US would be to use the feature to identify which trials were reinforced, and the target to determine when reinforcement was to occur.

An extension of the "conflict" notion claimed simply that occasion setting occurs *whenever* the training contingencies permit the target cue to acquire conditioning more rapidly than the feature (e.g., Rescorla, 1986b) and does not necessarily depend on any special temporal, perceptual, or predictive relations.

The final and most specific guide was that of Rescorla (1988), who suggested that occasion setting is established to a cue if it (or its trace) is present when a stimulus with an inhibitory component is reinforced. In FP discriminations, excitation acquired to A on $XA \rightarrow$ US trials is extinguished on A-alone trials, presumably as a consequence of some inhibitory process. Consequently, on $XA \rightarrow$ US trials, X will be reinforced in the presence of a cue with an inhibitory component. Because A is more likely to form excitatory associations with the US in serial procedures (in which A is more contiguous with the US than is X) than in simultaneous FP procedures (in which A and X are equally contiguous with the US, and hence X could overshadow A), A-alone trials are more likely to establish an inhibitory component to A in serial procedures. Consequently, serial procedures might be more likely to establish occasion setting to the feature cue than simultaneous procedures. However, within this view, *any* procedure that arranges for X to be reinforced in the presence of inhibition would be expected to establish occasion setting to X.

A.   TEMPORAL FACTORS

In our initial attempts to identify the properties of the serial procedure that were critical to the generation of occasion setting, we systematically varied each of the temporal parameters that differentiated the simultaneous and serial procedures that we had used previously. The serial and simultaneous procedures used by Ross and Holland (1981) and Holland and Lamarre (1984) differed in several ways. First, the features bore different temporal relations with the US. In these early experiments, we equated the target–US intervals across serial and simultaneous procedures; consequently, the feature–US intervals differed. Second, the features and targets bore different temporal relations with each other. Although in the simultaneous procedures the two cues were coterminous, in the serial procedures both the onset and termination of the feature preceded the target cue.

In a series of experiments with Pavlovian appetitive FP procedures (Holland, 1986a; Holland, unpublished data; Ross & Holland, 1981), we examined the effects of the intervals between feature and reinforcer on-

sets, between feature and target onsets, between feature and target terminations, and between feature terminations and target onset. In all these
experiments, the feature cues were visual and the targets were auditory.
Consequently, simple conditioning to the feature was indexed by rear and
quiet food cup behaviors, and occasion setting was assessed by head jerk
behavior during the target.

1. Feature–US, Feature–Target, and Target–US Intervals

Ross and Holland (1981) and Holland (unpublished) examined the effects
of the feature–reinforcer and/or feature–target interval on simple conditioning and occasion setting in FP training. Those experiments maintained
a constant 5 sec houselight feature and 5 sec tone target and varied the
feature–reinforcer (and hence the feature–target) interval. Figure 9 shows
asymptotic responding indicative of occasion setting (head jerk behavior)
and simple conditioning (rear and quiet food cup behaviors) to the feature
as a function of the feature–reinforcer interval. First, simple conditioning
was greater with shorter intervals. Second, although occasion setting was
minimal with shorter intervals, it was substantial over a broad range of
longer intervals, including those that supported only minimal conditioning.
Indeed, the incidence of occasion setting increased over the same range of

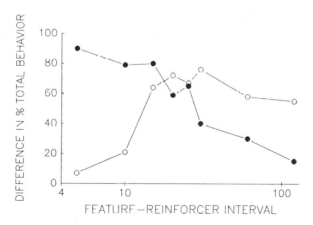

Fig. 9. Asymptotic levels of occasion setting (open circles) and conditioning (filled circles) as a function of feature–reinforcer interval (in seconds) in FP discrimination training.
Occasion setting is indexed as the difference between the frequency of head jerk behavior
during the target on compound trials and on target-alone trials. Conditioning is indexed as the
difference between the frequency of rear and quiet food cup behaviors during the feature and
during empty, prefeature intervals. The data given for the 5, 10, 15, 20, 25, and 30 sec
intervals are from Ross and Holland (1981) and those for 30, 60, and 120 sec intervals are from
an unpublished experiment.

intervals that simple conditioning decreased (providing some credence for the conflict model).

Another, previously unpublished, experiment examined the effects of the target–US interval and attempted to separate the effects of feature–US and feature–target intervals. In that experiment, nine independent groups of rats received serial FP training with a 5 sec houselight as feature and a tone, of varying durations, as target. Across the nine groups, all combinations of 5, 10, and 15 sec target–reinforcer and 0, 5, and 10 sec feature–target intervals were represented. In one set of three groups, the houselight and tone had simultaneous onsets (0 sec interval); in a second set of three groups, the houselight preceded the tone by 5 sec; and in a final set of three groups, the houselight preceded the tone by 10 sec. Within each of these sets of groups, the tone was 5, 10, or 15 sec in duration. Food reinforcement was delivered at the termination of the tone. Thus, in each group the feature–reinforcer interval was the sum of the feature–target and target–reinforcer intervals.

Figure 10 shows asymptotic performance during the target cues as a function of the target–US (abscissa) and feature–target (parameter) intervals. Occasion setting was clearly affected by feature–target interval, with considerably more differential responding with longer than with shorter intervals. Conversely, for each feature–target interval, the target–reinforcer interval, and hence the feature–reinforcer interval as well, had

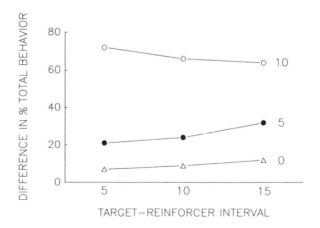

Fig. 10.   Asymptotic responding in FP discriminations as a function of target–reinforcer interval (abscissa, in seconds) and feature–target intervals (parameter, in seconds). The ordinate measure indicates the difference between responding during the target cues on reinforced compound trials and on nonreinforced target-alone trials. The data are from a previously unpublished experiment.

no reliable effect (within the range examined). Thus, the feature–target interval appeared critical to the establishment of occasion setting.

2. Termination Asynchrony

Other experiments (e.g., Holland, 1986a) showed that the relation of the feature's termination to the target played some role as well. For example, in one experiment (Holland, 1986a, Experiment 2) we compared acquisition of FP discrimination performance when the feature ended either prior to target onset (and thus an empty "gap" interval separated feature and target), simultaneously with target onset, or together with target termination, over three different feature–target intervals (10, 15, and 20 sec).

In that experiment we found substantial facilitatory effects of introducing a gap between feature termination and target onset relative to the other two arrangements, which did not differ. Interestingly, the substantial differences in occasion setting observed were not accompanied by reciprocal differences in simple conditioning to those features. Thus, without assuming that our measure of occasion setting is simply more sensitive to strength differences than our measure of conditioning differences, the conflict notion fared poorly.

It must be noted however, that we obtained a somewhat different pattern of data when we examined the effects of introducing gaps in an FN discrimination procedure, which used a shock reinforcer and a conditioned suppression measure. In that experiment (Lamarre & Holland, 1985), we found that introducing a gap *slowed* the acquisition of the discrimination. Nevertheless, these data may not contradict the appetitive data just described. First, the intervals used (30–120 sec) in the conditioned suppression study were much longer; gap effects might well interact with interval length. Second, although the appetitive FP procedure permits distinguishing simple conditioning and occasion setting controlled by the feature in terms of response form, responding observed in the conditioned suppression situation may have been the consequence of either simple inhibition (which might be hurt by the introduction of a gap), occasion setting, or both.

On the whole, the results of our experiments on temporal variations were consistent with the "discontinuity" notion. Increases in the feature-target interval and the introduction of gaps between feature and target would enhance the likelihood that the target and US would be grouped together and decrease the chance that the feature would be grouped with the target or US alone, thus encouraging the feature to gain conditional control over responding engendered by the target–US association.

These data are consistent with the inhibition notion, too. All these manipulations might be anticipated to affect the extent to which the target CS acquires excitation and consequently is subject to inhibitory processes on intermixed target-alone trials. The more of an inhibitory component possessed by a target, the more likely its feature will come to control occasion setting. However, we have no independent evidence for these variations in inhibitory component strength.

Support for the conflict model was mixed. Although the data in Fig. 10 show that occasion setting and simple conditioning were reciprocally related over one part of the range, considerable variation in occasion setting occurred in Holland's (1986a) Experiment 2 (just described) when there was little variation in the amounts of conditioning within the same range.

3. Relative Time Intervals

Also consistent with the discontinuity hypothesis are the effects of variations in the intertrial interval (ITI) on the occurrence of occasion setting. Casually speaking, the more isolated the target–reinforcer pair is from the *next* feature, the more likely that pair will be coded together. Thus, separating serial compound trials by larger ITIs might be anticipated to enhance the acquisition of occasion setting.

I recently examined the effects of variations in the ITI (as well as in the feature–target interval) on serial FP learning, using a discrete-trial operant lever press situation in which the events and sessions were identical to those used in our Pavlovian experiments, but in which the rats were required to press a lever during the target cue to receive the reinforcer. Although it is far from clear that the discrete-trial operant situation is comparable to the Pavlovian procedures that I have been discussing, Holland (1991a) has shown that that procedure generates transfer, extinction, and counterconditioning effects similar to those described earlier for Pavlovian procedures. That is, relative to simultaneous training, training with serial compounds resulted in less transfer and smaller effects of extinction and counterconditioning.

In our experiments that investigated ITI effects, rats received target-alone trials, and serial compounds comprising a 5 sec visual cue followed by an empty interval and then a 5 sec auditory target cue. The rats received sucrose for each lever press made during the target cue on serial compound trials. In different groups of rats, the feature–target intervals were 10 sec or 20 sec and the intertrial intervals averaged 1, 2, 4, or 8 min.

The top panel of Fig. 11 shows the number of trials to reach a discrimination criterion for each ITI (abscissa) and feature–target interval (parameter). For both feature–target intervals, the discriminations were learned more rapidly with the longer ITIs; however, the trend was far more obvious in subjects trained with the longer (20 sec) feature–target interval. In

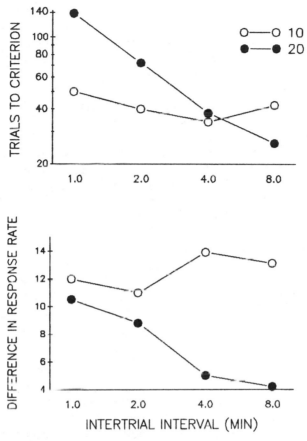

Fig. 11. (top panel) Number of reinforced compound trials needed for rats' performance to reach a criterion of 35% difference in the percentage of trials on which a response occurred during the target on reinforced compound trials minus that on target-alone trials. Each session included six reinforced compound trials. The parameter signifies the feature–target interval. (bottom panel) The effects of feature extinction on responding during the targets on serial feature → target compound trials. The measure plotted is the difference in response rate (responses/min) between performance during a test session prior to feature extinction and performance during an identical test session after feature extinction. Larger numbers indicate greater losses in compound responding as a result of feature extinction. The parameter indicates the feature–target interval (in seconds).

all conditions, acquisition of responding on reinforced trials occurred very rapidly (within a session or two); differences in performance among the conditions reflected differences in the rates of loss of responding on non-reinforced trials. Thus, these temporal variables likely affected discrimination learning rather than simple conditioning of the feature.

To evaluate the extent to which the responding shown in Fig. 11 reflected occasion setting rather than some other discrimination learning process, I next examined the effects of feature extinction on discrimination performance in these rats. The bottom panel of Fig. 11 summarizes the results of postextinction performance tests. First, note that extinction had greater deleterious effects on discrimination performance with the shorter feature–target interval than with the longer interval. This difference suggests that simple conditioning of the feature contributed substantially to performance with the shorter feature–target intervals, and that the longer feature–target intervals primarily yielded occasion setting. Recall that in this procedure the source of responding—feature– or target–US associations—cannot be identified by its form, as in the Pavlovian appetitive experiments.

Second, although the ITI had little influence on the effects of extinction with the short (10 sec) feature–target interval, with the longer (20 sec) feature–target intervals, extinction had substantially smaller effects as the ITI increased. Thus, with the longer feature–target intervals implicated in occasion setting, not only were the discriminations solved more easily with long ITIs, but also those solutions were more likely to involve occasion setting when long ITIs were used.

B. NONTEMPORAL FACTORS

Although temporal variables clearly had major impact on the occurrence of occasion setting in our experiments with rat subjects, Rescorla (e.g., Rescorla, 1989) found little evidence that the nature of FN discrimination learning in pigeon autoshaping studies was affected by the serial vs. simultaneous distinction. Outcomes characteristic of occasion setting were found in either case. Interestingly, although the rate of acquisition of simultaneous FN discriminations was greater than that of serial discriminations, even that difference was shown to be more the result of performance effects than of differences in the rate of learning. Thus, temporal factors cannot be universal determinants of occasion setting. So, we examined the effects of a variety of nontemporal factors, including element similarity, intensity, and reinforcement history on the occurrence of occasion setting in our procedures.

1. Context

Perhaps the most significant "perceptual discontinuity" evident in typical conditioning experiments is that between the punctate cues typically used as CSs and the contextual cues in which those CSs are embedded. Several authors (e.g., Balaz, Capra, Hartl, & Miller, 1981; Bouton, 1984; Bouton & King, 1986; Bouton & Swartzentruber, 1986; Grahame, Hallam, Geier,

& Miller, 1990; Swartzentruber 1991; Swartzentruber & Bouton, 1988) have suggested that contextual cues often act in ways that are reminiscent of the action of occasion setters. For example, analogs of the countercon- ditioning/extinction experiments described earlier show the ability of con- textual cues to modulate responding to discrete CSs to be independent of the contexts' simple excitatory or inhibitory relations with the reinforcer. Similarly, when the contributions of contexts' simple associative relations with the reinforcer are eliminated, transfer of contextual cues' modulating power is limited in ways similar to the limitations on transfer after occasion setting with explicit occasion setting cues (see Sections IV,B,1 and IV,B,2).

Furthermore, Swartzentruber (1991) recently found that context cues and punctate cues trained explicitly as occasion setters provided redun- dant information in a blocking design, but context cues and simple punctate CSs did not. Prior training of X as an occasion setter $(X \rightarrow A+/A-/X-)$ in one context blocked the ability of a novel context to acquire contextual control of responding when that novel context and X together signaled the reinforcement of A. Similarly, prior context learning blocked subsequent acquisition of occasion setting to X in that context. In neither case did contextual control and the simple excitatory powers of X mutually interfere. Reasoning that procedures that interact in this manner share more properties than those that do not, Swartzentruber concluded that contextual control of responding often is more characteristic of occa- sion setting than of simple conditioning.

It is worth noting that in Swartzentruber's (1991) experiments, contex- tual control of responding to a CS was established by explicit discrimina- tion between the consequences of that CS in different contexts, analogous to the explicit discrimination procedures used in occasion setting experi- ments with discrete cues. On the other hand, other experiments that have suggested relations between contextual control and occasion setting (e.g., Bouton & Swartzentruber, 1986; Swartzentruber & Bouton, 1988) have used nondifferential procedures, procedures that have not been observed to establish occasion setting when discrete cues are used as stimulus elements. At present, there still is controversy about the necessary condi- tions for the acquisition of conditional contextual control (e.g., Grahame et al., 1990; Lovibond, Preston, & Mackintosh, 1984).

2. Feature–Target Similarity

If occasion setting is enhanced by manipulations that place psychological distance between the feature and target, while maintaining the relation between target and reinforcer, then occasion setting should be best when feature and target are most dissimilar. Arranging similarity relations between feature and target would encourage association between those cues, "bridging the temporal gap" between them, or perhaps configuring feature and target to form a new, unique cue that could be directly associated with the reinforcer, reducing the likelihood of occasion setting. Lamarre and Holland (1987), who measured the conditioned suppression of lever pressing of rats, and Holland (1989a), who measured appetitive Pavlovian responding of rats, found that the use of similar-modality feature and target cues slowed the acquisition of serial FN and FP discriminations (respectively).

3. Target Intensity

The conflict view claimed that a feature acquired occasion setting when it was better correlated with reinforcement than a target that was more contiguous with reinforcement. Extending that reasoning, I supposed that a feature might acquire occasion setting when it was better correlated with reinforcement than another cue that was more associable with the US for reasons other than temporal factors. Holland (1989c), using Pavlovian appetitive conditioning procedures, examined the acquisition of simultaneous FP discriminations as a function of the intensity of the target cue. I reasoned that if the feature cue was more salient than the target, feature–reinforcer associations would form, as in previous experiments. But if the target cue was considerably more intense than the feature, strong target–reinforcer associations would form and overshadow conditioning to the weaker feature, despite the equivalent reinforcer contiguity of the feature and target and the superior predictive relation of the feature. The feature then would come to modulate the action of the already established target–reinforcer unit, just as in serial FP discrimination training.

When a weak–moderate intensity auditory cue was used as the target with a visual feature, the rats solved the discrimination by acquiring feature–reinforcer associations, as in our previous simultaneous FP discrimination experiments. That is, responding to the compound comprised mostly rearing and quiet food cup behavior (characteristic of the visual feature cue), and that responding was abolished by nonreinforced presentation of the feature alone (extinction). Conversely, when the target was a high-intensity auditory cue, the rats apparently adopted an occasion setting strategy: responding during the compound included substantial head jerk behavior (which was not observed on auditory-only trials) and was immune to the effects of feature extinction (Young & Pearce, 1984, report a similar finding). As in previous experiments (Section II,D), the effects observed with compounds that included different intensity noises were shown to depend on the intensity of the noises at the time of training, not that at the time of testing.

These outcomes are consistent with both the casual conflict notion and Rescorla's (1988) more precise statement. A more intense target would acquire more excitatory strength on compound trials, paving the way for its acquisition of a stronger inhibitory component on nonreinforced target-alone trials.

4. Target Training

The various guiding hypotheses also suggested that occasion setting might be encouraged or discouraged by explicit manipulation of the association of the individual elements of the compound cue with the reinforcer. For example, if occasion setting depends on the formation of a target–reinforcer unit (which is in turn modulated by the feature), then pretraining of the target–reinforcer relation might be anticipated to enhance the acquisition of occasion setting. Not only would this procedure provide a head start on the formation of this relation, but the absence of the feature cue removes a major source of interference (overshadowing) of conditioning to the target during normal FP training, and the lack of nonreinforced target trials eliminates the decremental effects of those trials. Thus, pretraining of the target would provide substantially greater opportunity to establish this necessary unit than the standard FP procedure. Furthermore, from Rescorla's (1988) perspective, this procedure would insure that at the time of initial nonreinforced presentations of the target, it would be highly conditioned, hence permitting its development of an especially strong inhibitory component.

Several studies examined the effects of target pretraining. Most clear cut were the results of Rescorla (1986b), who found substantial enhancement of a feature's occasion-setting power in simultaneous FP training in pigeon autoshaping. Ross (1983) found a suggestion of a similar enhancement in appetitive Pavlovian serial FP in rats, although the effect was not statistically reliable.

Perhaps most interesting were the results of Holland (1989c), who examined the effects of prior target–reinforcer training on the acquisition of occasion setting in simultaneous FP learning in rats. In that experiment, the feature was a visual cue and the target was either a low- or a high-intensity auditory cue. Without pretraining of the target, only simple conditioning of the visual feature was observed when the low-intensity target was used, but occasion setting was observed when the high-intensity target was used (see Section III,B,3). If occasion setting is produced whenever the target has the opportunity to be conditioned prior to the feature, or when nonreinforced target presentations produce a substantial inhibitory component, then this prior target training should favor occasion setting regardless of the intensity of the target used. But to the extent that occasion setting is engendered by perceptual relations between the feature and target cues, then pretraining might be anticipated to have a facilitatory effect only under perceptual conditions adequate for occasion setting (i.e., with the intense target). Indeed, pretraining facilitated occasion setting only with the intense target.

However, separate target–reinforcer pairings can only benefit occasion setting up to a point. Consider, for example, the consequences of continuing those pairings into FP discrimination training itself. In the extreme case, that of replacing the nonreinforced target trials with reinforced ones, Davidson & Rescorla (1986) with rats and Rescorla (1985) with pigeons found little evidence for occasion setting. This outcome is hardly surprising from either Rescorla's inhibition perspective (the target would not acquire an inhibitory component) or a conflict hypothesis (the target was a better predictor than the feature both in terms of contingency and contiguity), but it does restrict the perceptual and modified conflict views somewhat. Apparently, perceptual discontinuities or differences in the rates of acquisition to target and feature alone are insufficient for the development of occasion setting: the feature must also be a better predictor of the reinforcer than the target. Several investigations of the effects of the relative predictiveness of feature and target bear out this claim. First, reinforced presentations of the serial compound, without also presenting nonreinforced target trials, do not yield occasion setting in the rat appetitive conditioning situation (e.g., Holland & Ross, 1981). Second, Holland (1986b) found no evidence of occasion setting when a serial feature–target compound was reinforced on half of its presentations, and the target alone was reinforced on half of its presentations. And third, in unpublished experiments, I have found no evidence for occasion setting with 25% or 75% of both types of trials reinforced. It is worth noting that with all these partial reinforcement schedules, the target acquired its strength more rapidly than the feature. Similarly, although no independent tests of inhibition were made, it could be argued that these schedules provided ample opportunities both for the target to acquire an inhibitory component (the target was nonreinforced after a history of reinforcement) and for the feature to be reinforced in the presence of that target CS.

Paradoxically, Rescorla (1988) has reported that prior training of the target as a conditioned inhibitor, that is, as A in a $B+/BA-$ procedure, also enhances X's acquisition of occasion setting in an $XA+/A-$ procedure in pigeon autoshaping. This outcome is predicted straightforwardly by Rescorla's account for the acquisition of occasion setting: explicit establishment of inhibition to the target would obviously maximize the chance that the feature would be reinforced in the presence of an inhibitory target. However, it is not clear to me how any of the other guides would anticipate this finding.

5. *Feature Training*

Several studies indicate that manipulations that enhance conditioning of the feature in FP discriminations tend to diminish occasion setting. For example, in Section III,A I discussed temporal variables that affected conditioning and occasion setting in opposite manners. Similarly, Ross (1983) and Rescorla (1986b) showed that prior feature–reinforcer pairings interfered with the acquisition of occasion setting to that feature. It might be argued that the acquisition of conditioning to the feature directly interferes with its ability to acquire occasion setting, for example, from the perceptual view, by encouraging the grouping of feature and reinforcer, at the expense of the feature → (target → US) grouping. Alternately, there may be some other inherent competitive relation between conditioning and occasion setting, such that a feature may have only so much signal value to distribute among potential signaling functions.

A simpler account for these effects, however, is that prior training of the feature merely blocks the formation of the target–reinforcer associations demanded by each of the characterizations of the conditions necessary for the acquisition of occasion setting. This view is supported by Rescorla (1986b), who found that feature pretraining had deleterious effects only if that pretraining resulted in blocking of target–reinforcer associations. When blocking effects were minimized by explicit pretraining of the target as well, the feature readily acquired occasion setting. In fact, Rescorla (1991) has demonstrated that under some circumstances feature–reinforcer pairings can *enhance* the establishment of occasion setting, probably by increasing attentional processing of the feature. Thus, there seems to be little justification to assume any inherent competition between occasion setting and conditioning powers of a cue.

Several authors have investigated the effects of contemporaneous *non-*reinforced presentations of the feature as well. Holland (1989a, 1989b) and Ross and Holland (1981, 1982) found that occasion setting was acquired equally readily with serial positive patterning ($X \to A+/X-/A-$) and serial FP discriminations. At the same time, feature–reinforcer (and also feature–target) associations were substantially weaker as a consequence of those nonreinforced feature presentations. Thus, the occurrence of a consistent feature–reinforcer or feature–target relation does not seem critical for the acquisition of occasion setting. Of course, our experiments involved only minimal degrading of those relations, ranging from 25% to 50% of all features being followed by targets, so it remains to be seen whether the acquisition of occasion setting is wholly immune to these effects. But suffice it to say that within a range in which considerable variation in feature conditioning occurs there is no observable variation in the rate of occasion setting, just as was the case with the temporal variables discussed in Section III,A.

All in all, occasion setting was most commonly observed under temporal and nontemporal conditions that would seem to encourage perceptual grouping of the target and reinforcer on compound trials but at the same time arrange for the feature to be a better predictor of the reinforcer than the target. Many but not all of these conditions arrange for the reinforcement of the feature in the presence of a target with a strong inhibitory component. Thus, although each of the hypotheses that guided this search has merit, the precise determinants of occasion setting remain unspecified.

IV. Content of Learning in Occasion Setting

Perhaps the most compelling question about any learning process concerns its content. Just how is the organism changed when it acquires occasion setting: what is the nature of the internal representation of information in occasion setting? In this section I first review the relation between occasion setting and simple association that was discussed in Section II. As a point of departure I take simple representations of knowledge in Pavlovian conditioning (e.g., Rescorla, 1974), in which internal representations of CS and US events are linked by excitatory and inhibitory associative links, which permit a CS to generate CRs by activating the US representation (e.g., Fig. 7). Next I consider a variety of possible loci for the modulatory action of occasion setters within that representational scheme and suggest some alternative schemes. Finally I introduce a configural alternative to occasion setting and contrast the predictions and implications of configural and occasion setting perspectives.

A. Relation of Occasion Setting to Conditioning

Section II of this article described many examples of how responding ascribed to occasion setting differed from that usually attributed to conditioning (excitatory or inhibitory), focusing on differences in response form, the effects of counterconditioning and extinction, and differences in transfer to other target cues. Section III showed further that behavior attributed to simple conditioning and occasion setting was affected differently by many experimental manipulations, such as changes in the feature–reinforcer interval and prior training. Finally, considerable evidence for the independence of cues' occasion-setting and response-eliciting properties was presented.

This distinction is also supported by the results of some brain lesion experiments that used our appetitive conditioning procedure. Ross, Orr, Holland, & Berger (1984) found that in serial FP discriminations, lesions of the hippocampal formation destroyed the acquisition of occasion setting to X but had no effect on the acquisition of simple conditioning to that cue. More recently, Jarrard and Davidson (1991) replicated this finding but provided evidence that the locus of neural damage was probably not the hippocampus proper. Regardless of the effective lesion site, however, these results indicate an anatomical as well as functional independence of simple conditioning and occasion-setting functions.

B. HIERARCHICAL ORGANIZATION

Our early research was guided by the idea that the independence of occasion setting and simple conditioning was most easily understood if associative and occasion-setting links acted at different loci. Consider the simple-minded portrayal of the representation of FN $A+/X \rightarrow A-$ conditioning episodes in Fig. 12A. In this diagram, CRs are produced when a CS

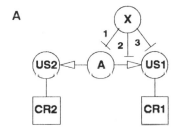

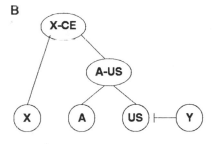

Fig. 12. (A) Diagram of alternative representations after initial $A \rightarrow \mathrm{US1}/X \rightarrow A-$ serial FN training and subsequent pairings of A with US2. The arrows represent excitatory associations, and the barred lines 1, 2, and 3 represent potential loci of X's negative occasion-setting effects (see text). (B) Diagram of a hierarchical representation in which X serves as an occasion setter and Y is a simple inhibitor. Circles represent simple stimulus representations and ellipses portray higher-order control elements.

(*A*) activates a US representation by virtue of excitatory associations. Ross and Holland (1981) suggested that whereas simple excitation and inhibition acted directly on the US representation, occasion setting acted on the *A*–US association (link 1 in Fig. 16A). A single feature could easily have an inhibitory relation with the *A*–US association and an excitatory relation with the US representation.

Alternatively, *X* might reduce responding to *A* by modifying processing of *A* itself, say, by reducing the sensitivity of the *A* representation to stimulation by *A* itself (link 2 in Fig. 12A). This modification of the effectiveness of the target CS might be profitably described in terms of attentional models of conditioning, which attribute a variety of stimulus selection effects to conditioning-dependent changes in the processing of CSs. Casually speaking, contingencies that favor occasion setting might be those that permit *X* to direct attention toward or away from *A*.

Conversely, Rescorla (1985) argued that both exciters and occasion setters act directly on the US representation, but by different means. Whereas exciters elicit CRs by activating the US representation, occasion setters are linked to the US representation with a separate modulatory link, which transiently raises or lowers the US representation's sensitivity to activation by its associates (link 3 in Fig. 13A). Thus a single feature might have at the same time both an excitatory association and an inhibitory modulatory link with the US representation.

1. CS and US Specificity of Occasion Setting

Most of our attempts to localize the action of occasion setters involved transfer strategies (see Rescorla & Holland, 1977, for an exposition of the logic of such transfer testing in the context of a different question). Our initial transfer experiments, described earlier in Section II,C (see Fig. 8), were designed to investigate the CS specificity of occasion setting. If occasion setters acted by modulating the activity of the US representation, as Rescorla suggested, then they should alter responding to any cue associated with that US. However, in the experiments described previously, we found that features trained within serial FN and FP discriminations failed to modulate responding conditioned to separately trained target cues. Consequently, we concluded that, at least in our preparation, occasion setters did not act directly on the US representation but instead acted either directly on the CS representation or on the CS–US association itself.

Our next experiments attempted to distinguish between the latter alternatives. If occasion setters acted on the CS–US association, then their action should be US specific as well as CS specific. Thus, if *A* were paired with a new US (US2 in Fig. 13A) after the completion of occasion setting training, then X should have no power to modulate responses based on A's associations with the new US. However, if X modulated attention to A, then X would reduce the likelihood of A's eliciting any response conditioned to it, regardless of US.

Holland (1985, 1989d) first trained serial FN ($X \rightarrow A - /A +$) discriminations with either food or shock US, and then separately paired A with the other reinforcer. Subsequent transfer tests showed that although X retained its ability to modulate any remaining responding that was based on A's association with the training US, it had no effect on responding due to A's associations with the new US. Later experiments (Holland, 1989d) showed a similar pattern when the two USs were food pellets and a liquid sucrose solution.

This US specificity implied that X acted on the CS–US association itself, rather than on the representation of A. Consequently I suggested (Holland, 1983, 1985) that occasion setting might be well described in terms of a simple hierarchical model of inhibitory effects offered by Estes (1972, 1973). In that model, associations are represented as control elements that link representations of the individual events. Thus, in an $A + /X \rightarrow A -$ discrimination, the connection between representations of A and the US is mediated by an A–US control element. Furthermore, as a consequence of serial FN training, a higher order control element linking X and the A–US control element is established (Fig. 13B); X modulates responding normally elicited by A by suppressing the activity of that control element. I suggested that procedures that establish occasion setting are those that especially encourage the formation of these hierarchically organized representations of conditioning episodes. Other procedures, like simultaneous FN discriminations, promote the formation of associations between representations of the individual events themselves (the Y–US element in Fig. 13B). I then speculated that occasion setting might be a link between simple Pavlovian association and more complex learning, and that it might provide a model system for the study of hierarchical control.

2. Within-Category Transfer of Occasion Setting

This particular hierarchical model demanded substantial CS and US specificity of occasion setting, consistent with all the transfer test data I have described in this article so far. Unfortunately for my optimistic speculations just cited, Rescorla (e.g., 1985) reported substantial transfer of occasion setters' powers across target CSs in autoshaping experiments with pigeons. Our next task was to reconcile these observations of transfer with our consistent failure to find transfer.

Although species and preparation differences were an obvious potential source of the discrepancy, Lamarre (1984) and Lamarre and Holland (1987) sought a procedural origin. Two major procedural differences seemed reasonable candidates for the origin of the different outcomes: the number of discriminations trained, and the nature of the transfer target's training. The transfer experiments in our laboratory all involved initial training of a single discrimination, followed by appropriate training of a target cue, and concluded with transfer testing. Conversely, Rescorla typically trained two discriminations in each subject contemporaneously and then examined the power of each occasion setter to modulate responding in the presence of the other target.

We thought it possible that whereas training of a single discrimination would establish modulatory links between X and the A–US association (as we posited), training of multiple discriminations might encourage a more global representation, akin to a learning set. Similarly, we thought that the like treatment of targets in Rescorla's experiments might also encourage transfer between them. Lamarre (Lamarre, 1984; Lamarre & Holland, 1987) investigated the contribution of these factors to transfer, using a serial FN discrimination procedure with rats in a conditioned suppression preparation. Rats were first trained with either one or two serial FN discriminations. Subjects that received only one serial FN discrimination also received other treatments of a second excitor (for example, in one experiment, separate groups of rats received presentations of a consistently reinforced cue, a partially reinforced cue, or a simultaneous FN discrimination). Transfer tests were then conducted in all groups. Next, a third excitor was separately trained in all subjects, either by partially reinforcing it, or by first training it, then extinguishing it, and then retraining it. All these procedures gave the target a history of both reinforcement and nonreinforcement. Finally, transfer tests were again administered.

Figure 13 shows the results of one of these experiments as well as those of an analogous appetitive conditioning experiment in which all subjects received training with two serial FN discriminations and, concurrently, a third excitor (Holland, 1989d). The results of both experiments were clear: X's ability to modulate responding to its target transferred readily (but not perfectly) to the target of the other serial FN discrimination, but only minimally to the other kinds of targets.

These outcomes reconciled the apparent differences in Rescorla's and our data but shed little light on the locus of occasion setters' action. Lamarre and I (1987) posed two alternative accounts for the occurrence of transfer to targets of other occasion setters, but not to other cues. Our first proposal maintained the claim that occasion setting acts on particular CS–US associations. Following Jenkins (1963), we suggested that like

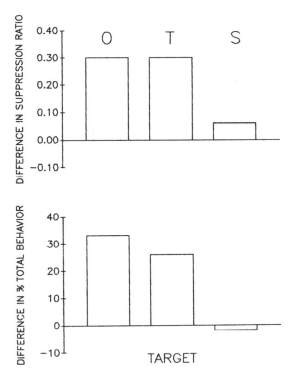

Fig. 13. Transfer test performance as a function of target training. Values indicate the difference in responding during a target when it was preceded by the X feature and when it was not. The bars labeled O show performance with the original target, those labeled T show performance with the target trained with the other feature, and those labeled S show performance when the target had been separately reinforced. The data in the top panel are from Lamarre and Holland (1987); those in the bottom panel are from Holland (1989d).

treatment of cues enhances generalization among them. When occasion setters are followed by targets of other occasion setters, enhanced confusion between the features and between the targets conspire to enhance apparent transfer, even if the occasion setters are acting on specific CS–US associations. Unfortunately, in the absence of a specific theory of generalization and a mechanism whereby contingencies that generate occasion setting would modify that generalization, this account is little more than a redescription of the data.

Our second account involved a claim that occasion setting training involves access to multiple memory systems (e.g., Holland, 1990). Within this view, simple conditioning and occasion setting involve separate memory systems. As a consequence of exposure to simple conditioning procedures, representations of individual events and of the excitatory and inhibitory associations among those events are stored in a lower-level memory system. But under circumstances that generate occasion setting, information about those events and their relations is also represented in another memory system, which features conditional "if–then" relations (e.g., Hirsh, 1980). We assumed further that transfer is more likely to occur within systems than between systems. Simple inhibition transfers readily across cues of a variety of training histories because all cues are represented in the simple system, but transfer of negative occasion setting occurs only among those cues that have themselves been involved in occasion setting, because only those cues are represented in the conditional system. Similarly, because transfer across systems is minimal, the simple associative strength of a cue can be largely independent of the strength or valence of its occasion-setting relations with the same events in the conditional system.

A recent series of experiments considered how information about occasion setting discriminations is represented in the conditional system. Figure 14 illustrates the first, an elaboration of the Estes-like representation shown in Fig. 12B. In this version, the conditional system includes control elements that gate simple-system associations between target CSs and the USs, and higher-order control elements that link the occasion setting features and the A–US1 and B–US1 control elements.

In order to account for the observed transfer among targets of occasion setters in the structure shown in Fig. 14, it is necessary to assume substantial generalization or class equivalence among the control elements and/or higher-order control elements. That is, for X to exert influence over responding based on B–US1 associations, either the X–CE and Y–CE

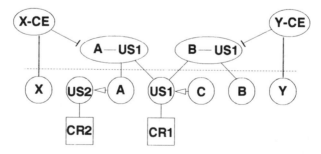

Fig. 14.   Diagram of a representation of conditioning episodes in Holland (1989d, Experiment 3), in which hierarchically organized control elements (ellipses) that relate to CS–US associations are represented in a conditional memory system as a consequence of occasion setting training. The elements above the dotted line reside in the conditional system and those below the dotted line are represented in the simple system.

higher-order control elements or the A–US1 and B–US1 control elements must be relatively interchangeable. Note that such greater generalization would apply only within the conditional system and would not affect performance generated within the simple system. Thus, a given target–US control element might be a suitable target for the action of other occasion setters, but representations of individual CSs and USs in the simple system would not be (e.g., C or US2 in Fig. 14.)

Consider first the application of this framework to Holland's (1989d) Experiment 3, in which reinforced presentations of a simple excitor, $C+$, were intermixed with training on two serial FN discriminations: $X \rightarrow A-/A+$, $Y \rightarrow B-/B+$, $C+$, using either a food pellet or sucrose US (US1). X and Y were of different modalities, and the modalities and identities of A, B, and C were counterbalanced. After discrimination training, the rats received continued pairings of B with the same US1 that was used in discrimination training. However, A was paired with the other US (US2; either sucrose or food pellets). C was paired with the original US1 in half the subjects and with the new, transfer US2 in the other half. Finally, the ability of X and Y to modulate responding in the presence of A, B, and C was examined in transfer tests.

As a consequence of the discrimination training procedures, all of the features, CSs, and USs would be represented in the simple memory system. Additionally, because of the occasion setting contingencies, A–US1 and B–US1 control elements and X–(A–US1) and Y–(B–US1) higher-order control elements would be established in the conditional system. Thus, the occasion-setting powers of X and Y should transfer readily to responding gated by the A–US1 and B–US1 control elements, that is, to responding elicited by A and B based on those cues' associations with US1.

However, because neither C nor US2 was involved in an occasion setting discrimination, control elements linking C and US1, C and US2, or A and US2 would *not* be represented in the conditional system. Instead, associations among those elements would be represented only in the simple system. Consequently, the occasion-setting powers of X and Y should not modulate responding based on C–US1, C–US2, or A–US2 associations.

The results mirrored those predictions (bottom panel of Fig. 13). First, Y maintained its ability to suppress responding based on $B \rightarrow$ US1 associations (the bar labeled O). Second, responding based on those $B \rightarrow$ US1 associations was also suppressed by X (the bar labeled T), indicating transfer of X's occasion-setting power to another target that had also been trained as a target of an occasion setter. Third, neither X nor Y suppressed responding during C (the bar labeled S), which was never presented within an occasion setting discrimination. Fourth, neither X nor Y suppressed responding to A that was based on A's associations with US2, which was also never presented within an occasion setting discrimination (not shown in Fig. 13). Thus, the results of this experiment were consistent with the scheme portrayed in Fig. 14: occasion setters only modulated responding that was mediated by control elements in the conditional system, which were presumably established only by occasion setting discriminations.

Our next experiment (Holland, 1989d, Experiment 4) expanded on these findings by examining whether negative occasion setting transfers across these same two USs if control elements involving each of them were represented in the conditional system, that is, if they were both trained within discriminations known to produce occasion setting. It should be noted that Holland (1989d, Experiment 1) found that simple conditioned inhibition, established with simultaneous FN procedures, transferred across these two USs.

Rats were first trained with two serial FN discriminations, with two different USs: $X \rightarrow A-/A \rightarrow$ US1, $Y \rightarrow B-/B \rightarrow$ US2. (Note that these two USs, food pellets and sucrose solution, which were delivered to different locations in the chamber, supported recognizably different CRs.) After separate pairing of a third excitor C with US1, a transfer test examined X's and Y's abilities to suppress responding to A, B, and C.

Figure 15A adapts the hierarchical framework of Fig. 14 to portray the associative structure that would be established by the procedures of this experiment (Holland, 1989d, Experiment 4). Both A–US1 and B–US2 units are represented in the conditional system and thus might serve as equivalent targets for modulatory action of X and Y. But C–US2 units would not be formed, and hence neither X nor Y should modulate responding elicited by C.

Consistent with the framework shown in Fig. 15A (and with the results of the previous experiment), neither X nor Y affected responding elicited by C. Furthermore, transfer of X's and Y's negative occasion-setting powers to the targets that had been paired with the other US was nearly complete (top panel of Fig. 16). Therefore, transfer of occasion setting across both CS target and US was observed, but only if the transfer target and reinforcer had themselves been part of an occasion setting discrimination, and hence control elements linking those events had been established in the conditional system. Accordingly, in this experiment responding mediated by *any* target–US control element represented in the conditional system seemed to be an appropriate locus for the action of occasion setters.

Combined with the results of Holland's (1989d) Experiments 1–3, these results support the general notion that transfer *within* the simple or condi-

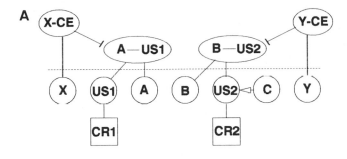

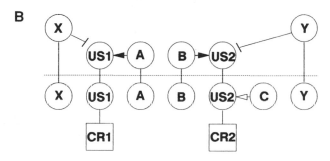

Fig. 15. Alternative representations of occasion setting in Holland's (1989d) Experiment 4. A, a representation in which CS–US association control elements are represented in a conditional memory system as a consequence of occasion setting training; B, individual events are represented in that system. In both panels, the elements above the dotted line reside in the conditional system, and those below the dotted line reside in the simple system.

tional systems is greater than transfer *between* those systems. The frameworks shown in Figs. 14 and 15A capture this intuition by contrasting relations among representations of individual events in the simple system with relations among control elements, represented in the conditional system. However, neither this notion of differential transfer nor the data already presented demand that *hierarchical control elements* are established.

Figure 15B portrays a conditional system that functions in the manner described by Rescorla (1985), that is, with no hierarchical organization of targets and reinforcers into control elements, but including representations of all the individual events involved in occasion setting discriminations. In this framework, occasion setters act not by activating CS–US control elements but by altering the sensitivity of the US representation (in the conditional system) to activation by targets also represented in that system. Thus, targets of other occasion setters would be appropriate

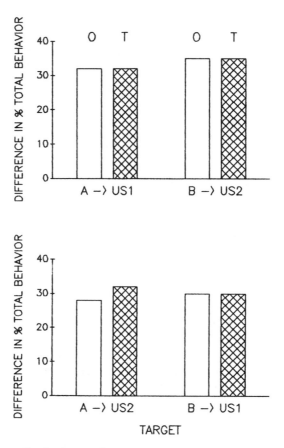

Fig. 16.   Responding in the transfer tests of Holland's (1989d) Experiment 4. Top panel shows responding in the first test and bottom panel shows responding in the second test, after reversal training. The open bars represent responding during targets when they were preceded by the features originally trained with those targets, and the hatched bars show responding during targets when they were preceded by the transfer features trained with the other targets. All entries reflect the differences in responding during the targets on target-alone and feature-target trials.

targets of transfer, but exciters not part of occasion setting discriminations would not be, because they are not represented in the conditional system. Accordingly, in Fig. 15B, *A, B,* US1, and US2 are all individually represented in the conditional system and thus should all be eligible for transfer (as observed in the experiments just described). But *C* was represented only in the simple system and hence would not be an acceptable target of *X*'s and *Y*'s occasion-setting powers (as observed).

An extension of Holland's (1989d) Experiment 4 contrasted the frameworks represented in Figs. 15A and 15B. In it, I asked whether transfer of negative occasion setting across CSs and USs demanded that specific target–reinforcer control elements be established in the conditional system (as suggested in Fig. 15A) or merely that the targets and reinforcers all be individually represented in the conditional system (Fig. 15B).

Immediately after the transfer test just described (results in the top panel of Fig. 16), the *A* and *B* targets were separately paired with the US that had been originally paired with the other target, that is, *A* was paired with US2 and *B* with US1 (reversal training). Then another transfer test was administered.

As in the previous transfer test, both *X* and *Y* suppressed responding elicited by both *A* and *B* (bottom panel of Fig. 16). What is especially notable about this finding is that in this final test the two targets *A* and *B* elicited responding based on associations, *A*–US2 and *B*–US1, for which control elements would not have been established in the conditional system in the original training: neither pair had been involved as a target–reinforcer unit in an occasion setting discrimination. Accordingly, as a result of the initial occasion setting training, the individual target and US events were apparently represented in the conditional system, permitting subsequent simple pairing of those targets and USs to establish associations within the *conditional* system. If occasion setting training had established only *A*–US1 and *B*–US2 control elements in the conditional system, then subsequent *A*–US2 and *B*–US1 pairings would not have been sufficient to establish *A*–US2 and *B*–US1 control elements, and no transfer would have been observed.

Thus, the scheme shown in Fig. 15B, which emphasizes the representation of individual events in the conditional system, seems more adequate than the scheme shown in Fig. 15A, which focuses on target–reinforcer units. Of course, to say that higher-order target reinforcer units *need* not be represented does not demand that they *must* not be represented. With a few exceptions (e.g., the experiment just described), transfer of occasion setting is not complete, even in Rescorla's laboratory (e.g., Rescorla, 1987). Indeed, in experiments that examined transfer after serial feature *positive* discriminations (Holland, 1989a), we found substantial decrements when a target cue was replaced by the target from another serial feature positive discrimination (but still more transfer than to cues not trained as targets of occasion setters). The lack of complete transfer might be indicative of the representation of specific target–reinforcer associations or control elements as well as of individual events (e.g., Colwill & Rescorla, 1990).

3.   Independence of Positive and Negative Occasion Setting

We have come from an initial hypothesis that occasion setters act on particular CS–US associations to one that allows for broad generality across both CSs and USs, but only those represented in a particular memory system as a consequence of particular training experiences. Recent experiments that used the discrete trial operant procedure described earlier (Section III,A,3) explored further the limitations or rules of transfer within this conditional memory system.

All the previous experiments considered the transfer of occasion setting across targets and reinforcers that had been involved in the same kind of occasion setting. That is, a feature from one FP discrimination was asked to modulate responding to targets of another FP discrimination, or a feature from one FN discrimination was asked to modulate responding to a target from another FN discrimination. If transfer of occasion setting is indeed general across all events represented in the conditional system, then features from FP discriminations might also be expected to modulate responding elicited by cues trained as targets of FN discriminations, and vice versa.

In the first experiment in this series, Javier Morell trained both an FP and FN discrimination in the same subjects ($X \rightarrow A+/A-, B+/Y \rightarrow B-$), in which the X and Y features were of different modalities, and the identities of A and B were counterbalanced. Transfer tests assessed X's and Y's abilities to modulate responding to the other targets. To make possible the observation of both suppressive and facilitatory effects of the features on both targets, prior to one set of transfer tests Morell reinforced A and nonreinforced B until responding occurred during both at an intermediate level. Although X still enhanced responding to A and Y suppressed responding to B, X had no effects on responding to B and Y had no effects on responding to A. This absence of transfer implied substantial independence of positive and negative occasion setting.

Morell also examined the effects of a simultaneous XY compound on responding to A and B in those subjects. If X's and Y's occasion-setting powers summed (subtractively), then the compound should engender intermediate levels of responding to both A and B. But if only X can act on A and only Y can act on B, then the XY compound would affect responding to A the same way X-alone affects it (facilitating it) and should affect responding to B the same way Y-alone affects it (suppressing it). Morell found the latter outcomes, further strengthening the idea that positive and negative occasion setting are quite independent (cf Wilson & Pearce, 1989). (It is worth noting here that Rescorla, 1987, in a similar experiment, but using a target cue that was an acceptable target of both positive and negative occasion setting, found the XY compound to produce effects intermediate to those of X and Y alone).

Holland (1991) and Holland and Reeve (1991) explored a similar question in a somewhat different context. Consider a discrimination in which a feature cue serves as a positive occasion setter for responding to one target and as a negative occasion setter for responding to another target, $X \rightarrow A+/A-$, $X \rightarrow B-/B+$. If occasion setters act by altering the sensitivity of the US representation to activation by target cues (Rescorla, 1985), or if they act indiscriminately on any target of another occasion setting discrimination (Holland, 1989d), then this discrimination should be very difficult. From Rescorla's (1985) perspective, X would have to both raise and lower the US representation's sensitivity to activation, making the discrimination impossible, without adding some mechanism of CS specificity to that view. From Holland's (1989d) perspective, if both A and B were appropriate targets for both the positive and negative occasion setting powers that X might develop, then X's explicitly trained facilitatory influence on A would be countered by its transferred suppressive influence, and its explicit suppressive influence on B would be countered by its transferred facilitatory influence. To the extent that transferred powers are weaker than explicitly trained ones, the discrimination would be possible but relatively difficult.

In fact, the ambiguous discrimination was learned readily. Acquisition of both components of the ambiguous discrimination, that is, $X \rightarrow A+/A-$ and $X \rightarrow B-/B+$, was at least as rapid as in the analogous positive patterning $X \rightarrow A+/A-/X-/B+$ and negative patterning $X+/A-/X \rightarrow B-/B+$ discriminations (in which each of the three cues bore the same individual relations to reinforcement as in the ambiguous discrimination).

Three accounts for this rapid acquisition of the ambiguous discrimination come to mind. First, as Holland (1983) suggested, occasion setters may act on specific target–reinforcer associations. Thus, X could readily facilitate responding based on the A–US association and suppress responding based on the B–US association. Unfortunately, our transfer data (Section IV,B,2) showed such a view to be untenable in the case of separate learning of FP and FN discriminations: substantial transfer occurred to targets of other FP and FN discriminations respectively. A second possibility relies on Morell's finding that positive and negative features do not transfer their action to stimuli trained as targets of the other kind of discrimination (negative and positive, respectively). Perhaps occasion setters act on any cues represented in the conditional memory system, except that positive and negative occasion setting functions are somewhat independent. Third, and least satisfying, it is possible that ambiguous discriminations involve a different sort of learning process from the occasion setting found in FP and FN discriminations, yet another memory system in which, for example, transfer occurs only among other cues also involved in ambiguous discriminations.

Holland (1991) considered these alternatives by examining transfer among the features and targets of ambiguous, FP, and FN discriminations. All subjects received training on a primary ambiguous discrimination $X \to A+/A-$, $X \to B-/B+$ in addition to one of four other secondary treatments. Those secondary treatments were an FP discrimination, $Y \to C+/C-$, an FN discrimination, $Y \to C-/C+$, another ambiguous discrimination, $Y \to C+/C-$, $Y \to D-/D+$, or a pseudodiscrimination, $Y \to C\pm/C\pm$, in which both serial compound and target-alone trials were reinforced on half their presentations and nonreinforced on the other half. Then all rats received transfer tests, which assessed responding to all combinations of the X and Y features and A, B, C (and in one case, D) targets. Finally, as in Morell's experiment, another set of transfer tests was administered after responding to the B cue alone was adjusted to intermediate levels (by either reinforcing it or nonreinforcing it in the various groups), so that both facilitation and suppression was observable).

The results of the transfer tests were clearcut. First, in the initial transfer tests, there was mutual transfer between analogous features from the ambiguous, FP, and FN discriminations (top panel of Fig. 17). That is, the primary ambiguous X feature facilitated responding during the secondary C targets of another ambiguous discrimination and of an FP discrimination and suppressed responding during the D target of the secondary ambiguous discrimination and during the C target of the secondary FN discrimination. X did not, however, affect responding to the partially reinforced C target of the pseudodiscrimination. Furthermore (bottom panel of Fig. 17), responding to the A target of the primary ambiguous discrimination was facilitated by the Y feature from both the secondary ambiguous and FP discriminations, and responding to the B target of the primary ambiguous discrimination was suppressed by the Y feature from both the secondary ambiguous and FN discriminations. Neither primary target's responding was affected by the Y feature from the pseudodiscrimination.

Second, even after responding to A and B was brought to intermediate levels, the secondary FP feature had no effect on the primary B target, and the secondary FN feature had no effect on responding to the primary A target (not shown). Thus, the FP feature only modulated responding to the target of the positive $X \to A+/A-$ component of the ambiguous discrimination, and the FN feature only modulated responding to the target of the negative component $X \to B-/B+$ of the ambiguous discrimination. Fur-

AMBIGUOUS FEATURE

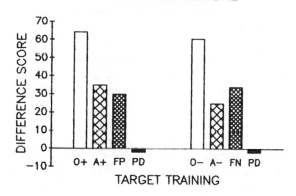

TARGET TRAINING

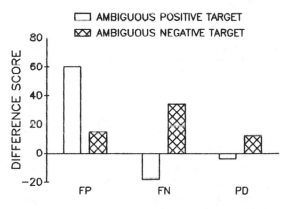

TRANSFER FEATURE TRAINING

Fig. 17. Responding during transfer tests of Holland's (1991) Experiment 1. The left four bars of the top panel show responding on tests with the primary ambiguous feature and either its original positive target (*O*), the other ambiguous positive target (*A+*), the feature-positive target (FP), or the pseudodiscrimination target (PD). The right four bars show responding on tests with the primary ambiguous feature and either its original target (*O−*), the other ambiguous negative target (*A−*), the feature-negative target (FN−), or the pseudodiscrimination target (PD). The bottom panel shows responding during the positive and negative targets of the primary ambiguous discrimination when preceded by the features from either the feature-positive discrimination (FP), feature-negative discrimination (FN), or pseudodiscrimination (PD).

thermore, regardless of the level of responding established to A and B, the secondary ambiguous feature Y only facilitated responding to A and suppressed responding to B.

These transfer data indicate that the ambiguous feature acquired transfer properties very similar to those normally possessed by positive and negative occasion setters from FP and FN discriminations: it enhanced responding to targets of FP discriminations, suppressed responding to targets of FN discriminations, and had no effect on targets of a pseudo-discrimination (that is, a "separately trained cue"). Furthermore, analogous to Morell's results, positive and negative occasion-setting functions in the ambiguous discriminations seemed quite independent: (1) although positive targets from the ambiguous and FP discriminations were more or less interchangeable, and negative targets from the ambiguous and FN discriminations were comparable, there was no transfer from positive to negative or vice versa; (2) acquisition of both positive and negative occasion-setting functions to X was no more difficult than the acquisition of only one (Holland & Reeve, 1991). Thus, within the systems pictured in Fig. 15, all events involved in occasion setting discriminations are represented in the higher level system, but the system is somehow compartmentalized to isolate positive and negative occasion setting functions (that partition is not shown in Fig. 15).

4.   Functional Equivalence of Features and Targets

A related question that arises is whether feature and target events are interchangeable or are coded with unique properties. Here the answer seems straightforward. In several unpublished experiments, I have examined the effects of presenting target → feature, target → target, and feature → feature compounds after serial FP discrimination training. In no case did I see any evidence of modulatory activity. Thus there was no evidence for equivalence relations (e.g., Sidman, 1986) between feature and target in serial FP discriminations: we observed neither reflexivity (an event did not modulate responding to itself) nor symmetry (a target did not modulate responding to a feature). Rescorla (1985) reported a similar set of outcomes in pigeon autoshaping.

5.   Conditions for Establishing Target Representations in
Conditional System

Section III was concerned with the conditions under which feature cues acquired occasion-setting properties. Another question concerns the conditions under which CSs become appropriate targets for the action of occasion setters. The data presented in Section IV,B,2 indicate that it is sufficient that a cue be trained as a target of another occasion setter with similar-valence relation with the reinforcer. However, is that training necessary? Most data (e.g., Bouton & Swartzentruber, 1986; Holland, 1986b; Rescorla, 1985) are consistent in indicating that some treatments do *not* endow cues with the ability to serve as such a target (e.g., consistent or partial reinforcement). However, the evidence on at least two other kinds of target is mixed.

Rescorla (1985) suggested that any cue that has both excitatory and inhibitory components would serve as an appropriate target for modulation by positive occasion setters. One potential transfer target then would be a compound cue, one element of which was excitatory and the other of which was explicitly trained as an inhibitor. Using a pigeon autoshaping preparation, Rescorla (1987) found that a positive occasion setter established in a serial FP discrimination, $X \rightarrow A+/A-$, readily facilitated responding in the presence of a simultaneous YB compound, which had been previously trained using a simultaneous FN procedure, $B+/YB-$. Conversely, using analogous procedures with the Pavlovian appetitive conditioning procedure with rats, Holland (1986b) found no evidence for transfer to a cue trained in that fashion.

Another potential transfer target is a cue that is first trained and then extinguished; many theorists have claimed that extinction involves the acquisition of countervailing inhibitory associations. However, in my laboratory, responding to a trained and extinguished stimulus is unaffected by feature presentation after serial Pavlovian appetitive FP or positive patterning discrimination training (e.g., Holland, 1983, 1986b, 1989a, 1989b). On the other hand, other investigators (e.g., Davidson & Jarrard, 1989; Davidson, Aparicio, & Rescorla, 1986; Rescorla, 1985) routinely find occasion setters (or context cues, Bouton & Swartzentruber, 1986) to enhance responding to extinguished cues. Similarly, Holland (1991a) found reliable (but not complete) transfer to an extinguished cue in a discrete-trial operant lever pressing procedure. I have no account for this discrepancy. But it is clear that to the extent that events such as those just described are acceptable targets of occasion setters, my claims about the necessity of occasion setting training for representation in a conditional memory system are invalid.

The character of my claims might be salvaged by assuming that occasion setting training is implicit in the procedures just described. For example, Bouton & Swartzentruber (1986) argued that the operations of training and extinction establish a CS as a target of an occasion setter, which can be identified as the "context of reinforcement," thus permitting its representation in the conditional system. Or, one could simply claim that any cue that has both excitatory and inhibitory associations is represented in that system. However, in that case, it is not obvious why conditioning and extinction would be sufficient, but not partial reinforcement. All in all, it probably adds little to propose multiple memory systems until the rules for entry into each system are more clearly specified and the nature of event coding within each system is more clear.

C. APPLICATION TO OPERANT CONDITIONING

The notion of occasion setting probably originated in early attempts to contrast the action of Pavlovian CSs with that of operant discriminative stimuli (e.g., Skinner, 1938). Operant discriminative stimuli (Sd's) are often described as setting the occasion for responding based on the response–reinforcer contingency. Indeed, the simplest procedure for establishing an operant Sd is analogous to the Pavlovian serial positive patterning procedures $X \rightarrow A+/A-/X-$ used by Davidson and Rescorla (1986), Holland (1989a), and Ross and Holland (1982) to establish a Pavlovian occasion setter. Presentation of the Sd (X), if followed by a response A, is followed by reinforcement, but neither presentation of the Sd in the absence of a response nor the occurrence of the response in the absence of the Sd produces the reinforcer. Furthermore, Colwill and Rescorla (1990) recently provided considerable evidence that such hierarchical Sd– (response–reinforcement) associations play a role in operant performance.

Some data also indicate that Pavlovian occasion setters and operant Sds share properties not shared by simple CSs and Sd's. Davidson, Aparicio, and Rescorla (1988), using a rat appetitive conditioning procedure, and Colwill and Rescorla (1986), using a pigeon autoshaping procedure, found that cues trained as Pavlovian occasion setters facilitated operant responding considerably more than did cues trained as simple Pavlovian exciters. Similarly, Davidson et al. (1988) found that a cue trained as an operant Sd also facilitated responding to a cue that had been trained as the target of a Pavlovian occasion setter.

These analyses imply that even a simple Sd is an occasion setter. In a series of discrete-trial operant conditioning experiments (e.g., Holland, 1991a, 1991b; Holland & Reeve, 1991), we arranged Pavlovian occasion setting relations among CSs but demanded additionally that an operant response be made in the presence of to-be-reinforced cues. Our findings were similar to those obtained previously in Pavlovian experiments: extinction, counterconditioning, and transfer effects were dependent on the temporal arrangement of feature and target cues: cues trained as features in simultaneous FP, FN, or ambiguous $(XA+/A-, XB-/B+)$ discriminations did not act as occasion setters, whereas those trained in serial compounds did. At first glance, these data conflict with those of Davidson et al.

(1988) and Colwill and Rescorla (1986), which suggested that even simple Sd's can act as occasion setters. In this context, it must be recalled that in my discrete-trial experiments, the target cues were always operant Sd's. Consequently, the Pavlovian feature → (target–reinforcer) relations arranged a four-term feature → [target → (response → reinforcer)] relation. Perhaps the stimulus control acquired by the feature in four-term relations like these differs from that in the three-term relations I have described here, as suggested by Sidman (1986). The study of higher-order occasion setting, in which occasion setting relations themselves are made contingent on the previous occurrence or nonoccurrence of a higher-order feature (e.g., Arnold, Grahame, & Miller, 1991) is likely then to be a valuable model for analysis of higher-level operant relations.

D. CONFIGURAL ALTERNATIVES

An alternative account for many of the phenomena I have been discussing minimizes the role of special modulatory processes like occasion setting and emphasizes instead the conditioning of compound stimulus configurations (e.g., Pearce, 1987; Wilson & Pearce, 1989, 1990; Young & Pearce, 1984). Within such theories, a compound cue XA is not treated as the combination of elements X and A but as a unique stimulus. Various summation and stimulus selection phenomena are due to the generalization of excitation and inhibition between the compound and stimuli that other theories would describe as its elements. For example, within Pearce's (1987) theory, in an FP ($XA+/A-$) discrimination procedure, the XA compound acquires excitation. To the extent that XA's excitatory strength generalizes to A, A will be nonreinforced in the presence of excitation and consequently will acquire inhibitory strength until its generalized inhibitory and direct excitatory strengths sum to 0. Meanwhile, the inhibitory strength accrued to A will also generalize to XA, permitting further excitatory conditioning of XA.

Coupled with simple assumptions about the rules of that generalization (casually speaking, the more salient A is than X, the more XA will resemble A than X), these theories can account for many (but not all) of the phenomena described in this article. In this section I consider, from the perspective of Pearce's (1987) configural model of conditioning, the three basic findings I used to distinguish occasion setting from simple conditioning: response form, counterconditioning/extinction, and transfer effects.

At first glance, to the extent that configural processes are viewed as perceptual processes, attributing occasion-setting phenomena to configuring seems to go against two basic observations already noted here: first, that occasion setting is more likely when serial, rather than simultaneous, feature and target cues are used, and second, that solution of serial FP and FN discriminations is enhanced by the use of features and targets of different stimulus modalities, rather than of similar modalities (Holland 1983, 1989a; Lamarre & Holland, 1987). Casually speaking, one might anticipate configuring of two cues to be more likely in just the opposite circumstances, when they are coincident in time and when they are of the same modality. However, within Pearce's theory it is not a question of the subject's being more or less likely to configure a particular compound: compounds are *always* configured. Variables like similarity and temporal relations instead affect the amount of generalization between the compound configuration and the stimuli other theorists would refer to as its elements.

1. Response Form

Consider first a serial FP discrimination, $X \to A+/A-$. The $X \to A$ compound at the time of reinforcement might be redescribed as a serial combination of X and a simultaneous compound, "X's trace + A". Because A is likely to be more salient than X's trace, this compound is likely to resemble A more than X.[1] Thus, the form of responding observed during this portion of the serial compound (i.e., during what I describe as the target) is likely to be characteristic of responding generated by cues with A's physical characteristics and will generalize substantially to A-alone. Consequently, the response during the target cue would have the form I attribute to target–reinforcer associations, and the serial discrimination would be relatively difficult (it usually is, e.g., Ross & Holland, 1981). Similarly, the reinforced compound would generalize less to X alone, and relatively lower levels of simple conditioning to that cue might be anticipated.

In a simultaneous $XA+/A-$ discrimination, the form of responding during XA would also be determined by the physical characteristics of that compound. If XA resembles X more than A (i.e., if X is more salient than A), then the form of the response conditioned to the compound should be more like that observed to X. Furthermore, that strength should generalize to X-alone, so that responding to the feature alone should be substantial (i.e., performance should reflect what I describe as feature–reinforcer associations). Conversely, relatively little strength should generalize to A,

---

[1] Wilson and Pearce (1990) offered a somewhat different suggestion for why serial compounds should generalize more to the target cue than do simultaneous compounds. They claimed that serial presentations permitted more opportunity for habituation of the feature, reducing its salience. I prefer my version because it permits accurate statements about the form of responding observed over the course of the compound (feature specific at cue onset, followed by target-specific response forms later).

so the simultaneous FP discrimination should be easier than a serial discrimination with the identical elements (as Ross & Holland, 1981, noted), and A would acquire little inhibitory strength.

If, however, XA resembles A more than X (i.e., if A is more salient than X), then a different outcome would be anticipated. The form of the response to XA would be more like that seen to A if it were conditioned alone (i.e., what I would describe as reflecting target–reinforcer associations). Further, conditioned excitation to XA would generalize more to A and less to X. Inhibition would accrue to A on nonreinforced A trials and generalize to XA, permitting further excitatory conditioning of XA. That excitation would again generalize little to X but considerably to A. Consequently, although the discrimination would be relatively difficult, asymptotically XA would be a strong excitor, X a weak excitor, and A a net neutral cue. This pattern of data, identical to that predicted for *serial* FP discriminations, is consistent with what Holland (1989b) observed when very salient A cues were used, except for the predicted difficulty of the discrimination.

Thus, this configurational theory captures the major aspects of the differences in response form observed in various FP discriminations, without recourse to a modulatory process. Furthermore, it does so without having to assume that configuring is more likely with serial than with simultaneous compounds. Temporal variables have their effects not by especially encouraging a configural process but by modifying the similarity of the compound to the feature and target elements: arranging the cues serially, and placing gaps between them (both of which encourage the pattern of data I describe as indicating occasion setting), reduce the relative salience of the feature, enhancing the generalization between compound and target.

However, Pearce's (1987) theory is unable to deal with a more obvious issue in the determination of response form in discriminations involving compounds. Ross and Holland (1981) and Holland (1989a) examined $XA+/A-$ simultaneous FP discriminations in which the identities of X and A were counterbalanced. That is, all subjects received reinforced presentations of the same auditory-visual compound stimulus. Some received additional nonreinforced presentations of the auditory cue and others received nonreinforced presentations of the visual cue.

Within Pearce's (1987) theory, the XA compound acquires excitation, which is displayed in the presence of X and/or A individually only as a consequence of generalization. Thus, the form of responding to the reinforced XA compound should be determined by that compound's physical properties and should not be affected by which element was separately nonreinforced. However, Holland (1989a) and Ross and Holland (1981) found that if the visual element was nonreinforced, responding to the compound was characteristic of its auditory feature element, and if the auditory element was nonreinforced, responding to the compound was characteristic of its visual feature. Furthermore, if neither element was separately nonreinforced (Ross & Holland, 1981), the compound exhibited behavior characteristic of both of its elements. These and some other more detailed aspects of response form (see Holland, 1989b, for a more detailed discussion) are inconsistent with Pearce's (1987) theory but are predicted from views that recognize distinct conditioning and modulating functions.

2. Counterconditioning/Extinction

Within Pearce's theory, compounds are unique cues that acquire excitatory and/or inhibitory strengths independent (except for generalization) of those of their elements. Thus it is hardly surprising that under many circumstances posttraining manipulation of the associative strength of the feature alone may have relatively little effect. For example, in FP discriminations, if XA resembled A more than X (as with serial FP discriminations, or if A was more salient than X), then X would possess relatively little generalized excitatory strength. Consequently, posttraining nonreinforced X presentations would have little opportunity to generate conditioned inhibition, which in turn would be unlikely to generalize to XA. With serial discriminations or simultaneous discriminations with salient A cues, then, those X presentations would be anticipated to have little effect on responding to the compound. Conversely, with simultaneous FP discriminations with less salient A cues, XA would generalize substantially to X. X would then accrue substantial inhibitory tendencies, which in turn would generalize substantially to XA, reducing its net strength. Both these sets of predictions are supported in the data (e.g., Holland, 1989b; Young & Pearce, 1984). Analogous predictions can be derived for the case of excitatory counterconditioning of the features after FN discrimination training.

3. Transfer

Given the simple assumption made in the previous two sections, that the target portion of a serial compound resembles the target alone more than the feature alone, Pearce's (1987) theory can account for the basic differences in transfer observed with serial and simultaneous FP and FN discriminations. The more the compound resembles the target, the more generalization decrement will occur when the training target is replaced with a test target, because the test compound will be very different from the training compound (casually speaking, because they share only a weak feature). Thus there will be less transfer after serial FP and FN discrimination training than after simultaneous training, in which the training and test compound generalize substantially (casually, because they share a salient feature).

However, without further assumptions, Pearce's theory is unable to deal with observations that transfer of occasion setting is affected by the nature of target training (e.g., Holland, 1989a, 1989c, 1989d; Lamarre & Holland, 1987; Rescorla, 1985; Wilson & Pearce, 1990). Within that theory, generalization from compounds to individual cues is solely the function of physical similarities among those cues, so an X trained as an occasion setter with an A target should affect responding to B similarly regardless of B's training. To deal with these data, Lamarre and Holland (1987) and Wilson and Pearce (1990) suggested that training cues in similar fashions enhances generalization between them (e.g., Jenkins, 1963), a reasonable, but post hoc, contribution.

Unfortunately, it is not clear how even that additional notion helps deal with other aspects of the effects of target training on transfer. For example, Holland (1989a, 1989b) found that adding extra nonreinforced feature presentations to a serial FP discrimination procedure enhanced transfer to cues trained as targets in such discriminations but severely reduced that transfer if added to simultaneous FP discriminations. If serial FP discriminations show reduced transfer relative to simultaneous FP discriminations because the separate presentations of X within the serial compound make that cue relatively less salient, then separate nonreinforced presentations should reduce that salience even more and hence *reduce* the amount of transfer, as found with simultaneous compounds. Other, related problems are described by Holland (1991b); most notably, in contrast to our data, the model predicts that explicit discrimination training is often not necessary for the display of many of the phenomena we attribute to occasion setting. At any rate, as Wilson and Pearce (1990) note, it remains to be seen how notions of enhanced generalization, and indeed assumptions about how compounds of different temporal arrangements differ, can be incorporated more formally into Pearce's (1987) model.

4. Utility of Configural Models

In summary, a reasonably well specified configural view, like Pearce's (1987), can provide a useful counterpoint to views that propose new stimulus control functions, like mine and Rescorla's (e.g., 1985). Many of the basic aspects of the data I have described as compelling an occasion setting view are compatible with such a configural view as well. The mere passing of two or three tests does not guarantee that a modulatory process has been demonstrated.

However, more detailed aspects of the data described, many of them predicted from various models of occasion setting, are difficult to handle within configural theories without a variety of ad hoc assumptions. In general, it is fair to say that the results of our experiments with simultaneous compounds tend to conform more to Pearce's predictions than the results of our experiments with serial compounds. In several cases, although our simultaneous data were consistent with the theory's predictions, our results with simultaneous and serial compounds were diametrically opposed, as was the case in Holland's (1989a) observations that the use of similar feature and target cues enhanced $XA+/X-/A-$ learning but hurt $X \rightarrow A+/X-/A-$ learning, and that adding $X-$ trials reduced transfer in simultaneous FP procedures but enhanced it in serial FP procedures. It is unlikely that fine-tuning of such models will be sufficient to anticipate such differences, which I believe reflect qualitative differences between configural and occasion-setting processes.

Despite these faults, Pearce's model has much to recommend. First, although I have objected to its simplistic assumptions about generalization functions, and the necessity for making many post hoc assumptions to deal with the body of data discussed here, those latter assumptions are no more arbitrary than the extensive revisions to my original hierarchical occasion setting model (Holland, 1983). Furthermore, once the assumptions are made, at least semiquantitative predictions follow directly from the model. Most useful would be the development of configurally based models that make use of more sophisticated generalization functions than the elementary one adopted for simplicity's sake by Pearce (1987) and that represent quantitatively the temporal, intensity, and similarity relations among the cues, which are now dealt with by nonquantitative statements about how those variables affect relative salience.

V. Conclusion

Certain training procedures endow stimuli with the ability to modulate the action of other stimuli. Although a good model is not close at hand, this occasion-setting function seems conceptually and empirically distinguishable from simple conditioning and configural processes in many ways. Indeed, under many circumstances the occasion-setting and simple conditioning powers of a single cue may be quite independent.

Recent research has implicated the involvement of modulatory processes like occasion setting in a broad array of conditioning phenomena, for example, the development of contextual control of behavior, conditioned inhibition, superconditioning, latent inhibition, reinstatement of responding after extinction, and conditional discrimination learning (e.g., Holland, 1990; Rescorla, 1991; Swartzentruber, 1991). Indeed, Rescorla (1985, 1991) favors a view in which a pair of modulatory processes, facilitation and inhibition (which correspond to my positive and negative occasion setting) complement a single associative processes, excitation. The suggestion that inhibitory phenomena parallel not excitation but facilitation (positive occasion setting) would force a major reevaluation of basic conditioning models, given the substantial role conditioned inhibition has played in those theories (e.g., Pearce & Hall, 1980; Rescorla & Wagner, 1972). Clearly, the development of more precise models of occasion setting, which specify the interactions between modulatory, configural, and simple conditioning processes, is crucial to the understanding of simple learning processes.

My suggestion of multiple levels of representation of the events involved in conditioning procedures brings up the possibility of multiple modulatory processes as well. For example, despite the many parallel findings from my appetitive conditioning procedure with rats and Rescorla's autoshaping procedures, it is not at all clear that comparable modulatory processes are involved. Although temporal variables play a critical role in the acquisition of modulatory powers in my preparation, they seem largely unimportant in autoshaping (Rescorla, 1989). Furthermore, although in our Pavlovian preparations, temporal variables clearly affected the content of learning (that is, the critical temporal parameters were those in effect at the time of learning, rather than those at the time of performance testing), we have preliminary evidence that at least some differential acquisition and transfer phenomena in our discrete trial operant procedure are generated at the time of performance (Coldwell and Holland, unpublished data). Similarly, although I have demonstrated clear distinctions between negative occasion setting and simple inhibition, Rescorla's data (1985, 1987, 1989, 1991) give little evidence for a separate, nonmodulatory inhibitory process. And, although in our Pavlovian preparations a partially extinguished cue is not an adequate target of either positive or negative occasion setter, Rescorla routinely uses a cue with that history as a target of both. Interestingly, in our discrete trial operant procedure, an extinguished cue (but not a partially reinforced cue) served effectively as a target of occasion setting (e.g., Holland, 1991a).

I have emphasized very specific modulatory processes, which in some circumstances are highly stimulus specific and which are sensitive to details of the training history of their targets. But there is a long history of modulatory processes in conditioning that are construed as more general. For example, a major claim of two-process theory (e.g., Rescorla & Solomon, 1967) is that Pavlovian conditioned emotional states modulate ongoing operant responding. Others have noted that these conditioned emotional responses might equally modulate the acquisition and performance of other Pavlovian responses as well. For example, Konorski (1967) proposed that CS–US pairings led to the development of separate associations between CS representations and two kinds of US representations, one being primarily affective in nature and one being primarily sensory-motor. Activation of the affective representation not only generated certain kinds of CRs, but also modulated the performance of CRs mediated by the sensory-motor representation.

Wagner and Brandon (1989) presented a model of Pavlovian conditioning ("AESOP"), which follows Konorski in assuming that stimuli produce multiple representations in memory. Associations with sensory-perceptual representations of a US produce discrete CRs, whereas associations with emotive representations of that US produce diffuse responses often characterized as preparatory or emotional. Although AESOP assumes similar mechanisms for the acquisition of excitation and inhibition for each class of associations, the parametric characteristics of that learning might well differ. Thus, AESOP provides ready accounts for the frequently observed dissociations (e.g., Schneiderman, 1972) between the rates of learning and sensitivity to temporal relations seen with different response measures (often obtained concurrently). Furthermore, within this model, associations with the emotive representations can modulate the elicitation of discrete responses mediated by associations with the sensory-perceptual representation. Recently, Brandon and Wagner (1991) suggested that such modulation of discrete CRs by separable emotional CRs may be the basis of phenomena I have described as indicating occasion setting. They examined the elicitation of discrete eyeblink CRs by brief CSs in the presence of CSs trained with longer CS–US intervals, which did not themselves elicit eyeblink CRs but presumably did elicit modulatory, emotive CRs. For example, in one experiment, rabbits received training on an $X \rightarrow A+/Y \rightarrow A-$ discrimination, in which responding was observed to occur more frequently during A on $X \rightarrow A+$ trials than during A on $Y \rightarrow A$ trials. After separate partial reinforcement of another brief CS, B, until it elicited eyeblink CRs, the effects of the long-duration X and Y cues on eyeblink responding to B were assessed in transfer tests. X enhanced responding to B and Y suppressed it, indicating general transfer of the modulatory properties of the X and Y cues.

As Brandon and Wagner (1991) recognized, although such data provide evidence that emotional CRs may modulate the elicitation of discrete CRs, they may reflect processes unrelated to the occasion setting phenomena I have described. For example, the partial reinforcement training procedure used to establish responding to Brandon and Wagner's target stimulus does not generate an acceptable target in our conditioning preparations.

Similarly, consistent with AESOP, Brandon and Wagner (1991) found that special discriminative procedures were unnecessary to establish modulatory powers to the long-duration cue; indeed, a simple $A+/B-$ procedure endowed A with more powerful modulatory properties than did the $XA+/YA-$ procedure. But neither Rescorla (1985) nor I (e.g., Holland, 1985, 1991) has observed cues trained outside conditional discriminations to acquire occasion-setting powers. Finally, Rescorla's (1986a) and my (Holland, 1989b, 1989c) observations that repeated nonreinforced presentations of occasion setters have no effect on their modulatory powers are clearly at odds with AESOP, which attributes modulatory powers to simple associations conditioned to the occasion setter (unless one makes the readily tested assumption that the extinction rate parameters for emotional associations are extremely low).

Nevertheless, Wagner and Brandon (1989) illustrate how notions of modulation can be integrated within a quantitative model of Pavlovian conditioning. Furthermore, Wagner and Donegan (1989) have attempted to relate AESOP's functions to known features of the neurobiology of the rabbit's conditioned eyeblink. A similar specification for principles of occasion setting would be of great value. I suspect future models of Pavlovian conditioning will incorporate notions of multiple stimulus representation both at the level of general properties, as assumed in AESOP, and more specific features, as is implicit in accounts like Holland's (1990), Finally, it would not be surprising if the rules for interactions among stimulus representations differed from level to level, nor if those interactions went beyond simple arithmetic summation of element strength (e.g., Pearce, 1987).

Acknowledgments

The research described in this article was supported by grants from the National Science Foundation and the National Institute of Mental Health. I thank Javier Morell for permission to describe his data, and Marie Crock for her considerable technical assistance in the course of this project.

References

Arnold, H. M., Grahame, N. J., & Miller, R. R. (1991). Higher-order occasion setting. *Animal Learning & Behavior, 19,* 58–64.

Balaz, M. A., Capra, S., Hartl, P., & Miller, R. R. (1981). Contextual potentiation of acquired behavior after devaluing direct context–US associations. *Learning and Motivation, 12,* 383–397.

Bouton, M. E. (1984). Differential control by context in the inflation and reinstatement paradigms. *Journal of Experimental Psychology: Animal Behavior Processes, 10,* 56–74.

Bouton, M. E., & King, D. A. (1986). Effect of context on performance to conditioned stimuli with mixed histories of reinforcement and nonreinforcement. *Journal of Experimental Psychology: Animal Behavior Processes, 12,* 4–15.

Bouton, M. E., & Swartzentruber, D. (1986). Analysis of the associative and occasion-setting properties of contexts participating in a Pavlovian discrimination. *Journal of Experimental Psychology: Animal Behavior Processes, 12,* 333–350.

Brandon, S. E., & Wagner, A. R. (1991). Modulation of a discrete Pavlovian conditioned reflex by a putative emotive conditioned stimulus. *Journal of Experimental Psychology: Animal Behavior Processes, 17,* 299–311.

Colwill, R. M., & Rescorla, R. A. (1986). Associative structures in instrumental learning. In G. H. Bower (Ed.), *The psychology of learning and motivation* (Vol. 20, pp. 55–104). San Diego: Academic Press.

Colwill, R. M., & Rescorla, R. A. (1990). Evidence for the hierarchical structure of instrumental learning. *Animal Learning & Behavior, 18,* 71–82.

Davidson, T. L., Aparicio, J., & Rescorla, R. A. (1988). Transfer between Pavlovian facilitators and instrumental discriminative stimuli. *Animal Learning & Behavior, 16,* 285–291.

Davidson, T. L., & Jarrard, L. E. (1989). Retention of concurrent conditional discriminations in rats with ibotenate lesions of the hippocampus. *Psychobiology, 17,* 49–60.

Davidson, T. L., & Rescorla, R. A. (1986). Transfer of facilitation in the rat. *Animal Learning & Behavior, 14,* 380–386.

Davis, M. (1984). The mammalian startle response. In R. C. Eaton (Ed.), *Neural Mechanisms of startle behavior* (pp. 287–351). New York: Plenum Press.

Estes, W. K. (1972). An associative basis for coding and organization in memory. In A. W. Melton & E. Martin (Eds.), *Coding processes in human memory* (pp. 161–190). Washington, D. C.: V. H. Winston.

Estes, W. K. (1973). Memory and conditioning. In F. J. McGuigan & D. B. Lumsden (Eds.), *Contemporary approaches to conditioning* (pp. 265–286). Washington, DC: Winston.

Grahame, N. J., Hallam, S. C., Geier, L., & Miller, R. R. (1990). Context as an occasion setter following either CS acquisition and extinction or CS acquisition alone. *Learning and Motivation, 21,* 237–265.

Hirsh, R. (1980). The hippocampus, conditional operations, and cognition. *Physiological Psychology, 8,* 175–182.

Holland, P. C. (1977). Conditioned stimulus as a determinant of the form of the Pavlovian conditioned response. *Journal of Experimental Psychology: Animal Behavior Processes, 3,* 77–104.

Holland, P. C. (1983). Occasion-setting in Pavlovian feature positive discriminations. In M. L. Commons, R. J. Herrnstein, & A. R. Wagner (Eds.), *Quantitative analyses of behavior: Discrimination processes* (Vol. 4, pp. 183–206). New York: Ballinger.

Holland, P. C. (1984a). Differential effects of reinforcement of an inhibitory feature after serial and simultaneous feature negative discrimination training. *Journal of Experimental Psychology: Animal Behavior Processes, 10,* 461–475.

Holland, P. C. (1984b). The origins of Pavlovian conditioned behavior. In G. Bower (Ed.), *The Psychology of Learning and Motivation* (Vol. 18, pp. 129–173). Englewood Cliffs, NJ: Prentice-Hall.

Holland, P. C. (1985). The nature of inhibition in serial and simultaneous feature negative discriminations. In R. R. Miller & N. E. Spear (Eds.), *Information processing in animals: Conditioned inhibition* (pp. 267–297). Hillsdale, NJ: Erlbaum.

Holland, P. C. (1986a). Temporal determinants of occasion setting in feature positive discriminations. *Animal Learning & Behavior, 14,* 111–120.

Holland, P. C. (1986b). Transfer after serial feature positive discrimination training. *Learning and Motivation, 17,* 243–268.

Holland, P. C. (1989a). Acquisition and transfer of conditional discrimination performance. *Journal of Experimental Psychology: Animal Behavior Processes, 15,* 154–165.

Holland, P. C. (1989b). Feature extinction enhances transfer of occasion setting. *Animal Learning & Behavior, 17,* 269–279.

Holland, P. C. (1989c). Occasion setting with simultaneous compounds in rats. *Journal of Experimental Psychology: Animal Behavior Processes, 15,* 183–193.

Holland, P. C. (1989d). Transfer of negative occasion setting and conditioned inhibition across conditioned and unconditioned stimuli. *Journal of Experimental Psychology: Animal Behavior Processes, 15,* 311–328.

Holland, P. C. (1990). Forms of memory in Pavlovian conditioning. In J. L. McGaugh, N. M. Weinberger, & G. Lynch (Eds.), *Brain organization and memory: Cells, systems, and circuits* (pp. 78–105). New York: Oxford University Press.

Holland, P. C. (1991a). Acquisition and transfer of occasion setting in operant feature positive and feature negative discriminations. *Learning and Motivation, 22,* 366–387.

Holland, P. C. (1991b). Transfer of control in ambiguous discriminations. *Journal of Experimental Psychology: Animal Behavior Processes, 19,* 113–124.

Holland, P. C., & Lamarre, J. (1984). Transfer of inhibition after serial and simultaneous feature negative discrimination training. *Learning and Motivation, 15,* 219–243.

Holland, P. C., & Reeve, C. E. (1991). Acquisition and transfer of control by an ambiguous cue. *Animal Learning & Behavior, 19,* 113–124.

Holland, P. C., & Ross, R. T. (1981). Within-compound associations in serial compound conditioning. *Journal of Experimental Psychology: Animal Behavior Processes, 7,* 228–241.

Jarrard, L. E., & Davidson, T. L. (1991). On the hippocampus and learned conditional responding: Effects of aspiration versus ibotenate lesions. *Hippocampus, 1,* 103–113.

Jenkins, J. J. (1963). Mediated associations: Paradigms and situations. In C. N. Cofer & B. S. Musgrave (Eds.), *Verbal behavior and verbal learning* (pp. 210–245). New York: McGraw-Hill.

Konorski, J. (1967). *Integrative activity of the brain.* Chicago: University of Chicago Press.

Lamarre, J. (1984). *Stimulus control in Pavlovian feature negative discriminations.* Unpublished doctoral dissertation. University of Pittsburgh.

Lamarre, J., & Holland, P. C. (1985). Acquisition and transfer of feature negative discriminations. *Bulletin of the Psychonomic Society, 23,* 71–74.

Lamarre, J., & Holland, P. C. (1987). Acquisition and transfer of serial feature negative discriminations. *Learning and Motivation, 18,* 319–342.

Lovibond, P. F., Preston, G. C., & Mackintosh, N. J. (1984). Context specificity of conditioning, extinction, and latent inhibition. *Journal of Experimental Psychology: Animal Behavior Processes, 10,* 360–375.

Moore, J. W., Newman, F. L., & Glasgow, B. (1969). Intertrial cues as discriminative stimuli in human eyelid conditioning. *Journal of Experimental Psychology, 79,* 319–326.

Pearce, J. M. (1987). A model for stimulus generalization in Pavlovian conditioning. *Psychological Review, 94,* 61–75.

Pearce, J. M., & Hall, G. (1980). A model for Pavlovian learning: variations in the effectiveness of conditioned but not of unconditioned stimuli. *Psychological Review, 106,* 532–552.

Rescorla, R. A. (1969). Pavlovian conditioned inhibition. *Psychological Bulletin, 72,* 77–94.

Rescorla, R. A. (1974). A model of Pavlovian conditioning. In V. S. Rusinov (Ed.), *Mechanisms of formation and inhibition of conditional reflex* (pp. 25–39). Moscow: Academy of Sciences of the USSR.

Rescorla, R. A. (1985). Conditioned inhibition and facilitation. In R. R. Miller and N. E. Spear (Eds.) *Information processing in animals: Conditioned inhibition* (pp. 299–326). Hillsdale, NJ: Erlbaum.

Rescorla, R. A. (1986a). Extinction of facilitation. *Journal of Experimental Psychology: Animal Behavior Processes, 12,* 16–24.

Rescorla, R. A. (1986b). Facilitation and excitation. *Journal of Experimental Psychology: Animal Behavior Processes, 12,* 325–332.

Rescorla, R. A. (1987). Facilitation and inhibition. *Journal of Experimental Psychology: Animal Behavior Processes, 13,* 250–259.

Rescorla, R. A. (1988). Facilitation based on inhibition. *Animal Learning & Behavior, 16,* 169–176.

Rescorla, R. A. (1989). Simultaneous and sequential conditioned inhibition in autoshaping. *Quarterly Journal of Experimental Psychology, 41B,* 275–286.

Rescorla, R. A. (1991). Separate reinforcement can enhance the effectiveness of modulators. *Journal of Experimental Psychology: Animal Behavior Processes, 17,* 259–269.

Rescorla, R. A., & Holland, P. C. (1977). Associations in Pavlovian conditioned inhibition. *Learning and Motivation, 8,* 429–447.

Rescorla, R. A., & Solomon, R. L. (1967). Two process learning theory: Relationships between classical conditioning and instrumental learning. *Psychological Review, 74,* 151–182.

Rescorla, R. A., & Wagner, A. R. (1972). A theory of Pavlovian conditioning: Variations in the effectiveness of reinforcement and nonreinforcement. In A. H. Black & W. F. Prokasy (Eds.), *Classical conditioning II* (pp. 64–99). New York: Appleton-Century-Crofts.

Ross, R. T. (1983). Relationships between the determinants of performance in serial feature positive discriminations. *Journal of Experimental Psychology: Animal Behavior Processes, 9,* 349–373.

Ross, R. T., & Holland, P. C. (1981). Conditioning of simultaneous and serial feature-positive discriminations. *Animal Learning & Behavior, 9,* 293–303.

Ross, R. T., & Holland, P. C. (1982). Serial positive patterning: Implications for "occasion-setting." *Bulletin of the Psychonomic Society, 19,* 159–162.

Ross, R. T., Orr, W. B., Holland, P. C., & Berger, T. W. (1984). Hippocampectomy disrupts acquisition and retention of learned conditional responding. *Behavioral Neuroscience, 98,* 211–225.

Schneiderman, N. (1972). Response system divergencies in aversive classical conditioning. In A. H. Black & W. F. Prokasy (Eds.), *Classical conditioning II* (pp. 341–376). New York: Appleton-Century-Crofts.

Sidman, M. (1986). Functional analysis of emergent verbal classes. In T. Thompson & M. D. Zeiler (Eds.), *Analysis and integration of behavioral units* (pp. 2133–2145). Hillsdale, NJ: Erlbaum.

Skinner, B. F. (1938). *The behavior of organisms.* New York: Appleton-Century.

Swartzentruber, D. (1991). Blocking between occasion setters and contextual stimuli. *Journal of Experimental Psychology: Animal Behavior Processes, 17,* 163–173.

Swartzentruber, D., & Bouton, M. E. (1988). Transfer of positive contextual control across different conditioned stimuli. *Bulletin of the Psychonomic Society, 26,* 569–572.

Wagner, A. R., & Brandon, S. E. (1989). Evolution of a structured connectionist model of Pavlovian conditioning (AESOP). In S. B. Klein & R. R. Mower (Eds.), *Contemporary learning theories: Pavlovian conditioning and the status of traditional learning theory* (pp. 149–189). Hillsdale, NJ: Erlbaum.

Wagner, A. R., & Donegan, N. H. (1989). Some relationships between a computational model (SOP) and a neural circuit for Pavlovian (rabbit eyeblink) conditioning. In G. Bower (Ed.), *The Psychology of Learning and Motivation* (Vol. 23, pp. 157–203). New York: Academic Press.

Wilson, P. N., & Pearce, J. M. (1989). A role for stimulus generalization in conditional discrimination learning. *Quarterly Journal of Experimental Psychology, 41B*, 243–273.

Wilson, P. N., & Pearce, J. M. (1990). Selective transfer of responding in conditional discriminations. *Quarterly Journal of Experimental Psychology, 42B*, 41–58.

Young, D. B., & Pearce, J. M. (1984). The influence of generalization decrement on the outcome of a feature positive discrimination. *Quarterly Journal of Experimental Psychology, 36B*, 331–352.

PAIRINGS IN LEARNING AND PERCEPTION: PAVLOVIAN CONDITIONING AND CONTINGENT AFTEREFFECTS

Shepard Siegel
Lorraine G. Allan

I. Introduction

The fact . . . that demonstrations of intrasensory conditioning are difficult to obtain makes the McCollough Effect even more interesting for both students of vision and of conditioning. (Murch, 1977, p. 322)

The study of associations between two sensory events has a long history (e.g., Brogden, 1939; Karn, 1947), and there has been renewed interest in this area (e.g., Rescorla, 1980; Rescorla & Durlach, 1981). The consequence of the pairing of sensory events is of interest to perception researchers, as well as to learning researchers. Such pairing is the central feature of a well known perceptual phenomenon, the McCollough effect. In this article, we attempt to integrate these two research traditions.

II. The McCollough Effect

An aftereffect of color which depends on the orientation of lines in the test field may be obtained by presenting a horizontal grating of one color alternately with a vertical grating of a different color. (McCollough, 1965, p. 1115)

127

In 1965 Celeste McCollough described an orientation-contingent color aftereffect. The phenomenon, now known as the McCollough effect (ME), results from pairing orientation stimuli with colors. During an "induction" period, an observer inspects two colored grids that alternate every few seconds. In the typical arrangement the grids are complementarily colored and orthogonally oriented. For example, one grid could be constructed of alternating black and green horizontal bars, and the other grid could be constructed of alternating black and red vertical bars. Following such induction, complementary color aftereffects contingent on bar orientation are noted—black and white assessment grids appear colored. In this example, the white spaces between the black horizontal bars appear pinkish, and the white spaces between the black vertical bars appear greenish.

McCollough's (1965) report inspired research in many laboratories. Techniques were developed for objective assessment of illusory color (e.g., Allan, Siegel, Toppan, & Lockhead, 1991; Riggs, White, & Eimas, 1974), and results of numerous experiments provided considerable information about the ME. We now know that the ME is very robust and may be seen in adult humans, young children (e.g., Meyer, Coleman, Dwyer, & Lehman, 1982), monkeys (Macquire, Meyer, & Baizer, 1980), and pigeons (Roberts, 1984).

The ME captured the interest of perception researchers for many reasons. The ME is similar to simple color aftereffects, which have been investigated for many years, but differs from such simple aftereffects in dramatic ways. A simple aftereffect is seen when one looks at a colored field, say green, for some minutes, then looks at an achromatic field. For some seconds, the achromatic field will appear to be tinged with a color complementary to that of the colored inspection field; the achromatic field will appear pinkish in this example. In contrast to simple aftereffects, ME induction yields *two* aftereffects, neither of which is apparent unless the subject is presented with the appropriate orientation stimulus. Investigators have also been fascinated by the extraordinary persistence of the ME. There are reports that it lasts for hours, days, and perhaps even weeks (see Jones & Holding, 1975). Although there are various interpretations of the ME, an especially intriguing possibility is that it represents an instance of Pavlovian conditioning.

III. Pavlovian Conditioning and the ME

At the very least, it is clear that describing the McCollough and related effects in the terminology of classical conditioning leads to viable predictions across a wide variety of experimental conditions. (Brand, Holding, & Jones, 1987, p. 316)

There is similarity in the pairing operation involved in ME induction and Pavlovian conditioning. This similarity was recognized soon after the ME was reported. The year after McCollough published her article, a conditioning interpretation of the ME was presented by Mary Viola, an undergraduate at Smith College (Viola, 1966).

Several vision researchers subsequently noted the similarities in operation and outcome, and offered (if somewhat tentatively) an associative interpretation of the ME. Gregory (1978) stated that "contingent aftereffects . . . show many of the characteristics of classical Pavlovian Conditioning" (p. 110), and Leppmann (1973) suggested that "a learning model analogous to classical conditioning appears to have considerable heuristic, if not explanatory, value" (p. 411). Others also noted parallels between the ME and more conventional CRs but often felt compelled to embed the associative explanation in a conceptual nervous system (see Skowbo, Timney, Gentry, & Morant, 1975).

In 1976 Murch provided the clearest conditioning account of the ME: "The lined grid in inspection functions as a conditioned stimulus (CS) while color functions as the unconditioned stimulus (UCS). As a result of the pairing of the CS (lined grid) with the UCS (color) a conditioned response (CR) develops so that the adaptive response of the visual system to the color is evoked by the lined grid" (p. 615).

IV. Effective Induction Stimuli

A simple conditioning model should predict that MEs can be generated for any clearly discriminable spatial stimulus. . . . This is too general; MEs appear to be limited to a small class of rather special patterns. (Dodwell & Humphrey, 1990, p. 79)

Most investigations of contingent color aftereffects have used McCollough's (1965) stimuli—horizontal and vertical grids (or perpendicularly oriented diagonal grids, such as 45° and 135°). Several investigators have suggested that, on the basis of the conditioning interpretation of the ME, elicitation of illusory color should follow induction with virtually any patterned stimuli (see Skowbo, 1984). Indeed, there are reports of color aftereffects contingent on visual features other than orientation, such as spatial frequency (Breitmeyer & Cooper, 1972; Leppmann, 1973; Lovegrove & Over, 1972; Stromeyer, 1972), movement direction (Hepler, 1968; Stromeyer & Mansfield, 1970), and dot size (MacKay & MacKay, 1975a). In evaluating this literature, Dodwell and Humphrey (1990) concluded that all stimuli that contingently elicit color aftereffects are "simple, repetitive, redundant, and highly predictable" (p. 83). Results of recent research, however, greatly expand the types of stimuli that can contingently elicit color aftereffects.

A. FORM STIMULI

Foreit and Ambler (1978) reasoned that, if MEs were CRs, they should be demonstrable with arbitrarily selected form stimuli, as well as orientation stimuli. They attempted to induce a contingent aftereffect with colored forms constructed from four line segments: a square constructed from red line segments, and a Greek cross constructed from green line segments (see Fig. 1A and 1B). They reported that their stimuli did not contingently elicit color aftereffects. They concluded, "the McCollough effect is sensitive to line orientation but not to form (line configurations)" (p. 301) and suggested that their results were contrary to a conditioning interpretation of the ME. Recent summaries of the ME literature have argued that the aftereffect is not a Pavlovian conditioning phenomenon because, if it were, it would be expected that chromatic patterns of the sort used by Foreit and Ambler (1978) should be effective (see Skowbo, 1984).

Foreit and Ambler (1978) evaluated the aftereffect with a color matching procedure that is not as sensitive as more recently developed techniques. Siegel, Allan, and Eissenberg (1992) assessed the effectiveness of Foreit and Ambler's (1978) forms with the psychometric–function shift procedure (Allan et al., 1991). They demonstrated that, following chromatic presentation of the square and Greek cross used by Foreit and Ambler (1978), a form-contingent color aftereffect was clearly detectable.

Although the square and the Greek cross used by Foreit and Ambler (1978) occupy the same proportion of the display, they vary in size; the

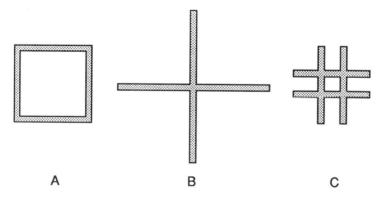

A   B   C

Fig. 1.   Forms constructed of four line segments of equal length used in demonstrations of form-contingent color aftereffects (Siegel et al., 1992). Copyright © 1992 by The American Psychological Association. Reprinted by permission.

horizontal and vertical extent of the cross is twice that of the square. Siegel et al. (1992), in another experiment evaluating form-contingent color aftereffects, alternated a different cross with the square. A "tic-tac-toe" cross (see Fig. 1C) was constructed from the square by moving each side toward the middle; thus, both the proportion of the display occupied by the segments and the extent of the two forms were the same. In this experiment, there was again clear evidence that the forms could contingently elicit color aftereffects.

Siegel et al. (1992) reported further evidence that stimuli constructed of identical elements can, like orientation stimuli, contingently elicit illusory color. Two novel forms were arbitrarily selected—an upright and an inverted isosceles triangle, constructed of three line segments. During aftereffect induction, these triangles were alternately upright (base on bottom) and inverted (base on top). The line segments that formed the triangle were green when the triangle pointed in one direction and red when pointed in the other direction. A triangle direction–contingent color aftereffect was demonstrated.

B. Frame Lightness

Siegel et al. (1992) also reported a new contingent color aftereffect, induced by pairing color with a feature of the stimulus that does not have the characteristics of either orientation or form—the lightness of a surrounding frame. During induction of this new aftereffect, complementary colors were paired with the lightness of a frame surrounding the colored area. For example, for some subjects induction consisted of alternate presentations of a green "picture" (a square stimulus in the middle of the computer monitor) surrounded by a white "frame" (the remainder of the monitor screen) and a red picture surrounded by a black frame.

A frame lightness–contingent color aftereffect was clearly demonstrated; thus, following induction with white-framed green pictures and black-framed red pictures, colorless assessment pictures presented in the white frame appeared pinkish, and colorless assessment pictures presented in the black frame appeared greenish. Siegel et al. (1992) reported that the frame lightness–contingent color aftereffect, like the orientation–contingent color aftereffect, displayed substantial retention; it persisted for at least 24 hr.

C. Words

Allan, Siegel, Collins, and MacQueen (1989) reported a very different color contingent aftereffect—illusory color seen on text. For example, in one of their experiments subjects were induced with the anagrammatical words SIREN and RINSE, one word being constructed of green letters and the other of red letters. Following induction, a contingent color aftereffect was observed on words constructed of colorless letters; the word that was red during induction appeared greenish, and the word that was green during induction appeared pinkish. Within a conditioning interpretation of color contingent aftereffects, word is the CS. These data are consistent with earlier reports that words can serve as CSs (e.g., Razran, 1961).

D. Constraints on Effective Stimuli

Results of research summarized above indicate that many stimuli can, following pairing with color, contingently elicit illusory color. It is not the case, however, that a contingent color aftereffect will be seen following pairing of *any* stimulus with color. Some orientation stimuli appear to be especially effective (e.g., high contrast grids) and others relatively ineffective (e.g., isoluminant grids). Similarly, some letter strings will elicit illusory color (e.g., letter strings that form meaningful words), but others do not (e.g., letter strings that do not form meaningful words). Perhaps most intriguing, some stimuli can contingently elicit illusory color even if they have never been paired with color. This ME, seen with noninduced stimuli, has been termed the "indirect ME" (Dodwell & Humphrey, 1990).

1. Isoluminant Grids

Although the ME is readily seen following induction with high contrast grids (alternating black and colored bars), no ME is seen following induction with isoluminant grids (alternating gray and colored bars) (e.g., Allan et al., 1991; Mikaelian, 1980). The failure of isoluminant grids to support an ME might be interpreted as contrary to a conditioning analysis, but there is another explanation. In some conditioning preparations, certain CSs are better than others at eliciting CRs. Such selective associability is characteristic of many conditioning preparations (e.g., flavor stimuli, but not exteroceptive stimuli, will be associated readily with gastrointestinal illness; see Domjan, 1983). A number of investigators have suggested that selective associability may also be a feature of contingent aftereffects (Allan & Siegel, 1986; Harris, 1980; Siegel & Allan, 1985; Westbrook & Harrison, 1984).

Constraints on illness-induced aversion learning may result from the organization of the innate connections of the gustatory and visceral systems (Garcia, Hankins, & Rusiniak, 1974). Similarly, constraints on contingent color aftereffects may result from the organization of innate connections between luminance- and color-perception systems (e.g., Livingstone & Hubel, 1987).

2. Nonwords

As summarized above, Allan et al. (1989) reported that words can contingently elicit color aftereffects. However, when exposed to these same chromatic letter strings in a different order, such that they did not form words, no contingent color aftereffects were induced. For example, although alternate chromatic presentations of SIREN and RINSE induce contingent color aftereffects, alternate chromatic presentations of ENSRI and RENIS do not. Siegel et al. (1992) suggested that this result may also be another manifestation of selective associability.

3. The Indirect ME

Two chromatic grids are not necessary for the induction of an orientation-contingent color aftereffect (e.g., Allan & Siegel, 1991; Humphrey, Dodwell, & Emerson, 1989). Following repeated presentations of a single chromatic grid, for example, green horizontal, an achromatic horizontal grid appears pinkish. Such aftereffect induction with a single chromatic grid sometimes results in illusory color on the orthogonal grid orientation as well, even though this orthogonal grid was not presented during induction. Such an "indirect ME" (Dodwell & Humphrey, 1990) is observed if, following induction with only a green horizontal grid, an achromatic vertical grid appears greenish.

Whether or not the indirect ME is acquired (i.e., whether or not the vertical assessment grid appears green in the above example) depends on what is alternated between the repeated presentations of the induction grid (green-horizontal, in the example). An indirect ME is obtained if a color complementary to the induction color (i.e., a homogeneous red stimulus) is presented between occurrences of the green-horizontal grid. An indirect ME is also obtained if the interpolated stimulus is achromatic (black or white) (Allan & Siegel, 1991).

a. Stimuli That Elicit the Indirect ME. The indirect ME is noted only on grids orthogonal to the induction grid. For example, after induction with a green-horizontal grid, a vertical grid is seen as greenish, but no illusory color is seen on a 135° grid (Allan & Siegel, 1991; Humphrey et al., 1989).

Dodwell and colleagues (see Humphrey et al., 1989) suggested that contingent color aftereffects are most readily elicitable by global vector-fields specified in the Lie transformation group theory of visual perception (named after the Norwegian mathematician, Sophus Lie). Patterns described by Lie transformations are orthogonal—if superimposed on each other their contours will be perpendicular at every point of intersection. Thus, pairs of grids differing in orientation by 90° (e.g., horizontal and vertical grids, or 45° and 135° grids) are "Lie derivatives" (Humphrey et al., 1989, p. 97); so is the pair constructed of concentric circles and radial lines (like the spokes of a wheel), and the pair constructed of 90° and 45° oriented rectangular hyperbolae.

Humphrey et al. (1989) hypothesized that the indirect ME results from a shift in contour coding activity to the alternative Lie derivative, combined with the complemental color of the homogeneous field. According to this analysis, repeated presentation of a colored orientation stimulus results in a decrease in sensitivity of coding mechanisms for this orientation. When the orientation stimulus is terminated, there is a compensatory increase in activity of coding mechanisms for the orthogonal orientation, and this orthogonal orientation activity is paired with the color of the homogeneous field interpolated between each presentation of the induction stimulus. As indicated, an indirect ME is obtained if the color of the homogeneous field is the complement of the induction color. In these circumstances, the alternative Lie derivative pattern is functionally paired with the complement of the color of the induction pattern. According to this interpretation, the indirect ME, in common with the direct ME, results from the pairing of orthogonal patterns with complementary colors. For example, consider the situation in which a green-horizontal grid is alternated with a homogeneous red field. When the green-horizontal grid is terminated, there is an increase in activity of the alternative Lie derivative—vertical. This vertical coding activity is paired with the red field. Thus, although only the green-horizontal grid is presented in induction, the subject is functionally induced with both green-horizontal and red-vertical grids.

To explain the fact that an indirect ME is also obtained when an achromatic field is interpolated between presentations of the induction grid, Humphrey et al. (1989) additionally hypothesized that the indirect ME could result from a shift in contour coding activity combined with a color afterimage. Consider the example in which a green horizontal grid is alternated with a homogeneous achromatic field. During intervals when the achromatic field is presented, the coding for the orthogonal orientation (vertical) is effectively paired with the complementary color afterimage (pink) of the just-terminated green grid, and the resulting aftereffect on vertical would be green.

b. The Indirect ME and the Conditioning Interpretation of the ME. The conditioning interpretation of the ME is as relevant to the indirect ME as to the direct ME, since both appear to result from similar processes. The results of indirect ME experiments suggest, however, that there is something special about certain patterns. That is, perhaps it is not coincidental that Lie derivatives have been used in most ME research— rather, they have been used because they work very well.

The fact that some patterns are better than others in inducing the ME is similar to findings that high contrast grids are better than low contrast grids. That is, Lie derivatives may represent a category of stimuli highly associable with color. However, just as selective associability is often not absolute (e.g., with sufficient training, exteroceptive stimuli *can* be associated with gastrointestinal distress; Best, Best, & Henggeler, 1977), so the selective associability of Lie derivatives with color is not absolute. As documented earlier, many stimuli that are not Lie derivatives can, following pairing with color, contingently elicit aftereffects. Even Dodwell and colleagues do not claim that all MEs are interpretable within the framework of Lie transformation theory (Dodwell & Humphrey, 1990). Indeed, they have demonstrated contingent color aftereffects that are not readily interpretable by their model (Dodwell & O'Shea, 1987, see Note added in proof, p. 579).

V. Evidence for the Pavlovian Conditioning Analysis of the ME

Taken as a whole, the evidence in the present analysis does not seem to support the hypothesis that MEs are classically conditioned responses. (Skowbo, 1984, p. 224)

A close look at the conditioning literature leads us to conclude that the characteristics of contingent aftereffects are consistent with classical conditioning data. (Allan & Siegel, 1986, p. 398)

Having analyzed Allan and Siegel's evidence, I find little in their article that strongly supports a classical conditioning model of MEs. (Skowbo, 1986, p. 397)

Some features of ME generation are suggestive of classical conditioning, but others definitely are not. (Dodwell & Humphrey, 1990, p. 79)

As indicated by the above quotations, there has been considerable debate concerning the conditioning basis of the ME. We suggest that Dodwell and Humphrey's (1990) recent summary of the debate—"the result is pretty much a draw" (p. 79)—although conciliatory, is incorrect. There are now many findings indicating that the ME is best understood as a CR.

A. Parallels between CRs and MEs

A conditioning interpretation of contingent color aftereffects is supported by demonstrations that manipulations of the putative CS and UCS have conditioning-like effects. Skowbo (1984) and Allan and Siegel (1986) enumerated various similarities between the operations that modulate the strength of conditioning and those that modulate the magnitude of the ME.

1. Extinction

Generally, CR magnitude decreases if the CS is repeatedly presented in the absence of the UCS. If the ME is a CR, it too should evidence such extinction. That is, repeated presentations of the grid following ME induction should decrease the aftereffect. Several investigators have reported that this occurs (e.g., Riggs et al., 1974; Savoy, 1984; Skowbo, 1988; Skowbo & Clynes, 1977; Skowbo, Gentry, Timney, & Morant, 1974). Indeed, as suggested by Skowbo (1984), any decrement in the ME over time may be due (at least in part) to extinction resulting from incidental exposure to environmental stimuli containing repeated-line patterns. This hypothesis is supported by findings indicating that the ME decays relatively little during sleep or when the eye is occluded (MacKay & MacKay, 1975b, 1977).

2. Spontaneous Recovery

Following a rest period, extinguished CRs typically display some recovery. The phenomenon, termed *spontaneous recovery,* has also been noted with the ME (e.g., Skowbo, 1988; Skowbo & Clynes, 1977).

3. Latent Inhibition

Generally, CR acquisition is faster with a novel CS than with a preexposed CS. The phenomenon, termed *latent inhibition,* has also been noted with the ME. That is, preinduction exposure to achromatic grids decreases the magnitude of the ME when chromatic grids are subsequently presented during ME induction (e.g., Skowbo, 1988).

B. COMPOUND CONDITIONING AND THE ME

The development of a CR is not the inevitable result of CS–UCS pairings. This is seen in *compound conditioning,* conditioning in which at least two CSs simultaneously signal the UCS. It is well established that the effectiveness of any one of the CSs in becoming associated with the UCS depends on the characteristics of the stimuli with which this CS is compounded. These compound conditioning effects may be seen in phenomena such as "blocking" and "overshadowing" (see Kamin, 1969; Pavlov, 1927, pp. 142–143 and 269–270; Rescorla & Wagner, 1972).

1. Blocking of the ME

If a particular CS (say, CS_A) has been associated with a UCS, and CS_A is subsequently compounded with a second CS (say, CS_B), with this

$CS_A + CS_B$ compound still being paired with the UCS, little is learned about CS_B. That is, prior training with one component of a compound will *block* the conditioning of a second component; in this example, CS_A blocks CS_B.

Skowbo (1984) suggested that, on the basis of the conditioning analysis, MEs (like other CRs) should be subject to blocking. Westbrook and Harrison (1984) demonstrated blocking, using a modified version of the contingent–aftereffect induction procedure. Subsequently, Siegel and Allan (1985) reported blocking of the ME with the procedure typically used to induce the aftereffect. They induced the ME with diagonal patterns (CS_A) prior to continued aftereffect induction with a compound grid consisting of diagonal and horizontal-vertical components $(CS_A + CS_B)$. They found that the prior CS_A induction attenuated the aftereffect elicited by CS_B. These results have been confirmed by others (Brand et al., 1987; Sloane, Ost, Etheriedge, and Henderlite, 1989).

2. Unblocking of the ME

An influential model of many phenomena of compound Pavlovian conditioning, including blocking, is the Rescorla-Wagner model (Rescorla & Wagner, 1972). On the basis of this model, increasing the intensity of the UCS between the first and second phases of the blocking experiment should lead to unblocking; that is, something should be learned about the CS_B–UCS relationship. There is evidence that unblocking occurs in Pavlovian conditioning (e.g., Kamin, 1969), and Brand et al. (1987) demonstrated the phenomenon with the ME. After establishing blocking, Brand et al. (1987) increased the intensity of the putative UCS (i.e., the saturation of the color) and demonstrated unblocking; the added CS element now contingently elicited illusory color.

3. Overshadowing of the ME

In the case of blocking, CS_A is pretrained prior to being compounded with CS_B, and subjects learn little about CS_B. Sometimes, even if there is no prior training of an element of a compound CS, subjects still learn little about one of the elements. This occurs when one element is more *salient* than the other (other things being equal, a subject trained with a more salient CS will learn more rapidly than a subject trained with a less salient CS). If CS_A is more salient than CS_B, the effect of pairing a UCS with the $CS_A + CS_B$ compound will be to strongly associate CS_A with the UCS, with little associative strength developing between CS_B and the UCS (CS_A overshadows CS_B). Indeed, less will be learned about CS_B than if this less salient CS alone had been paired with the UCS (rather than as a component of the compound CS).

In addition to demonstrating blocking, Siegel and Allan (1985) demonstrated overshadowing of the ME. For the stimulus patterns used in this experiment, the diagonal grids (CS_A) were more salient than the horizontal-vertical grids (CS_B); that is, for any given amount of aftereffect induction, a group induced with CS_A acquired a stronger aftereffect than a group induced with CS_B. As expected, on the basis of a conditioning analysis of the ME, for subjects induced with a $CS_A + CS_B$ compound grid, CS_A overshadowed CS_B. Overshadowing of the ME has also been reported by Brand et al. (1987).

4. Overprediction and the ME

The usual way to decrease the strength of a CS–UCS association is to present the CS without the UCS (i.e., extinction). The Rescorla-Wagner model, however, suggests procedures for weakening the association even though the UCS is presented. This weakening can be accomplished by training two CSs individually with the same UCS, such that the association between each CS and the UCS is asymptotic; the subject receives many CS_A–UCS pairings and many CS_B–UCS pairings. If the subject subsequently receives presentations of a compound CS formed of $CS_A + CS_B$, with the compound being paired with the UCS, the strength of conditioning for each element decreases. That is, continued pairing of the two CSs with the UCS, albeit with the CSs now compounded, causes a loss of associative strength for each element. Such *overprediction* effects have been demonstrated in a variety of conditioning preparations (Kremer, 1978; Rescorla, 1970; Wagner, 1971). Using horizontal-vertical and diagonal grids as CS_A and CS_B elements, Sloane et al. (1989) recently demonstrated that overprediction can be observed with the ME.

C. CORRELATIONAL MANIPULATIONS AND THE ME

As first discussed by Skowbo and Forster (1983), if the ME represents an instance of Pavlovian conditioning, correlational[1] manipulations should affect the perceptual illusion much as they affect other CRs. Generally, decreasing the correlation between a CS and a UCS decreases the strength of conditioning. Such a decrease in correlation typically is effected by

[1] In the learning literature, CS–UCS correlation is often referred to as CS-UCS "contingency." In this article we use the term "correlation" to refer to the statistical relationship between the CS and UCS, so as not to confuse this relationship with the "contingent" color aftereffect.

UCS presentations interpolated between paired CS–UCS presentations (see Rescorla & Wagner, 1972). On the basis of a conditioning analysis of the ME, presentation of the putative UCS (homogeneous chromatic stimuli) between presentations of the putative CS (chromatic grids) should degrade the perceptual illusion. Skowbo and Forster (1983) reported that this manipulation did not influence the magnitude of the ME and suggested that their results were contrary to a conditioning account of the phenomenon.

Skowbo and Forster's (1983) results were subsequently confirmed by Siegel and Allan (1987). Siegel et al. (1992) recently proposed an explanation for the failure of correlational manipulations to affect the ME, inspired by the Rescorla-Wagner model. According to this model, associations between the experimental context and interpolated UCSs develop in parallel with CS–UCS associations. The reason why interpolated UCSs decrease the strength of conditioning is that the context–UCS association competes with, and blocks, the CS–UCS association (see Rescorla & Wagner, 1972). In the typical ME preparation, presentations of the putative UCS (homogeneous chromatic stimuli) between presentations of colored grids would not promote the development of context–color associations that would compete with the grid–color association. There is no distinctive context; interpolated homogeneous chromatic stimuli, green and red, are simply presented in the middle of a black screen. As summarized by Siegel and Allan (1987), "the inability of experimental context cues to become associated with chromatic stimuli would render the contingency [correlation] manipulation ineffective" (p. 284).

Recently, Tiffany, Maude-Griffin, and Drobes (1991) similarly discussed the importance of a "superordinate experimental context" (p. 58) in experiments evaluating the effects of CS–UCS correlation in conditioning. The frame lightness–contingent aftereffect, described earlier, provides a technique for presenting such a superordinate context during ME induction. Grid–color pairings can be presented in the context provided by the lightness of the frame surrounding the chromatic grid. Thus, both the context in which induction is conducted as well as the orientation stimulus specifically paired with color are effective as elicitors of illusory color.

Siegel et al. (1992) evaluated the effect of contingency manipulations on the ME, using frame lightness as a contextual cue. In their experiment, all subjects received green-horizontal and red-vertical grids appearing as pictures in white and black frames, respectively. As is the case in a typical conditioning experiment, the UCS (i.e., color) was paired with both the nominal CS (i.e., grid orientation) and the context (i.e., frame lightness). Subjects assigned to the low correlation group received additional presentations of only the chromatic stimulus in this context; that is, they received extra homogeneous colored stimuli paired with the same contextual cues present during grid–color pairings. Subjects assigned to the high correlation group did not have any additional exposure to color between chromatic grid presentations. The magnitude of the aftereffect contingently elicited by both the CS (grid orientation) and the context (frame lightness) was determined. The results of the experiment indicated that correlational manipulations affect the strength of the ME. Subjects in the low correlation group, who were exposed to intertrial chromatic stimuli, displayed smaller MEs than subjects in the high correlation group.

Decreasing the CS–UCS correlation in Pavlovian conditioning is hypothesized to retard learning because the intertrial UCSs become associated with context cues, and these context–UCS associations compete with the simultaneously forming CS–UCS associations (Rescorla & Wagner, 1972). This analysis of the decremental effects of decreasing CS–UCS correlation has been supported by the results of experiments in which the context–UCS association, as well as the CS–UCS association, was monitored. Increases in the former were associated with decreases in the latter (e.g., Kremer, 1974; Odling-Smee, 1975). Similar results were obtained by Siegel et al. (1992). Just as the context, as well as the nominal CS, is paired with the UCS for low correlation subjects in Pavlovian conditioning, so the frame, as well as the grid, was paired with the UCS for the low correlation subjects in the ME experiment. As in other Pavlovian conditioning preparations, there was an inverse relationship between the context–UCS association and the CS–UCS association. That is, high correlation subjects, who evidenced a relatively strong ME, evidenced a relatively weak frame lightness–contingent color aftereffect. Subjects in the low correlation group displayed weaker MEs and stronger frame lightness–contingent color aftereffects.

The results of Siegel et al. (1992) strongly implicate Pavlovian conditioning in the ME. Subjects assigned to the low correlation and high correlation groups received equivalent exposure to chromatic grids; they were exposed to the same chromatic grids, equally often, and at the same intervals. Nevertheless, low correlation subjects, who were exposed to colors in the absence of the grid, displayed weaker MEs than high correlation subjects. The fact that weaker MEs are seen in the group displaying the greater frame lightness–contingent aftereffect indicates that correlational manipulations affect the ME and other CRs via similar processes.

D.   Rehearsal Processes and the ME

There is evidence that the acquisition of an association between two stimuli requires a period following paired presentation during which the association is *consolidated* or *rehearsed:* "an interval free of interference from the occurrence of similar events (that is, events that would involve associative elements overlapping with those just established) or unusual disturbances of the nervous system such as those produced by electroconvulsive shock'' (Estes, 1970, p. 9). On the basis of an associative analysis of the ME, then, there must be a rehearsal period following chromatic grid presentation for the grid–color association to become established.

Although there are many events that may interfere with rehearsal and the acquisition of an association, they are generally effective to the extent that they are surprising (see Wagner, Rudy, & Whitlow, 1973). Presumably, such surprising events presented after conditioning trials demand attention and thus decrease the attention and rehearsal commanded by the paired conditioning stimuli on that trial. The work of Wagner et al. (1973) provided the inspiration for the manipulation of surprisingness in ME research. Wagner et al. (1973) evaluated the role of rehearsal in the acquisition of eyelid conditioning in the rabbit. Siegel and Allan (1990) applied their technique to evaluate the role of rehearsal in the acquisition of the ME.

1. Rehearsal and Posttrial Episodes

In the Wagner et al. (1973) experiments, rabbits were initially trained to discriminate two different CSs, one of which was paired with the UCS, a weak infraorbital shock that elicited eyelid closure. Thus, subjects received pairings of a CS_+ paired with the UCS, and CS_- not paired with the UCS. In a second phase of the experiment, all subjects received eyelid conditioning acquisition with yet a third CS (that is, subjects receive CS_{target}–UCS pairings). For some subjects, each CS_{target}–UCS trial was followed by a posttrial episode (PTE) that was *congruent* (i.e., an event consistent with the training in the first phase of the experiment). Examples of congruent PTEs are a CS_+–UCS pairing, or a CS_- presentation. For other subjects, each CS_{target}–UCS trial was followed by an *incongruent* PTE (i.e., an event inconsistent with the training in the first phase of the experiment). Examples of incongruent PTEs are a CS_-–UCS pairing, or a CS_+ presentation. The data of interest were the speed of acquisition of the CS_{target}–UCS association. Presumably, the incongruent PTEs would demand rehearsal and thus disrupt the consolidation of the CS_{target}–UCS association. Indeed, Wagner et al. (1973) reported that groups trained with congruent PTEs acquired the eyeblink conditional response faster than subjects trained with incongruent PTEs.

2. PTEs and the ME

In the ME situation, congruent and incongruent PTEs may be provided by presenting chromatic orientation stimuli that are either consistent or inconsistent with the subject's prior experience with chromatic grids. Consider, for example, ME induction in which a green diagonal grid of one orientation (e.g., 45°) alternates with a red grid of the orthogonal orientation (135°) during the first phase of the experiment. This Phase 1 induction provides stimuli that are used as PTEs in Phase 2. In Phase 2, subjects receive additional ME induction with different orientation stimuli—green horizontal and red vertical grids. The horizontal–vertical chromatic grid presentations constitute "target" aftereffect induction. Two groups differ with respect to the PTEs presented after each target grid in this second phase of the experiment. For one group each target grid presentation is followed by a congruent PTE (e.g., each horizontal green grid is followed by a 45° green grid, and each vertical red grid is followed by a 135° red grid). For a second group, each target grid presentation is followed by an incongruent PTE (e.g., each horizontal green grid is followed by a 135° green grid, and each vertical red grid is followed by a 45° red grid). If associative processes contribute to the ME, achromatic horizontal and vertical grids should elicit greater illusory colors in the congruent group than in the incongruent group. Just this finding was recently reported (Siegel & Allan, 1990).

VI. The ME's Cousins

There is an attractiveness to a theory that can subsume a variety of effects under a common mechanism. (Brandon, Bombace, Falls, & Wagner, 1991, p. 320)

The ME generally refers to color aftereffects contingent on orientation. On the basis of the conditioning interpretation of the ME, contingent aftereffects should be rather general. Indeed, as already discussed, there are color aftereffects contingent on many features other than orientation (e.g., spatial frequency, movement direction, dot size, form, and frame lightness). In fact, contingent color aftereffects are only one example of contingent aftereffects. The many contingent aftereffects that have been reported have been called *cousins* of the ME (Meyer, Jackson, & Yang, 1979).

An example of an ME cousin is movement contingent on color. That is, not only can color be made contingent on movement, but also vice versa. A color-contingent movement aftereffect is induced by selectively pairing two complementary colors with two movement directions (e.g., Bonnet, Le Gall, Lorenceau, 1984; Favreau, 1979; Favreau, Emerson, & Corballis, 1972; Mayhew & Anstis, 1972). For example, induction with a green spiral rotating clockwise alternating with a red spiral rotating counterclockwise results in illusory rotation contingent on color: a stationary green spiral appears to rotate counterclockwise and a stationary red spiral appears to rotate clockwise. Additional color aftereffects, contingent on features other than movement, have been reported (e.g., Held & Shattuck, 1971).

Some ME cousins do not involve color. An orientation-contingent achromatic aftereffect has been studied by a number of investigators (Allan & Tirimacco, 1987; Mikaelian, Linton, & Phillips, 1990; Over, Broerse, Crassini, & Lovegrove, 1974). During induction of the "achromatic ME," two orientations are selectively paired with two grays; e.g., horizontal with a relatively light gray and vertical with a relatively dark gray. In assessment, the perceived lightness of a gray is contingent on orientation; in this example, the same gray appears darker as part of a horizontal grid than as part of a vertical grid.

There are many demonstrations of achromatic contingent movement aftereffects. For example, selectively pairing two horizontal grids of different spatial frequencies with two movement directions induces a spatial frequency–contingent movement aftereffect (e.g., Mayhew & Anstis, 1972). Induction with a high spatial frequency grid moving upward and a low spatial frequency grid moving downward results in illusory movement contingent on spatial frequency: a stationary high spatial frequency grid appears to move downward and a stationary low spatial grid appears to move upward. Movement aftereffects contingent on a variety of features have been demonstrated (e.g., Anstis & Harris, 1974; Mayhew, 1973; Mayhew & Anstis, 1972; Walker, 1972).

In fact, contingent aftereffects are not even restricted to the visual modality. For example, Walker (1977, 1978; Walker & Shea, 1974) described contingent size aftereffects in the tactile modality. In one experiment, the subject was required to grasp, between the thumb and forefinger, the horizontal and vertical dimensions of a thin piece of Plexiglas™. During induction, the Plexiglas was rectangular (say horizontal shorter than vertical), and the subject alternately grasped the two dimensions. After induction, a square piece of Plexiglas felt rectangular: in this example, the square felt longer in the horizontal dimension than in the vertical dimension.

Other examples of nonvisual aftereffects involve the judgment of time. For example, the perceived duration of a tone can be made contingent on the pitch of the tone. During induction, two tones of different pitch and temporal extent are alternated (e.g., a low pitch short tone and a high pitch long tone). Such induction will result in a low pitch tone appearing longer than a high pitch tone of equal physical duration (Allan, 1984; Walker & Irion, 1979). Other types of contingent duration aftereffects have been demonstrated (Allan, 1984; Meyer, 1977; Meyer, Lawson, & Cohen, 1975; Meyer et al., 1979; Walker & Irion, 1979; Walker, Irion, & Gordon, 1981).

The cousins of the ME enumerated above are representative of the extended family of contingent aftereffects and do not include all members of the family. A parsimonious explanation of the ME should include the many, many cousins of the phenomenon. Pavlovian conditioning provides such a common explanation: "The only obvious way to cut down markedly on the number of special mechanisms is to find some way to ascribe all the different aftereffects to a common associative mechanism, capable of connecting any of a wide range of attributes of stimuli and perceptions" (Harris, 1980, p. 130). An association between orientation and chromatic stimuli is hypothesized to mediate McCollough's original contingent aftereffect. Associations formed between the other stimuli, paired during induction of the cousins, likely mediate these related aftereffects.

VII. Retention of the ME

These aftereffects may persist for an hour or more before fading completely. (McCollough, 1965, p. 1115)

When four more groups were subsequently tested at intervals up to 2,040 hr., the [McCollough] effect remained at better than half strength. (Jones & Holding, 1975, p. 323)

Although there may be some controversy about exactly how long the ME lasts, researchers agree that it lasts for a very long time. Some investigators have suggested that this substantial longevity of contingent color aftereffects contrasts with the very brief duration of simple color aftereffects (which typically last only for seconds). They argue that such persistence is characteristic of CRs and thus provides evidence for the associative nature of the ME (see Allan & Siegel, 1986). Other investigators have countered that this alleged difference between contingent and simple aftereffects results from "the mistaken belief that contingent aftereffects always last much longer than simple aftereffects. . . . Many simple aftereffects can last for hours, days, and even weeks" (Dodwell & Humphrey, 1990, p. 79). As Harris (1980) noted:

There are two possible conclusions. One is that all of these seemingly noncontingent aftereffects are actually contingent upon some undetermined attribute of the adapting stimulus or the experimental situation. The other is that *non*associative aftereffects can also be very persistent, and therefore longevity cannot be taken as evidence for an associative model of the McCollough Effect. (p. 131)

The first of these conclusions is quite tenable.

In many studies of "simple" aftereffects, the experimenters did not evaluate whether the aftereffect was contingent. That a contingency may have been established in such studies is suggested by the indirect ME experiments described earlier. The one-grid induction procedure is similar to procedures often used in induction of "simple" aftereffects. For example, Favreau (1979) induced subjects with a green spiral rotating clockwise. She found that a stationary green spiral appeared to rotate counterclockwise. This aftereffect was detectable as long as 96 hr after induction. Favreau (1979) suggested that her results indicated substantial retention of a simple noncontingent movement aftereffect; however, since she assessed the aftereffect only with a green stationary spiral, she had no way of evaluating whether the movement aftereffect was noncontingent or contingent.

Allan and Siegel (1991) showed not only that one-grid induction results in a contingent aftereffect, but also that the aftereffect following one-grid induction is long lasting. Some aftereffects that have been labeled as "simple" might really be contingent aftereffects. Understandably, then, some "simple" aftereffects are as long lasting as contingent aftereffects.

An anecdote told by Martin Taylor[2] illustrates nicely the potentially contingent nature of an aftereffect established in a manner similar to that used in many "simple" aftereffect studies. Taylor spent many months at his typewriter when writing his Ph.D. dissertation. He had a supply of cheap blue paper which he used for the many drafts he produced over this prolonged period. When he was ready to generate the final draft, he switched to regular white paper. On inserting the first sheet of white paper into his typewriter, Taylor was surprised to find that the paper appeared yellow rather than white. When he removed the paper from the typewriter, it was again white. The white paper appeared yellow *only* when in the typewriter! This typewriter-contingent color aftereffect (perhaps a distant cousin to the ME) illustrates that seemingly simple aftereffects are not so simple—they may be contingent on subtle stimuli paired with color.

VIII. Simultaneous Associations and the ME

It remains to be determined whether learning about simultaneously presented events (e.g., the form–colour combination) follows the same rules as those that have been adduced to explain how organisms learn about the causal relations between events. (Westbrook & Harrison, 1984, p. 316)

---

[2] Professor Taylor presented this observation at the 1990 meeting of LOVE (Lake Ontario Visual Establishment).

In most conditioning preparations, maximal conditional responding is seen if the CS and UCS are presented sequentially (the CS occurring before the UCS). Sequential presentation of grid and color, however, leads to a smaller ME than simultaneous presentation (Murch, 1976). Several investigators have suggested that the fact that simultaneous grid–color presentation is optimal for ME induction argues against the conditioning analysis of the ME (McCarter & Silver, 1977; Skowbo, 1984): "The strong aftereffects obtained in the simultaneous paradigm, as found by Murch and others, then, must be considered an instance of incompatability with conditioning phenomena" (McCarter & Silver, 1977, p. 317).

Since the ME is most pronounced when the grid and color are presented at the same time, there is some arbitrariness in the designation of one component of the induction stimulus (the grid) as the CS, and the other (color) as the UCS. This arbitrary labeling of CS and UCS has also been seen as presenting a difficulty for the conditioning interpretation of the ME:

> There is no a priori reason for assigning color to the role of the unconditioned stimulus, orientation to the conditioned stimulus, or vice versa. . . . The components identified as the conditioned and unconditioned stimuli in the McCollough paradigm are interchangeable, and therefore arbitrary. This is not an attribute of the stimuli in classical conditioning. (Dodwell & Humphrey, 1990, p. 79)

Traditional wisdom to the effect that Pavlovian conditioning is best with a successive arrangement of CS and UCS is based on the results of research with traditional conditioning preparations. In these preparations, a relatively neutral CS (e.g., tone or light) is paired with a very biologically significant UCS from a different sensory system (e.g., shock or food). Moreover, the CS is typically long, compared to the UCS. As suggested by several investigators (e.g., Domjan & Burkhard, 1986, p. 81; Rescorla & Holland, 1982), successive conditioning may not be superior to simultaneous conditioning when the CS and UCS are relatively weak, or are processed within the same sensory system, or are of the same duration.

Rescorla (1981) demonstrated that, in some types of animal conditioning preparations, simultaneous associations are more pronounced than successive associations, and concluded, "Substantial, important, and perhaps qualitatively different, learning occurs when stimuli are presented simultaneously" (p. 78). Similarly, Asch, Ceraso, and Heimer (1960) considered it likely that different processes may mediate the acquisition of simultaneous and sequential associations in humans. Several investigators applied this reasoning specifically to the ME (Murch, 1977; Siegel, Allan, Roberts, & Eissenberg, 1990; Westbrook & Harrison, 1984). The ME may best be understood as a result of processes unique to simultaneous associations.

Prevalent views of successive conditioning emphasize the role of the CS as a signal for the UCS—a relationship best described as *informative* or *predictive* (see Rescorla, 1981). In the case of simultaneously presented sensory events, subjects may form a unitary representation of the elements that form the compound perceptual stimulus, rather than form separate representations that are then associated (i.e., "coherence within units," rather than "coherence between units"; Asch et al., 1960). To give a common example, if you drink coffee sweetened with sugar, you do not learn that the sweet taste signals the coffee taste (or vice versa). Rather, you form a unitary representation of sweetened coffee. Neither of the two flavors is *the* CS or *the* UCS, although it can easily be demonstrated that a flavor–flavor association is formed (Rescorla, 1980). The ME might be another example of a simultaneous association.

There has been only one attempt to evaluate whether the ME displays any of the special attributes of a simultaneous association (Siegel et al., 1990). Based on results reported by Rescorla (1986) concerning simultaneous associations between visual stimuli in pigeons, Siegel et al. (1990) hypothesized that the ME may be attenuated by decreasing the spatial correlation between grid and color. This decreased spatial correlation can be accomplished by extending the color beyond the confines of the grid. Siegel et al. (1990) were wrong; the results provided no evidence that decreasing the spatial correlation between grid and color decreased the ME. In fact, the aftereffect was *increased* by such a manipulation.

As discussed by Siegel et al. (1990), the finding that the ME is greater following low spatial correlation induction than high spatial correlation induction suggests that the magnitude of the illusion is related to the quantity of color present at the time of grid presentation. That is, the demonstration that the ME is enhanced by increasing the *area* of color presented at the time of grid presentation is similar to earlier findings demonstrating that the ME is enhanced by increasing the *saturation* of the color (e.g., White, 1978). Siegel et al. (1990) concluded that spatial correlation manipulations were inappropriate for evaluating the conditioning analysis of the ME (because of the confounding between grid–color correlation and the quantity of color paired with the grid). Further research is needed to evaluate whether other procedures that have demonstrated the unique characteristics of simultaneous associations (Rescorla, 1981, 1986) may be applied to elucidate the associative basis of the ME.

IX. Relationship between Conditioning and Other
Interpretations of the ME

It is an open question whether they [contingent aftereffects] are due to cortical cells having shared functions, and being teased out by repeated stimulation; or whether they are due to some kind of adaptive learning during which orientation and colour become associated. (Gregory, 1978, p. 214)

Could it be that vision people are uneasy about associative models of the McCollough effect only because our notions about learning are out of date? (Harris, 1980, p. 134)

Evidence has been summarized that supports a conditioning interpretation of the ME. The conditioning interpretation may be contrasted with alternative interpretations. Some of these alternatives are based on hypothesized *adaptation* or *fatigue* of orientation detectors. Other theorists have suggested that the ME represents the operation of an *error correction device* (Andrews, 1964); following ME induction, achromatic grids seem colored because of the subject's tendency to reestablish the normal zero correlation between orientation and color.

A. DETECTOR FATIGUE

The discovery of the ME occurred at about the same time as exciting discoveries concerning the existence of visual cortical cells with special properties in cats (Hubel & Wiesel, 1962). Neurophysiologists demonstrated that some cells responded only to stimuli of a particular orientation. Such findings inspired interpretations of the ME that continue to be influential.

1. Edge Detectors

McCollough (1965) suggested that humans, like other animals, have separate mechanisms for detecting horizontal and vertical edges. She further speculated that these edge detectors are sensitive to color. A green-horizontal grid will adapt horizontal detectors to green light, and a red-vertical grid will adapt vertical detectors to red light. After ME induction, an achromatic horizontal grid will look pink because the green-adapted horizontal detectors respond with an attenuated green response (i.e., more red) to horizontal stimuli. Similarly, an achromatic vertical grid will look green because the red-adapted vertical detectors respond with an attenuated red response (i.e., more green) to vertical stimuli.

2. Color-coded Edge Detectors

McCollough (1965) proposed the existence of orientation detectors that respond to many colors but that display adaptation to a particular wavelength following exposure to that wavelength (during ME induction). Shortly after McCollough's report, evidence was reported that the monkey's visual cortex contained detectors that responded only to a particular combination of color and orientation (Hubel & Wiesel, 1968; Michael, 1978). McCollough's interpretation was modified to incorporate these so-called "double-duty" (color and orientation) detectors (see Harris, 1980). The ME was seen to provide psychophysical evidence that humans possessed color-coded edge detectors (e.g., horizontal-red, horizontal-green, vertical-red, and vertical-green). According to this analysis, during ME induction with green-horizontal and red-vertical grids, the detectors sensitive both to green and horizontal stimuli, and the detectors sensitive to red and vertical stimuli, are fatigued. The ME results because the fatigued green-horizontal detectors do not contribute to the processing of the achromatic horizontal assessment grid, and the fatigued red-vertical detectors do not contribute to the processing of the achromatic vertical assessment grid.

3. Evaluation of Detector Fatigue Models

Despite the fact that some form of detector fatigue model is still commonly invoked to explain the ME (e.g., Houck & Hoffman, 1986), there is considerable evidence contrary to such models. For example, the ME is noted even if the assessment grid is colored such that its spectral energy distribution does not overlap with either of the two, complementary induction colors (Murch, 1979). That is, the effect is seen even if the hypothesized edge detectors processing the induction grids are adapted to colors that are different than those processing the assessment grids.

More importantly, there are simply too many stimuli that can contingently elicit color aftereffects. It is unreasonable to postulate a detector for each of the myriad features of a chromatic display that subsequently contingently elicits illusory color (see Harris, 1980). In addition, as described above, color aftereffects can be contingently elicited by forms constructed of the same orientation components (Siegel et al., 1992). The fact that different illusory colors can be elicited by forms constructed of the same line orientations in different arrangements (see Fig. 1) makes existing formulations of orientation detector fatigue models of the ME untenable. Obviously, if an attempt were made to include the myriad ME cousins in a common explanation, specific double-duty detectors would have to be postulated for many different sensory systems. This model appears unwieldy.

B.   The ME as an Error Correction Mechanism

In 1964 Andrews presented an "error correcting theory" of perception. He suggested that illusions resulted from genetically determined error correction devices (ECDs)—systems that convert signals that contain errors to signals that are corrected. Such ECDs are crucial for veridical perception of the environment. They also result in what might be called "errors of correction." If exposed to an anomalous environment, ECD activity will induce perceptual alterations that attenuate the environmental alteration but may be seen as illusions in the normal environment.

Wolfe and O'Connell (1986) applied Andrews' (1964) concepts to visual aftereffects in general: "Adaptation to systemic changes in the retinal image grows out of the system's need for continuous recalibration" (p. 542). Dodwell and Humphrey (1990) invoked these concepts specifically to explain the ME. Normally the correlation between color and orientation is zero. This correlation is violated during ME induction, and the ECD biases the system to reestablish the zero correlation by moving the neutral point. If green-horizontal is presented in induction, for example, then the neutral point for green in the presence of horizontals is shifted by the ECD toward the overrepresented end of the color continuum (green). In assessment, when an achromatic horizontal grid is presented, white light, which was neutral before induction, is now on the red side of the neutral point, and the assessment figure will appear pinkish.

1.   Is the Error Correction Theory Associative?

In the elaboration of their error correction theory of the ME, Dodwell and Humphrey (1990) suggest that "the ME is established by a mechanism that detects stimulus correlations" (p. 82). Although they are not explicit about the manner in which the subject assimilates the correlation, they suggest that "processes of neural adaptation and perceptual learning that are akin to classical conditioning" (p. 79) do *not* explain the ME.

The study of the "mechanism that detects stimulus correlations," in both humans and nonhuman animals, is a matter of considerable research activity. There are two broad categories of explanations of the acquisition of such correlational information: (1) theories postulating that organisms extract statistical rules based on the probabilities or frequencies of the relevant events, and (2) theories postulating that apparent correlational learning is really the result of Pavlovian associations formed between *all* the various contiguously presented events in the conditioning situation.

On the basis of statistical rule theories, subjects act as computers; they calculate some relevant feature of the sequence of events (e.g., the difference between conditional probabilities of one event in the presence versus the absence of a second event) and respond differentially on the basis of the results of these calculations (see Allan & Jenkins, 1980, 1983). On the basis of contiguity learning theories, subjects associate the UCS with both the nominal CS and with contextual cues. According to one version of this contiguity analysis of correlational effects, correlational learning results because the expression of the CR is determined by the strength of the CS–UCS association, relative to the context–UCS association (e.g., Gibbon & Balsam, 1981; Miller & Schachtman, 1985). According to another influential contiguity theory, the Rescorla-Wagner model, the context–UCS association competes with and "blocks" the CS–UCS association (Wagner & Rescorla, 1972).

There is now abundant evidence that a simple contiguity model of Pavlovian conditioning is the appropriate way to evaluate the effects of correlational manipulations with infrahuman subjects (Papini & Bitterman, 1990). Similarly, human data "provide considerable evidence that the case for the application of conditioning theories to account for human contingency judgment is strong enough to merit serious consideration" (Shanks, 1985, p. 167). More recently, Shanks and colleagues (see Shanks, 1989; Shanks & Dickinson, 1987) presented an associative model for human judgments of correlation "that bears many similarities to one of the best-known animal learning models, the Rescorla and Wagner (1972) theory of Pavlovian conditioning" (Shanks, 1989, p. 27). We suggest that a correlational model of the ME is but a descriptive and shorthand presentation of a Pavlovian conditioning model.[3]

2. Correlation, Contiguity, Context, and Surprise

Previously described results attest to the advantage of using a specific conditioning model of the ME rather than a less well specified correlational model. For example, the ME is subject to blocking and PTE effects. Learning theorists have interpreted both blocking and PTE effects as evidence that events enter into associations to the extent that they are surprising. In the case of blocking, little is learned about the added element of a compound CS because the outcome of the conditioning trial is not surprising; it is already predicted by the pretrained element (Kamin, 1969; Rescorla & Wagner, 1972). In the case of PTEs, incongruent PTEs com-

---

[3] Viola (1966), in an undergraduate thesis, offered an account of the ME very similar to that subsequently presented by Dodwell and Humphrey (1990). Viola (1966) described her analysis as "a conditioning hypothesis" (p. 13).

mand rehearsal (and thus interfere with consolidation of an immediately preceding association) because they are surprising; they are inconsistent with pretraining contingencies (Wagner et al., 1973). Both phenomena suggest that the magnitude of the ME induced by presentations of target chromatic grids is affected by the degree of surprisingness of other chromatic grids that are presented either simultaneously or successively (blocking and PTE effects, respectively). There is no obvious provision in the error correction interpretation for the size of the ME to be affected by the degree to which other chromatic grids are unexpected.

Both Dodwell and Humphrey's (1990) and Pavlovian conditioning models of the ME suggest that decreasing the correlation between grid and color (by presenting colors between colored grid presentations) should decrease the ME. In the case of Dodwell and Humphrey, the ME results from the detection of the orientation–color correlation imposed during ME induction; thus anything that decreases this correlation (such as presenting colors in the absence of orientation stimuli) might be expected to decrease the aftereffect. However, their model does not explain why decreasing the grid–color correlation decreases the ME when effective context cues are provided (Siegel et al., 1992), but not when there are no such context cues (Siegel & Allan, 1987; Skowbo & Forster, 1983). In contrast, context cues are pivotal to influential models of Pavlovian conditioning (see Durlach, 1989).

In summary, there is considerable evidence in support of the conditioning analysis of the ME, and this evidence is not readily interpretable by views of the ME that do not acknowledge a role for associative processes. A further virtue of the conditioning interpretation is that it provides an answer to a question of enduring interest to ME researchers: "What purpose do MEs serve?" (Dodwell & Humphrey, 1990, p. 78).

X.   The Functional Significance of the ME

It is interesting to ask what the role is in normal perception of the mechanisms that produce the McCollough effect. Presumably, they do not exist simply to provide amusing perceptual demonstrations! (Harris, 1987, p. 168).

One would surely expect, however, that a system as elaborate and finely tuned to its environment as the human visual system would not have developed the mechanism that underlies MEs unless it served some useful purpose. It is amazing that so little effort has been made to develop a theory along these lines. (Dodwell & Humphrey, 1990, p. 79)

The conditioning interpretation of the ME is relevant to understanding the functional significance of the phenomenon. The ME, in common with other CRs, contributes to homeostatic functioning (Allan & Siegel, submitted; Allan, Siegel, & Linders, in press; Schull, 1979).

Pavlovian conditioning enables organisms to "make preparatory adjustments for an oncoming stimulus" (Culler, 1938, p. 136). Such preparatory responding has been demonstrated to importantly contribute to adaptation to repeatedly presented stimuli (see Poulos & Cappell, 1991; Siegel, 1991). For example, cues paired with drugs often elicit a drug-preparatory CR (Siegel, 1989)—that is, a compensatory CR opposite in direction to the drug effect. Such drug-compensatory CRs contribute to adaptation to repeated drug administrations (i.e., tolerance). Evidence for the contribution of compensatory CRs to tolerance is provided by demonstrations of situational specificity of tolerance (see Siegel, 1989)—tolerance is more pronounced in the presence of the usual drug-paired cues than in the presence of alternative cues. These drug-paired cues elicit drug compensatory CRs that mediate tolerance. Similarly, cues paired with thermic alteration elicit a temperature-compensatory CR (Hjeresen, Loebel, & Woods, 1982). This thermic CR likely contributes to adaptation to repeated temperature challenges, as revealed by the fact that there is situational specificity of thermic adaptation (Riccio, MacArdy, & Kissinger, 1991).

Color also adapts; continued exposure to a color results in desaturation of that color (e.g., Favreau & Corballis, 1976). Schull (1979) suggested that there is a common mechanism mediating adaptation to color and to other stimuli; a cue (such as orientation) associated with color elicits a color-compensatory CR (i.e., the ME), much as a cue associated with a drug elicits a drug-compensatory CR. Indeed, just as drug tolerance is more pronounced in the presence of drug-associated cues than in the presence of alternative cues, color adaptation is more pronounced in the presence of color-associated cues than in the presence of alternative cues (Allan et al., in press). For example, following presentations of a grid composed of alternating green and black horizontal bars, green is perceived as desaturated only in the presence of the horizontal grid, and not in the absence of a grid or in the presence of an alternative grid orientation.

As discussed by Allan et al. (in press), elucidation of parallels between the ME and other compensatory CRs, and between contingent adaptation to color and contingent adaptation to other stimuli (such as pharmacological or thermic stimuli), are relevant to understanding the functional significance of the ME: "The ME is a conditional-compensatory mechanism (like conditional compensation for a variety of other events) that is part of the system that attenuates the impact of repeatedly presented stimuli in a variety of modalities" (Allan et al., in press).

XI. Conclusion

The McCullough effect can be considered a paradigmatic case of compensatory conditioning, albeit within the visual system. (Schull, 1979, p. 78)

The relationship between associative and perceptual phenomena has been a matter of enduring interest. The purpose of this article has been to summarize the evidence indicating that the vocabulary, techniques, and theoretical analyses of Pavlovian conditioning are useful in understanding the phenomenon reported by McCollough over 25 years ago.

One virtue of the conditioning analysis of the ME is that it is integrative. There is an extensive literature on conditional compensatory responses in many systems. By viewing the ME as a color-compensatory CR, this literature is relevant to understanding the ME (Schull, 1979). Moreover, there are many contingent aftereffects, both visual and nonvisual. The conditioning interpretation is as relevant to (for example) a contingent temporal aftereffect as a contingent color aftereffect.

The conditioning interpretation of the ME makes unique, testable, and counterintuitive predictions about the phenomenon. Thus, the ME should be—and is—subject to blocking, unblocking, overshadowing, PTE effects, and so on. Although creative skeptics may interpret some of these findings as consistent with a nonassociative account of the ME (see Sloane et al., 1989), they would be hard pressed to incorporate all these findings in a parsimonious interpretation that does not acknowledge associative principles.

Finally, not only can conditioning principles elucidate the ME, but the ME may also help us to understand conditioning. For example, the aftereffect is maximal with simultaneous pairings. Associations formed from such simultaneous pairings may have unique characteristics (e.g., Rescorla, 1981), and the ME might provide a useful preparation to examine these characteristics.

Acknowledgments

Research from the authors' laboratory summarized in this article was supported by grants from the U. S. National Institutes of Mental Health and the Natural Sciences and Engineering Research Council of Canada. We thank James Debner and Thomas Eissenberg for their comments on earlier versions of this article. We also thank Gordon Hayman and Larry Roberts for orienting us to the ME.

REFERENCES

Allan, L. G. (1984). Contingent aftereffects in duration judgments. In J. Gibbon & L. G. Allan (Eds.), *Annals of the New York Academy of Sciences: Timing and time perception* (Vol. 423, pp. 116–130). New York: New York Academy of Sciences.

Allan, L. G., & Jenkins, H. M. (1980). The judgment of contingency and the nature of the response alternatives. *Canadian Journal of Psychology, 34,* 1–11.

Allan, L. G., & Jenkins, H. M. (1983). The effect of representations of binary variables on judgment of influence. *Learning and Motivation, 14,* 381–405.

Allan, L. G., & Siegel, S. (1986). McCollough effects as conditioned responses: Reply to Skowbo. *Psychological Bulletin, 100,* 388–393.

Allan, L. G., & Siegel, S. (1991). Characteristics of the indirect McCollough effect. *Perception and Psychophysics, 50,* 249–257.

Allan, L. G., & Siegel, S. (submitted). *McCollough effects as conditioned response: Reply to Dodwell and Humphrey.*

Allan, L. G., Siegel, S., Collins, J. C., & MacQueen, G. M. (1989). Color aftereffect contingent on text. *Perception and Psychophysics, 46,* 105–113.

Allan, L. G., Siegel, S., & Linders, L. M. (in press). Contingent adaptation to color. *Learning and Motivation.*

Allan, L. G., Siegel, S., Toppan, P., & Lockhead, G. R. (1991). Assessment of the McCollough effect by a shift in psychometric function. *Bulletin of the Psychonomic Society, 29,* 21–24.

Allan, L. G., & Tirimacco, N. T. (1987). An orientation-contingent achromatic aftereffect. *Bulletin of the Psychonomic Society, 25,* 54–55.

Andrews, D. P. (1964). Error-correcting perceptual mechanisms. *Quarterly Journal of Experimental Psychology, 16,* 104–116.

Anstis, S. M., & Harris, J. P. (1974). Movement aftereffects contingent on binocular disparity. *Perception, 3,* 153–168.

Asch, S. E., Ceraso, J., & Heimer, W. (1960). Perceptual conditions of association. *Psychological Monographs, 74,* No. 490, 1–48.

Best, P. J., Best, M. R., & Henggeler, S. (1977). The contribution of environmental non-ingestive cues in conditioning with aversive internal consequences. In L. M. Barker, M. R. Best, & M. Domjan (Eds.), *Learning mechanisms in food selection* (pp. 371–393). Waco, TX: Baylor University Press.

Bonnet, C., LeGall, M., & Lorenceau, J. (1984). Visual motion aftereffects: Adaptation and conditioned processes. In L. Spillman & B. R. Wooten (Eds.), *Sensory experience, adaptation, and perception* (pp. 561–582). Hillsdale, NJ: Erlbaum.

Brand, J. L., Holding, D. H., & Jones, P. D. (1987). Conditioning and blocking of the McCollough effect. *Perception and Psychophysics, 41,* 313–317.

Brandon, S. E., Bombace, J. C., Falls, W. A., & Wagner, A. R. (1991). Modulation of unconditioned defensive reflexes by a putative emotive Pavlovian conditioned stimulus. *Journal of Experimental Psychology: Animal Behavior Processes, 17,* 312–321.

Breitmeyer, B. G. & Cooper, L. A. (1972). Frequency-specific color adaptation in the human visual system. *Perception and Psychophysics, 11,* 95–96.

Brogden, W. J. (1939). Sensory preconditioning. *Journal of Experimental Psychology, 25,* 323–332.

Culler, E. A. (1938). Recent advances in some concepts of conditioning. *Psychological Review, 45,* 134–153.

Dodwell, P. C., & Humphrey, G. K. (1990). A functional theory of the McCollough effect. *Psychological Review, 97,* 78–89.

Dodwell, P. C., & O'Shea, R. P. (1987). Global factors generate the McCollough effect. *Vision Research, 27,* 569–580.

Domjan, M. (1983). Biological constraints on instrumental and classical conditioning: Implications for general process theory. In G. H. Bower (Ed.), *The psychology of learning and motivation* (Vol. 17, pp. 215–227). New York: Academic Press.

Domjan, M., & Burkhard, B. (1986). *The principles of learning and behavior* (2nd ed.). Monterey, CA: Brooks/Cole.

Durlach, P. J. (1989). Learning and performance in Pavlovian conditioning: Are failures of contiguity failures of learning or performance? In S. B. Klein & R. R. Mowrer (Eds.), *Contemporary learning theories: Pavlovian conditioning and the status of traditional learning theory* (pp. 19–59). Hillsdale, NJ: Erlbaum.

Estes, W. K. (1970). *Learning theory and mental development.* New York: Academic Press.

Favreau, O. E. (1979). Persistence of simple and contingent motion aftereffects. *Perception and Psychophysics, 26,* 187–194.

Favreau, O. E., & Corballis, M. C. (1976, December). Negative aftereffects in visual perception. *Scientific American, 235*(6), 42–48.

Favreau, O. E., Emerson, V. F., & Corballis, M. C. (1972). Motion perception: A color-contingent aftereffect. *Science, 176,* 78–79.

Foreit, K., & Ambler, B. (1978). Induction of the McCollough effect: I. Figural variables. *Perception and Psychophysics, 24,* 295–302.

Garcia, J., Hankins, W. G., & Rusiniak, K. W. (1974). Behavioral regulation of the milieu interne in man and rat. *Science, 185,* 824–831.

Gibbon, J., & Balsam, P. D. (1981). Spreading association in time. In C. M. Locurto, H. S. Terrace, & J. Gibbon (Eds.), *Autoshaping and conditioning theory* (pp. 219–253). New York: Academic Press.

Gregory, R. L. (1978). *Eye and brain: The psychology of seeing.* New York: McGraw-Hill.

Harris, C. S. (1980). Insight or out of sight? Two examples of perceptual plasticity in the human adult. In C. S. Harris (Ed.), *Visual coding and adaptability* (pp. 95–149). Hillsdale, NJ: Erlbaum.

Harris, J. P. (1987). Contingent perceptual aftereffect. In R. L. Gregory (Ed.), *The Oxford companion to the mind* (pp. 166–168). Oxford: Oxford University Press.

Held, R., & Shattuck, S. R. (1971). Color- and edge-sensitive channels in the human visual system: Tuning for orientation. *Science, 174,* 314–316.

Hepler, N. (1968). Color: A motion-contingent aftereffect. *Science, 162,* 376–377.

Hjeresen, D. L., Loebel, A. D., & Woods, S. C. (1982). Tolerance to cold room hypothermia and potential cross tolerance to ethanol. *Alcoholism: Clinical and Experimental Research, 6,* 145. (Abstract)

Houck, M. R., & Hoffman, J. E. (1986). Conjunction of color and form without attention: Evidence from an orientation-contingent color aftereffect. *Journal of Experimental Psychology: Human Perception and Performance, 12,* 186–199.

Hubel, D. H., & Wiesel, T. N. (1962). Receptive fields, binocular interaction and functional architecture in the cat's visual cortex. *Journal of Physiology, 160,* 106–154.

Hubel, D. H., & Wiesel, T. N. (1968). Receptive fields and functional architecture of monkey striate cortex. *Journal of Physiology, 166,* 994–1002.

Humphrey, G. K., Dodwell, P. C., & Emerson, V. F. (1989). Pattern-contingent color aftereffects on noninduced patterns. *Perception and Psychophysics, 45,* 97–109.

Jones, P. D., & Holding, D. (1975). Extremely long-term persistence of the McCollough effect. *Journal of Experimental Psychology: Human Perception and Performance, 1,* 323–327.

Kamin, L. J. (1969). Predictability, surprise, attention, and conditioning. In B. A. Campbell

& R. M. Church (Eds.), *Punishment and aversive behavior* (pp. 279–296). New York: Appleton-Century-Crofts.

Karn, H. W. (1947). Sensory preconditioning and incidental learning in human subjects. *Journal of Experimental Psychology, 37*, 540–544.

Kremer, E. F. (1974). The truly random control procedure: Conditioning to the static cues. *Journal of Comparative and Physiological Psychology, 86*, 700–707.

Kremer, E. F. (1978). The Rescorla-Wagner model: Losses in associative strength in compound conditioned stimuli. *Journal of Experimental Psychology: Animal Behavior Processes, 4*, 22–36.

Leppmann, P. K. (1973). Spatial frequency dependent chromatic after-effects. *Nature, 242*, 411–412.

Livingstone, M. S., & Hubel, D. H. (1987). Psychophysical evidence for separate channels for the perception of form, color, movement, and depth. *Journal of Neuroscience, 1*, 3416–3468.

Lovegrove, W. J., & Over, R. (1972). Color adaptation of spatial frequency detectors in the human visual system. *Science, 176*, 541–543.

MacKay, D. M., & MacKay, V. (1975a). Dichoptic induction of McCollough-type effects. *Quarterly Journal of Experimental Psychology, 27*, 225–233.

MacKay, D. M., & MacKay, V. (1975b). What causes decay of pattern-contingent chromatic after-effects? *Vision Research, 15*, 462–464.

MacKay, D. M., & MacKay, V. (1977). Retention of the McCollough effect in darkness: Storage or enhanced read-out? *Vision Research, 17*, 313–315.

Macquire, W. M., Meyer, C. E., & Baizer, J. S. (1980). The McCollough effect in rhesus monkey. *Investigative Ophthalmology and Visual Science, 19*, 321–324.

Mayhew, J. E. W. (1973). After-effects of movement contingent on direction of gaze. *Vision Research, 13*, 877–880.

Mayhew, J. E. W., & Anstis, S. M. (1972). Movement aftereffects contingent on color, intensity, and pattern. *Perception and Psychophysics, 12*, 77–85.

McCurtur, A., & Silver, A. (1977). The McCollough effect. A classical conditioning phenomenon? *Vision Research, 17*, 317–319.

McCollough, C. (1965). Color adaptation of edge detectors in the human visual system. *Science, 149*, 1115–1116.

Meyer, G. E. (1977). The effects of color-specific adaptation on the perceived duration of gratings. *Vision Research, 17*, 51–56.

Meyer, G. E., Coleman, A., Dwyer, T., & Lehman, I. (1982). The McCollough effect in children. *Child Development, 53*, 838–840.

Meyer, G. E., Jackson, W. E., & Yang, C. (1979). Spatial frequency, orientation and color: Interocular effects of adaptation on the perceived duration of gratings. *Vision Research, 19*, 1197–1201.

Meyer, G. E., Lawson, R., & Cohen, W. (1975). The effects of orientation-specific adaptation on the duration of short-term visual storage. *Vision Research, 15*, 569–572.

Michael, C. R. (1978). Color vision mechanisms in monkey striate cortex: Simple cells with dual opponent–color receptive fields. *Journal of Neurophysiology, 41*, 1233–1241.

Mikaelian, H. H. (1980). Effective luminance contrast as a parameter in contingent aftereffects. *Perception and Psychophysics, 27*, 531–536.

Mikaelian, H. H., Linton, M. J., & Phillips, M. (1990). Orientation-specific luminance aftereffects. *Perception and Psychophysics, 47*, 575–582.

Miller, R. R., & Schachtman, T. R. (1985). The several roles of context at the time of retrieval. In P. D. Balsam & A. Tomie (Eds.), *Context and learning* (pp. 167–194). Hillsdale, NJ: Erlbaum.

Murch, G. M. (1976). Classical conditioning of the McCollough effect: Temporal parameters. *Vision Research, 16*, 615–619.

Murch, G. M. (1977). A reply to McCarter and Silver. *Vision Research, 17*, 321–322.

Murch, G. M. (1979). The role of test pattern background hue in the McCollough effect. *Vision Research, 19*, 939–942.

Odling-Smee, F. J. (1975). The role of background stimuli during Pavlovian conditioning. *Quarterly Journal of Experimental Psychology, 27*, 201–209.

Over, R., Broerse, J., Crassini, B., & Lovegrove, W. (1974). Orientation-specific aftereffects and illusions in the perception of brightness. *Perception and Psychophysics, 15*, 53–56.

Papini, M. R., & Bitterman, M. E. (1990). The role of contingency in classical conditioning. *Psychological Review, 97*, 396–403.

Pavlov, I. P. (1927). *Conditioned reflexes* (G. V. Anrep, Trans.). London: Oxford University Press.

Poulos, C. X., & Cappell, H. (1991). Homeostatic theory of drug tolerance: A general model of physiological adaptation. *Psychological Review, 98*, 390–408.

Razran, G. (1961). The observable unconscious and the inferable conscious in current Soviet psychophysiology: Interoceptive conditioning, semantic conditioning, and the orienting reflex. *Psychological Review, 68*, 81–147.

Rescorla, R. A. (1970). Reduction in the effectiveness of reinforcement after prior excitatory conditioning. *Learning and Motivation, 1*, 372–381.

Rescorla, R. A. (1980). *Pavlovian second-order conditioning: Studies in associative learning.* Hillsdale, NJ: Erlbaum.

Rescorla, R. A. (1981). Simultaneous associations. In P. Harzem & M. D. Zeiler (Eds.), *Predictability, correlation, and contiguity* (pp. 47–80). New York: Wiley.

Rescorla, R. A. (1986). Two perceptual variables in within-event learning. *Animal Learning and Behavior, 14*, 387–392.

Rescorla, R. A., & Durlach, P. J. (1981). Within-event learning in Pavlovian conditioning. In N. E. Spear & R. R. Miller (Eds.), *Information processing in animals: Memory mechanisms* (pp. 81–111). Hillsdale, NJ: Erlbaum.

Rescorla, R. A., & Holland, P. C. (1982). Behavioral studies of associative learning in animals. In M. R. Rosenzweig & L. W. Porter (Eds.), *Annual Review of Psychology, 33*, 265–308.

Rescorla, R. A., & Wagner, A. R. (1972). A theory of Pavlovian conditioning: Variations in the effectiveness of reinforcement and nonreinforcement. In A. H. Black & W. F. Prokasy (Eds.), *Classical conditioning II* (pp. 64–99). New York: Appleton-Century-Crofts.

Riccio, D. C., MacArdy, E. A., & Kissinger, S. C. (1991). Associative processes in adaptation to repeated cold exposure in rats. *Behavioral Neuroscience, 105*, 599–602.

Riggs, L. A., White, K. D., & Eimas, P. D. (1974). Establishment and decay of orientation-contingent aftereffects of color. *Perception and Psychophysics, 16*, 535–542.

Roberts, J. E. (1984). Pigeons experience orientation-contingent chromatic aftereffects. *Perception and Psychophysics, 36*, 309–314.

Savoy, R. L. (1984). ''Extinction'' of the McCollough effect does not transfer interocularly. *Perception and Psychophysics, 36*, 571–576.

Schull, J. (1979). A conditioned opponent theory of Pavlovian conditioning and habituation. In G. H. Bower (Ed.), *The psychology of learning and motivation* (Vol. 13, pp. 57–90). New York: Academic Press.

Shanks, D. R. (1985). Continuous monitoring of human contingency judgment across trials. *Memory and Cognition, 13*, 158–167.

Shanks, D. R. (1989). Selective processes in causality judgment. *Memory and Cognition, 17*, 27–34.

Shanks, D. R., & Dickinson, A. (1987). Associative accounts of causality judgment. In G. H. Bower (Ed.), *The psychology of learning and motivation* (Vol. 21, pp. 229–261). New York: Academic Press.

Siegel, S. (1989). Pharmacological conditioning and drug effects. In A. J. Goudie & M. W. Emmett-Oglesby (Eds.), *Psychoactive drugs: Tolerance and sensitization* (pp. 115–180). Clifton, NJ: Humana Press.

Siegel, S. (1991). Feedforward processes in drug tolerance. In R. G. Lister & H. J. Weingartner (Eds.), *Perspectives in cognitive neuroscience* (pp. 405–416). New York: Oxford University Press.

Siegel, S., & Allan, L. G. (1985). Overshadowing and blocking of the orientation-contingent color aftereffects: Evidence for a conditioning mechanism. *Learning and Motivation, 16,* 125–138.

Siegel, S., & Allan, L. G. (1987). Contingency and the McCollough effect. *Perception and Psychophysics, 42,* 281–285.

Siegel, S., & Allan, L. G. (1990). Rehearsal processes and orientation-contingent color aftereffects. *Bulletin of the Psychonomic Society, 28,* 481. (Abstract)

Siegel, S., Allan, L. G., & Eissenberg, T. (1992). The associative basis of contingent color aftereffects. *Journal of Experimental Psychology: General, 121,* 79–94.

Siegel, S., Allan, L. G., Roberts, L., & Eissenberg, T. (1990). Effect of spatial contingency on the McCollough effect. *Perception and Psychophysics, 48,* 307–312.

Skowbo, D. (1984). Are McCollough effects conditioned responses? *Psychological Bulletin, 96,* 215–226.

Skowbo, D. (1986). McCollough effects as conditioned responses?: Reply to Allan and Siegel. *Psychological Bulletin, 100,* 394–397.

Skowbo, D. (1988). Interference with the McCollough effect via pre- and postinduction exposure to achromatic gratings: Time course and magnitude of aftereffect decrement. *Perception and Psychophysics, 44,* 295–303.

Skowbo, D., & Clynes, N. (1977). Decline and revival of McCollough effects following inspection of achromatic gratings *Perception and Psychophysics, 21,* 180–182.

Skowbo, D., & Forster, T. (1983). Further evidence against a classical conditioning model of McCollough effects. *Perception and Psychophysics, 34,* 552–554.

Skowbo, D., Gentry, T., Timney, B., & Morant, R. B. (1974). The McCollough effect: Influence of several kinds of visual stimulation on decay rate. *Perception and Psychophysics, 16,* 47–49.

Skowbo, D., Timney, B. N., Gentry, T. A., & Morant, R. B. (1975). McCollough effects: Experimental findings and theoretical accounts. *Psychological Bulletin, 82,* 497–510.

Sloane, M. E., Ost, J. W., Etheriedge, D. B., & Henderlite, S. E. (1989). Overprediction and blocking in the McCollough aftereffect. *Perception and Psychophysics, 45,* 110–120.

Stromeyer, C. F. (1972). Edge-contingent color aftereffects: Spatial frequency specificity. *Vision Research, 12,* 717–733.

Stromeyer, C. F., & Mansfield, R. J. W. (1970). Colored aftereffects produced with moving edges. *Perception and Psychophysics, 7,* 108–114.

Tiffany, S. T., Maude-Griffin, P. M., & Drobes, D. J. (1991). Effect of interdose interval on the development of associative tolerance in the rat: A dose–response analysis. *Behavioral Neuroscience, 105,* 49–61.

Viola, M. M. (1966). *Color adaptation contingent upon the geometry of the inducing stimulus.* Unpublished bachelor's thesis, Smith College, Northampton, MA.

Wagner, A. R. (1971). Elementary associations. In H. H. Kendler & J. T. Spence (Eds.), *Essays in neobehaviorism: A memorial volume to Kenneth W. Spence* (pp. 187–213). New York: Appleton-Century-Crofts.

Wagner, A. R. & Rescorla, R. A. (1972). Inhibition in Pavlovian conditioning: Application of a theory. In R. A. Boakes & M. S. Halliday (Eds.), *Inhibition and learning* (pp. 301–336). London: Academic Press.

Wagner, A. R., Rudy, J. W., & Whitlow, J. W. (1973). Rehearsal in animal conditioning. *Journal of Experimental Psychology Monograph, 97,* 407–426.

Walker, J. T. (1972). A texture contingent visual motion aftereffect. *Psychonomic Science, 28,* 333–335.

Walker, J. T. (1977). Orientation-contingent tactual size aftereffects. *Perception and Psychophysics, 22,* 563–570.

Walker, J. T. (1978). Simple and contingent aftereffects in the kinesthetic perception of length. *Journal of Experimental Psychology: Human Perception and Performance, 4,* 294–301.

Walker, J. T., & Irion, A. L. (1979). Two new contingent aftereffects: Perceived auditory duration contingent on pitch and on temporal order. *Perception and Psychophysics, 26,* 241–244.

Walker, J. T., Irion, A. L., & Gordon, D. S. (1981). Simple and contingent aftereffects of perceived duration in vision and audition. *Perception and Psychophysics, 29,* 475–486.

Walker, J. T., & Shea, K. S. (1974). A tactual size aftereffect contingent on hand position. *Journal of Experimental Psychology, 103,* 668–674.

Westbrook, R. F., & Harrison, W. (1984). Associative blocking of the McCollough effect. *Quarterly Journal of Experimental Psychology, 36A,* 309–318.

White, K. D. (1978). Studies of form-contingent color aftereffects. In J. C. Armington, J. Krauskopf, & B. R. Wooten (Eds.), *Visual psychophysics and physiology* (pp. 267–281). New York: Academic Press.

Wolfe, J. M., & O'Connell, K. M. (1986). Fatigue and structural change: Two consequences of visual pattern adaptation. *Investigative Ophthalmology and Visual Science, 27,* 538–543.

EVOLUTIONARY MEMORIES, EMOTIONAL PROCESSING, AND THE EMOTIONAL DISORDERS

Susan Mineka

I. Overview

In the past two decades, research deriving from several different traditions within experimental psychology has had a substantial impact on furthering understanding of the anxiety and depressive disorders—now commonly known as the emotional disorders. Thus, progress in the psychology of learning, motivation, attention, and memory has not only been substantial in its own right, but it has also contributed to knowledge about the myriad factors involved in the etiology and maintenance of these disorders. Over the past 15 years my own research has reflected an interest both in furthering knowledge about basic issues in the psychology of learning and motivation and in using this knowledge to help understand these important and relatively prevalent clinical disorders. This article reviews some of the major findings from three very different areas of research, each using paradigms and principles of experimental psychology to advance knowledge about the etiology and maintenance of the emotional disorders. For fears and phobias, some of the advances have stemmed from basic research on classical conditioning of fear which has illuminated what appear to be evolutionarily based constraints on the acquisition and retention of these disorders. For depression and other anxiety disorders, many of the advances have stemmed from basic research using an information-processing framework to explore the interaction between emotion and cognition. Although research from these different traditions has generally proceeded along independent and quite unrelated paths, attempts will be made to draw some possible parallels and links between them.

Let me first briefly overview the three major themes of the chapter in order to give a preliminary sense of the range of topics to be discussed and what some possible links between them may be. First, experiments are reviewed demonstrating that human and nonhuman primates have what could be called "evolutionary memories"[1] that play a role in determining which objects and situations are most likely to become the objects of fears and phobias. It seems likely that these evolutionary memories underlie selective associations in fear conditioning, which in turn mediate the nonrandom distribution of fears and phobias seen clinically (e.g., Seligman, 1971).

Second, several different lines of research on fear conditioning in animals suggest that memory processes affecting the acquisition and retention of fears serve to promote the maintenance and overgeneralization of fear with the passage of time (cf. Mineka & Tomarken, 1989, for a review). The possibility that these memory processes generally may have evolved along principles of adaptive conservatism is considered. That is, through natural selection fear may have come to be associated with conservative cognitive biases which, under ordinary circumstances, are more likely to promote the reinforcement, enhancement, or overgeneralization of fear rather than the forgetting of fear (Hendersen, 1985; Tomarken, 1988). Human research on judgmental biases associated with fear is reviewed which is also consistent with the idea of adaptive conservatism.

Finally, the question is also considered as to whether human research on anxiety and depression that has been conducted within the framework of an information-processing perspective on the emotion–cognition interaction can also profitably be viewed within a similar framework. In this context, highlights of research are reviewed showing that anxiety and depression are associated with cognitive biases for emotion-relevant material (e.g., MacLeod & Mathews, 1991; Mineka & Sutton, 1992; Mineka & Tomarken, 1989; Williams, Watts, MacLeod, & Mathews, 1988). Moreover, it is quite possible that the functions served by these cognitive biases are to reinforce, confirm, or even enhance the emotional states. Thus there is a possibility that the functions served by these cognitive

---

[1] The term "evolutionary memories" was suggested by James McGaugh to describe this phenomenon when he invited me to participate in a symposium at the American Psychological Society in 1991 on "Emotion and memory." A preliminary version of the ideas presented in this chapter was presented in that symposium, as well as in invited addresses at the American Psychological Association and the Society for Research in Psychopathology in 1991.

biases may parallel the adaptive conservatism principles thought to be operating with fear memories in animals and with the judgmental biases associated with phobic fears.

II. Selective Associations in Fear Conditioning: Evolutionary Memories?

A. BACKGROUND

Seligman (1971) and Marks (1969) systematized observations that fears and phobias do not tend to occur to a random arbitrary group of objects or situations associated with trauma. For example, many more people have phobias for snakes, spiders, heights, and enclosed spaces than for bicycles, stoves, knives, or cars, even thought the latter may be at least as likely to be associated with traumatic experiences or verbal warnings or both, during ontogeny. To account for these observations that certain "fear-relevant" stimuli appear to be the focus of a disproportionately large number of clinical fears and phobias, Seligman (1971), and later Öhman and his colleagues (e.g., Öhman, 1986; Öhman, Dimberg, and Öst, 1985, for reviews), argued that primates and humans may have a biologically based "preparedness" to easily associate certain kinds of objects or situations with aversive events. Their argument is that there may have been a selective advantage in the course of evolution for primates who easily acquired fears of certain objects or situations that may frequently have been dangerous or posed a threat to our early ancestors.

Human experiments on this topic—many from Öhman's lab—generally have involved comparisons of electrodermal conditioning (or sometimes heartrate conditioning) in two groups of subjects. A discriminative conditioning paradigm is typically used, with the CS+ being paired with mild electric shocks, and the CS− paired with the absence of shocks. For one group, both the CS+ and the CS− are fear-relevant stimuli (such as snakes or spiders, or angry faces), and for a second group both the CS+ and the CS− are fear-irrelevant stimuli (such as flowers or mushrooms, or happy faces). Many studies have shown that subjects conditioned with fear-relevant stimuli show superior discriminative conditioning (differential response to CS+ relative to CS−) as evidenced by markedly enhanced resistance to extinction, relative to what is seen in subjects conditioned with fear-irrelevant stimuli (e.g., Cook, Hodes, & Lang, 1986; Öhman, 1986; Öhman et al., 1985; Öhman, Fredrikson, Hugdahl, & Rimmö, 1976; although see McNally, 1987, for a review of several failures to find a fear-relevance effect). Furthermore, they have shown that this superior conditioning with fear-relevant CSs was not merely the result of subjects simply being predisposed to show larger responses to the fear-relevant stimuli, or of these CSs simply being more salient or prepotent. By using a discriminative conditioning paradigm in which the CS+ and the CS− are both fear-relevant, or both fear-irrelevant, their results and conclusions are based on superior discrimination of fear-relevant CS+'s and CS−'s, rather than simply on a greater conditioned response (CR) to a fear-relevant CS+. This same feature of their discriminative conditioning paradigm also helps to control for possible nonassociative sensitization effects (see also Mineka, 1985).

This series of experiments (along with some other experiments discussed below) constituted preliminary presumptive evidence that humans selectively associate certain fear-relevant stimuli with aversive outcomes. That is, certain CS–UCS combinations are more readily associable (CS_1–UCS_1) than are other combinations (CS_2–UCS_1). However, selective associations are also supposed to represent *experience-independent* association bias. Not surprisingly, then, one of the most controversial aspects of the human experiments on selective associations in fear conditioning has been whether such effects derive from phylogenetic factors or from ontogenetic factors (cf. Delprato, 1980). That is, do these effects derive—as hypothesized by Seligman and Öhman—from an evolutionarily based predisposition to acquire more easily fears of objects and situations that once posed a threat to our early ancestors, but that nevertheless are not instinctively feared? If this were true, then one could say that some sort of "evolutionary memories" underlie and mediate these selective associations in fear conditioning. Or do these effects simply derive—as suggested by Delprato—from the possibility that superior conditioning occurs to stimuli that people may have developed negative associations to in the course of their own development? This question cannot be addressed in human experiments, because the subjects all have prior ontogenetically based associations to the CSs used in the experiments. Moreover, it is not unreasonable to suspect that many more subjects may have negative ontogenetically based associations to the fear-relevant CSs typically used (such as snakes and spiders) than to many of the fear-irrelevant CSs used (such as flowers or mushrooms).

B.   SELECTIVE ASSOCIATIONS IN FEAR CONDITIONING: PRIMATE STUDIES

To circumvent these inherent limitations of human research on this topic, several years ago Michael Cook and I conducted a series of experiments at the Wisconsin Primate Laboratory using a primate model for the acquisition of phobic fears. The results of this series of experiments do strongly implicate phylogenetic factors—or the idea of evolutionary memories—in such selective associations in fear conditioning because the fear-relevant and fear-irrelevant stimuli that were used as CSs were totally novel stimuli, that is, stimuli with which none of the subjects had any prior experience. In these experiments laboratory-reared monkeys who were not initially afraid of snakes served as subjects in a discriminative observational fear conditioning paradigm. The models were wild-reared rhesus monkeys who showed an intense phobic-like fear of snakes (see Mineka, Keir, & Price, 1980, for results showing that wild-reared, but not lab-reared, monkeys exhibit a strong phobic like fear of snakes). In earlier experiments it had been repeatedly demonstrated that lab-reared monkeys would rapidly acquire an intense fear of snakes simply through watching a wild-reared model monkey behaving fearfully with snakes, and nonfearfully with other objects (e.g., Cook, Mineka, Wolkenstein, & Laitsch, 1985; Mineka, Davidson, Cook, & Keir, 1984). Moreover, the major determinant of the observer's level of acquired fear as measured following conditioning was the level of fear shown by the model during conditioning (see Mineka & Cook, in press, for details).

1. SN+FL−/FL+SN− Experiment

With regard to the question of selective associations it was important to determine whether the lab-reared monkeys would acquire fears of other more arbitrary objects with equal facility if they observed model monkeys behaving fearfully with those "fear-irrelevant" or arbitrary objects. The first experiment on this topic followed Öhman's early experiments by using toy snakes (SN) as the "prepared" or fear-relevant stimuli and artificial flowers (FL) as the "unprepared" or fear-irrelevant stimuli. To do the experiment correctly, it was necessary to be able to equate the model's fear performance (the nominal UCS) in the presence of flowers with his/her fear performance in the presence of snakes. This is because, as noted above, the major determinant of the level of snake fear acquired by the observer monkeys (the nominal conditioned response, CR) is the level of snake fear shown by the fearful models (Mineka & Cook, in press). Thus, it only makes sense to compare levels of conditioned responding to flowers versus snakes if there has been an equivalent UCS (model's fear performance) during conditioning, and yet this is not feasible to accomplish with live models. Therefore, we decided to use videotapes of fearful models, allowing the use of editing/splicing techniques to accomplish this equating of fear performances to snakes and flowers. We had first demonstrated that observer monkeys do indeed acquire an intense fear of snakes simply through watching, on a color video screen, a model behaving fearfully with live and toy snakes and nonfearfully with neutral objects (Cook & Mineka, 1990, Experiment 1). Knowing that the observer monkeys could acquire an intense fear through watching videotapes, it was then possible in the next experiment to proceed with making a videotape in which the model was in reality reacting fearfully to a snake, but in which—through state-of-the-art editing techniques—it looks as if the model is reacting to some other stimulus such as flowers. Thus it was possible to exactly equate the model's fear performance with the fear-relevant and the fear-irrelevant stimuli.

The notation is as follows: an abbreviation for a stimulus (here SN = snake, FL = flower) is followed by + if the model is shown reacting fearfully to that stimulus, by − if not. In the experiment using edited videotapes (Cook & Mineka, 1990, Experiment 2), the FL+SN− group watched videotapes of two different model monkeys reacting fearfully on some trials to flower stimuli (FL+), and nonfearfully on other trials to toy snake stimuli (SN−). The SN+FL− group watched videotapes of the same two model monkeys reacting fearfully to toy snake stimuli on some trials (matched to the FL+ trials for the FL+SN− group) and nonfearfully to flower stimuli on other trials (matched to the SN− trials for the FL+SN− group). The fear performance (as well as the nonfear performance) of the models that each group saw on the matched trials was identical. The groups differed only in whether the fear performance appeared to be elicited by a toy snake or by flowers, and vice versa for the nonfear performance. Each group had 12 sessions of observational conditioning, with each session involving a total of 12 min of exposure to the fearful models.

The results of this study suggested that there are indeed differences in conditioning of fear to snakes versus flowers. As seen in Fig. 1, the SN+FL− group did indeed acquire a significant fear of snakes (but not of flowers), as indexed by a significant increase from pretest to posttest in latency to reach for a food treat on the far side of the toy snake. By contrast, monkeys in the FL+SN− group, did not show significant acquisition of flower fear, as indexed by no increase in food reach latency in the presence of the flowers from pretest to posttest. Parallel results were found with fear or disturbance behaviors as a second index of fear (see Cook & Mineka, 1990, for details).

2. C+R−/R+C− Experiment

Another experiment (Cook & Mineka, 1989, Experiment 2) examined whether comparable differences in conditioning would occur when the two

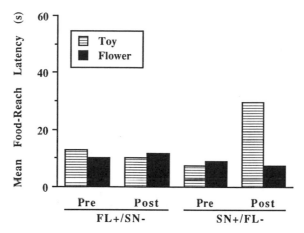

Fig. 1.   Mean food-reach latency in the presence of two stimulus objects (toy snakes and flowers) for the FL+/SN− and SN+/FL− groups at pretest and posttest (following conditioning). (Adapted from Cook & Mineka, 1990, as in Cook & Mineka, 1991.)

stimuli being compared were both animals, but animals that differed in fear relevance or preparedness. This was deemed important because flowers and toy snakes differ not only in fear-relevance but also in the degree to which they might be perceived as potentially animate (see Cook & Mineka, 1991, for a discussion of this issue). For this experiment, a toy crocodile (C) was used as the fear-relevant stimulus based on Öhman et al.'s (1985) hypothesis that reptiles are a prototypical fear-relevant stimulus for mammals because of the struggles that early mammalian species had with the then-dominant reptile class. A toy rabbit (R) was used as the fear-irrelevant stimulus. In other ways the paradigm was identical to that used for the snake and flower experiment. Paralleling the results with snakes and flowers, observer monkeys who watched models behaving fearfully with a toy crocodile did acquire a fear of the toy crocodile, but observers who watched models behaving fearfully with a toy rabbit did not acquire a fear of the toy rabbit. The results for disturbance behaviors as one index of fear are illustrated in Fig. 2; an identical pattern of results was also observed with food-reach latency as the index of fear.

   The results of these two experiments (and two others: Cook & Mineka, 1987, Experiment 2; 1989, Experiment 1) are certainly consistent with the requirements for demonstration of a selective association. However, by themselves they do not provide an adequate demonstration that the association is indeed selective. (See Cook & Mineka, 1990, 1991; LoLordo, 1979a, 1979b; LoLordo & Droungas, 1989, for the requirements of demonstrating selective associations.) In particular, it is necessary to demonstrate that the failure of fear conditioning to the fear-irrelevant stimuli

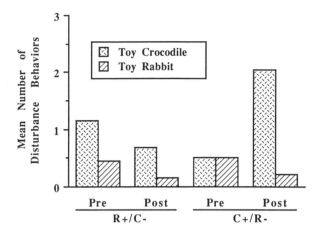

Fig. 2. Mean number of disturbance behaviors in the presence of two stimulus objects (toy crocodile and toy rabbit) for the R+/C− and C+/R− groups at pretest and posttest (following conditioning). (From Cook & Mineka, 1989.)

(flowers or toy rabbit) is specifically due to a failure of *fear* conditioning, and not due to a general lack of conditionability of these stimuli with alternative reinforcers. So, for example, if the fear-irrelevant stimuli were much lower in salience than the fear-relevant stimuli, this could potentially provide at least a partial account of the observed difference in conditionability to these stimuli (e.g., Mackintosh, 1974, chap. 2). In order to demonstrate a selective association, it was necessary to find an alternative reinforcer that would support a level of conditioning to the fear-irrelevant stimulus that was at least as strong as the conditioning to the fear-relevant stimulus (see LoLordo, 1979a, 1979b; LoLordo & Droungas, 1989).

3.   PAN Experiment with Appetitive Reinforcers

In order to address this requirement of demonstrating a selective association, an experiment was conducted using the same videotaped flower and toy snake stimuli as cues for an appetitive reinforcer (food treats). The design involved a discriminative operant procedure rather than a Pavlovian observational conditioning procedure because extensive pilot work had failed to provide a reliable paradigm for classical conditioning of appetitive responses in rhesus monkeys. In this experiment (Cook & Mineka, 1990, Experiment 3), monkeys were trained to solve appetitive, discrete-trial, simultaneous discriminations, one involving two fear-relevant stimuli (two different toy snakes), and the other involving two fear-irrelevant stimuli (two different flower arrangements). The stimuli were videotaped as in the fear conditioning experiments described above, and one from each category (snake and flower) was identical to the ones used in the SN+/FL− experiment (see Cook & Mineka, 1990, for details).

Because of the need to ensure that both snake and flower stimuli were used in solving the discrimination problems, the kind of discrimination problems that were used were PAN ambiguous cue problems (see Cook & Mineka, 1990, 1991, for a detailed rationale). With a PAN problem there are two kinds of trials—one with a positive cue and an ambiguous cue (PA trials), and one with a negative cue and an ambiguous cue (NA trials). The ambiguous cue (A) is nonrewarded when presented with the positive cue (P), and rewarded when presented with the negative cue (N). Thus, subjects must learn about both positive and negative stimuli because the problems cannot be solved through the use of the ambiguous cue alone. One PAN problem involved fear-relevant toy snakes, and the second PAN problem involved fear-irrelevant flowers; the ambiguous cues were geometric figures. For each problem it was the N cue which was identical to the one used in the SN+FL− experiment. The N cues were quite comparable in salience, size, and shape (both long and narrow—a stretched out, slightly sinuous toy snake and artificial flowers with a long stem). The P cues (which were new for this experiment) were also fairly comparable in salience, size, and shape (both round—a coiled snake and a circular arrangement of the flowers). A representation of these problems is given in Fig. 3.

Given the complexity of these problems, it is probably not surprising that many of the subjects found the solutions difficult or impossible. Indeed, of 13 subjects that were trained, only 6 ever attained an 80% correct criterion on all problems. Of the remaining 7 subjects, none achieved this criterion for any problem in spite of extensive training (at least 1000 trials), and none showed any tendency toward superior performance on particular problems. Of the 6 subjects who attained the 80% correct criterion on all problems, the rate of learning the discriminations was comparable with the flower and the toy snake stimuli. All 6 of these subjects acquired the discriminative operant when flowers were the P or the N stimuli in the problem. Of greatest importance were the results with the N stimuli (NA problems) because these were the same as the stimuli used in the SN+/FL− study. For the two NA problems (flower and snake), 4 out of the 6 subjects showed more rapid attainment of the criterion with the flower stimulus, and 2 with the snake stimulus (a nonsignificant difference). For the two PA problems, the numbers were reversed, with 2 out of 6 subjects showing more rapid attainment of criterion with the flower stimulus.

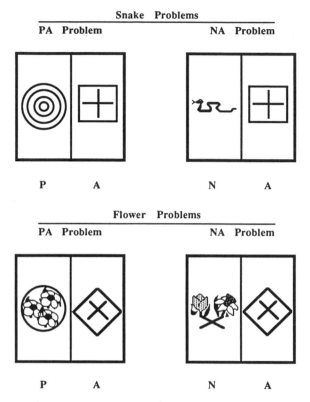

Fig. 3. Representation of snake and flower PAN problems (stimuli not drawn to scale). For the snake problems (top panels), the concentric circles represent a coiled rattlesnake model, and the depiction of a snake (with a forked tongue) represents the sinuous toy snake. For the flower problems (bottom panels), the circle enclosing three flowers represents a circular arrangement of mums, and the two flowers (each connected to a straight line) represent the two artificial flowers (including the stems). (From Cook & Mineka, 1990.)

4.   Summary of Primate Studies on Selective Associations

These results demonstrate that the videotaped flower stimuli were capable of supporting excitatory learning when an appetitive reinforcer was used and were fairly comparable in this regard to the videotaped toy snake stimuli. Taken together, the results of the PAN appetitive experiment and the results of the two experiments demonstrating a failure of fear conditioning to flower stimuli (Cook & Mineka, 1989, Experiment 1; 1990, Experiment 2) strongly imply a differential associability of fear-relevant CSs and vicariously observed UCSs (i.e., the fear responses of conspecifics). In other words, it does not appear that simple differential salience or discriminability of the two stimulus classes can account for the overall pattern of results. For example, if salience of the flower stimuli were lower than salience of the snake stimuli, then one would have expected subjects in the PAN problems to achieve criterion more rapidly on the snake problems. Instead, it appears that snakes are selectively associable with aversive outcomes.

C. CONCLUSIONS REGARDING THE MEDIATION OF SELECTIVE ASSOCIATIONS IN FEAR CONDITIONING

Similar conclusions had been drawn by Öhman et al. (1976) when they also attempted to meet the requirements for demonstration of a selective association with their electrodermal conditioning paradigm. In their research it also was not possible to develop a paradigm using an appetitive reinforcer that was exactly parallel to their paradigm using shock as a reinforcer (as is needed in order to meet the strict requirements for demonstration of a selective association). This is because there is no known appetitive UCS which supports electrodermal conditioning in human subjects. Nevertheless, in an approximation to this requirement, Öhman et al. (1976) did show that the superior conditionability of snake CSs occurred only with an aversive UCS, and not when a nonaversive reaction-time task was used. Unfortunately, however, little conditioning occurred with either category of CS using the nonaversive reaction time task, thus weakening the conclusions that can be drawn from that experiment. Thus, although both the human and the monkey research falls somewhat short of meeting the ideal and strict requirements for demonstrating a selective association (which would require the use of parallel paradigms—see Cook & Mineka, 1991; LoLordo 1979a, 1979b; LoLordo & Droungas, 1989, for discussion of these issues), the convergence of findings provides quite strong support for the idea that both monkeys and humans seem to selectively associate certain fear-relevant stimuli with aversive outcomes.[2]

----

[2] There is, however, one apparent difference between the results of these two sets of studies. In the monkey experiments the observed group differences were in acquisition, whereas in the human experiments, the group differences are usually found in resistance to extinction rather than in acquisition. Failure to find acquisition differences in the human electrodermal conditioning experiments may, however, reflect ceiling effects because acquisition generally occurs very rapidly with both fear-relevant and fear-irrelevant stimuli. Moreover, it is quite possible that extinction differences might have been obtained in the monkey experiments if it had been possible to compare rates of extinction. It was not, however, possible to compare rates of extinction when no significant acquisition had occurred to the fear-irrelevant stimuli. (See Cook & Mineka, 1991, for a further discussion of these apparent differences in the human and monkey studies.)

As noted earlier, in the case of the human experiments it is not possible to show that the selective associations result from experience-independent biases in associability, which is theoretically a requirement for the demonstration of selective associations (cf. Cook & Mineka, 1991). However, because the observer monkeys used in these experiments had no prior exposure to any of the objects used as conditioned stimuli, the requirement of demonstrating experience-independent biases in associability would appear to be met. Moreover, as discussed by Cook and Mineka (1990, 1991), a reasonably strong case can be made that phylogenetic factors are likely to account for the observed differences in the conditionability of fear to these objects. Nevertheless, we also noted that this conclusion concerning the phylogeny and adaptive function of such selective associations would be stronger if a comparative methodology was used (cf. Hailman, 1976; see also Domjan & Galef, 1983; Johnston, 1981). For example, it would be useful to compare acquisition of snake fear in two populations of primates—one that had evolved in an environment without dangerous reptiles and one that had coevolved with dangerous snakes. One would not expect the species that had evolved in the environment without dangerous snakes to show selective associability of snakes with fear if, indeed, this type of selective association represents an adaptive specialization shaped by natural selection (Cook & Mineka, 1990, 1991).

Furthermore, other important questions also remain because the mechanisms through which such selective associations are mediated are, as of yet, poorly understood. That is, it is not yet clear how a human or nonhuman primate "knows" or "recognizes" whether the stimulus or situation encountered as a signal for danger is fear-relevant, or fear-irrelevant, in the absence of any prior experience with that stimulus. One possibility for the mediation of such evolutionary memories is that primates may be endowed with complete hard-wired memory representations of prototypes for fear-relevant stimuli, much as representations of objects that are instinctively feared must be represented. An alternative, not necessarily mutually exclusive, possibility is that potentially phobic objects may share certain perceptual characteristics in common (e.g., Bennett-Levy & Marteau, 1984; Merckelbach, van den Hout, & van der Molen, 1987). For example, one correlational study with human subjects suggested that potentially phobic characteristics include strangeness or oddness on visual, auditory, and olfactory dimensions, and ratings of perceived uncontrollability and unpredictability (Merckelbach et al., 1987). Another study suggested that the relevant perceptual characteristics included "ugliness, sliminess, speediness, and suddenness of movement" (Bennett-Levy & Marteau, 1984, p. 40). Unfortunately, the results from this series of experiments with rhesus monkeys do not provide good evidence for the perceived characteristics alternative because videotaped artificial and inanimate stimuli were used as conditioned stimuli in each of the experiments. Thus, the stimuli did not have characteristics such as sliminess, peculiar odors, suddenness of movement, or unpredictability. Furthermore, because the lab-reared monkeys used as observers also had no prior experiences with the live counterparts of these stimuli (that is real snakes, flowers, crocodiles, or rabbits), one cannot even construct an argument for the perceived characteristics hypothesis based on a prior conditioning history as Bandura (1991) has attempted to do. Thus, at present there is no good evidence in favor of either the simple hard-wired hypothesis or the perceived characteristics hypothesis (see Cook & Mineka, 1989, for further discussion of this issue).

III. Cognitive Processes Contributing to the Overgeneralization of Fear

A. BACKGROUND

If natural selection has played a role in determining the kinds of objects and situations that are likely to become the sources of fear, some have suggested that perhaps it has also played a role in shaping the processes promoting the overgeneralization of fear that is known to often occur with the passage of time. Clinical observations have long suggested that a common characteristic of anxiety disorders (including phobias) in humans is a pronounced tendency to overgeneralize the range of objects or situations that pose a threat (e.g., Beck & Emery, 1985; Marks, 1987). Research on fear conditioning conducted with animals over the past 15 years has shown that a major variable moderating the development of overgeneralization is time since the last aversive conditioning experience. In general, these findings suggest that memory, and perhaps other cognitive processes, operate in such a manner so as to maintain and overgeneralize fear with the passage of time. Moreover, it is also interesting to consider the possibility that will be discussed below that these processes may have evolved along principles of adaptive conservatism (cf. Hendersen, 1985; Tomarken, 1988).

B. FOUR PHENOMENA CONTRIBUTING TO OVERGENERALIZATION OF FEAR

Four rather different phenomena from the fear conditioning literature in animals can be used to illustrate the convergence of processes that mediate the maintenance and overgeneralization of fear with time (see Mineka & Tomarken, 1989, for a related discussion). First, Riccio, Richardson, and

Ebner (1984) reviewed evidence showing that as the retention interval following aversive conditioning increases, the generalization gradient around the CS+ flattens. This flattening is caused not by lowering of fear to the CS+, but rather by an increase in fear to the generalization test stimuli. Riccio et al. argued that this probably occurs because of forgetting of the very specific attributes of the CS+ with increasing retention intervals.

Second, and relatedly, Hendersen, Patterson, and Jackson (1980) also showed that rats seem to forget specific UCS attributes with the passage of time. That is, the animals seem to remember that the CS signaled danger but to forget exactly what the characteristics of the danger (UCS) were. As a consequence, the animals behave in an increasingly conservative fashion in a wider range of frightening situations than they would have immediately following conditioning. When these two phenomena are considered together, the consequences of loss of memory with the passage of time for specific CS attributes *and* for specific UCS attributes seem to be that the animal shows fear-motivated behaviors in situations that it would not have immediately following conditioning. Describing these results, one could say that the animal has become increasingly conservative (Hendersen, 1985).

Third, Hendersen (1978) and Thomas (1979) have also shown that conditioned inhibitors of fear are forgotten with the passage of time to a much greater extent than are conditioned excitors of fear. One would expect that this forgetting of fear inhibition or safety signals would do nothing to dampen or counteract the increasing generalization of objects and situations to which fear is shown with the passage of time (Riccio et al., 1984). That is, if places or objects that were once safe and actively inhibitory of fear lose these properties with the passage of time, while places or objects that the organism had learned to fear are well retained and increasingly generalized, the combined effects of these processes would seem to cause "the animal to become more warily conservative" (Hendersen, 1985, p. 47).

A fourth and potentially related phenomenon has been explored by Bouton and his colleagues (e.g., Bouton, 1991; Bouton & Bolles, 1979, 1985; Bouton & Swartzentruber, 1991), who have shown that extinction of fear CRs is context specific. Thus, although fears conditioned to a CS in Context A will also be elicited in Context B, this generalization across contexts is not true for extinction. If fear of a CS is extinguished in a different context from the one in which it was conditioned, there is no generalization of the extinction of fear of the CS to the original, or to new contexts. Based on extensive research on this phenomenon, Bouton has argued that "Extinction does not cause unlearning, but instead gives the

CS a second, and therefore 'ambiguous' meaning" (Bouton, 1991, p. 436). In other words, memories for both the original conditioning and extinction experience are retained; depending on which memory is retrieved by the current context, fear will or will not be exhibited. These findings are important not only because they clearly demonstrate that extinction does not erase the original learning, but also because they show that the retention of the original memory of conditioning "can provide a powerful basis for relapse" (Bouton & Swartzentruber, 1991, p. 124) if the extinguished CS is encountered in a new context. It seems quite possible that this context specificity of fear extinction may also promote the maintenance of generalization of fear once it has occurred. That is, in theory, the effects of generalization of excitatory CSs discussed above could potentially be undone through repeated nonreinforced exposure to those generalized CSs (an extinction procedure). However, Bouton's work on context specificity of fear extinction suggests important limits on how quickly such undoing of generalization could occur, as well as on how stable it is likely to be.

The instability issue is also related to Bouton's (1991; Bouton & Swartzentruber, 1991) extension of this analysis of context specificity of fear extinction to explain the phenomenon of spontaneous recovery (Pavlov, 1927)—another phenomenon which may contribute to the overgeneralization of fear with the passage of time. By considering time as a kind of context, Bouton's analysis suggests that just as animals show specificity of extinction to the physical context in which extinction occurred, so too may they show temporal specificity of extinction; this leads, with the passage of time, to "spontaneous recovery" of previously extinguished fear. A similar phenomenon known as "the return of fear" is seen in phobic patients undergoing multiple sessions of exposure therapy (e.g., Grey, Sartory, & Rachman, 1979; Rachman & Lopatka, 1988). That fear does not generalize across physical or temporal contexts provides an even stronger case that these processes seem to promote overgeneralization of fear.

To summarize, it appears that with the passage of time a loss of memory for specific CS and UCS attributes results in animals showing fear-motivated behaviors in situations that they would not have immediately following conditioning. In addition, inhibitory fear CRs are forgotten with time, and extinction of fear CRs does not generalize across contexts. The robustness of generalization of conditioned excitatory effects, combined with the fragility of conditioned inhibitory and extinction effects, when considered together, may help to illuminate some of the factors contributing to the maintenance, enhancement, and overgeneralization of fears with the passage of time.

C. DOES ADAPTIVE CONSERVATISM UNDERLIE THESE FOUR PHENOMENA?

Why should fear memories operate this way? One possibility discussed first by Hendersen (1985), and later by Tomarken (1988), is that fear may be associated with an "adaptive conservatism." The idea is that in the course of natural selection, "the long-run cost to an organism that would be incurred by mistakingly treating a threatening stimulus as non-threatening" was probably much "greater than the cost that would be incurred by mistakingly treating a safe stimulus or situation as threatening" (Tomarken, 1988, p. 77; see also Beck & Emery, 1985, for a related argument). It may be for this reason, Tomarken argued, that "fear is associated with a 'conservative' perceptual and cognitive bias to perceive, remember, or interpret fear-relevant stimuli or situations as more threatening than they actually may be" (p. 77).

At present, the adaptive conservatism hypothesis is quite speculative and many of the predictions that it might make have never been tested. Indeed, Hendersen (1985) suggested that "the conservatism hypothesis is an appealing simple way to characterize the forgetting of fear, but it is probably wrong" (p. 49). He based this conclusion on evidence that with the passage of time, fear memories appear to become more generally malleable—sometimes increasing and sometimes decreasing in strength depending on what new information is encountered about the strength of the UCS. That is, exposure to stronger or weaker shocks than were involved in the original conditioning has larger effects on inflating or . deflating the fear memory when those shocks occur several months following conditioning than when they occur one day following conditioning (Hendersen, 1985). However, it should be noted that this is the only phenomenon noted by Hendersen that is an apparent exception to the principle that with the passage of time animals become "more warily conservative" (Hendersen, 1985, p. 47). This leads one to consider whether there is any difference between this phenomenon of generally increased malleability of fear memories with the passage of time and the other phenomena reviewed above that are consistent with the adaptive conservatism hypothesis. One obvious difference is that the phenomenon of increased malleability of fear memories is the only phenomenon discussed here involving new exposures to the UCS (stronger or weaker shocks) following conditioning. None of the other four phenomena summarized above involve exposure to new information about the intensity of the UCS following conditioning. Thus, it may be that the increase in general malleability of fear memories with time that Hendersen has observed (as opposed to increasing conservatism) only occurs in situations where such new information is encountered. Moreover, the retention of these inflated and deflated fear memories seen with Hendersen's paradigm has not been tested. Thus, it remains possible that with the passage of time the deflated fear memories might show spontaneous recovery to the original strength, as would seem to be predicted by the adaptive conservatism hypothesis.

IV. Cognitive Biases Promoting the Maintenance of Phobic Fears

Thus far, the only evidence that has been discussed bearing on the adaptive conservatism hypothesis has been from research using fear conditioning paradigms in animals. There is also, however, a substantial body of evidence consistent with the hypothesis stemming from human research on the emotion–cognition interaction. A major theme of this research for the past decade has been that emotions such as fear, anxiety, and depression have prominent effects on cognitive processing (e.g., MacLeod & Mathews, 1991; Williams et al., 1988), and that these effects would appear to serve the function of confirming, reinforcing, or enhancing the emotion (e.g., Mineka & Sutton, 1992; Mineka & Tomarken, 1989; Tomarken, 1988; Tomarken, Mineka, & Cook, 1989). The effects involve what Tomarken and I (1989) called "cognitive biases," which we defined as any selective or nonveridical processing of emotion relevant information. Several different general types of cognitive bias have been identified, including attentional biases, memory biases, and judgmental or interpretive biases, although as is discussed below there appear to be some differences in which types of bias are most closely associated with different types of emotions.

A. ATTENTIONAL BIAS

With regard to fears and phobias, there is at least preliminary evidence that attentional biases may be prominent. For example, Watts, McKenna, Sharrock, and Trezise (1986) compared spider phobics with nonphobic controls on a modified Stroop task in which subjects were asked to name the color of words from various categories, including neutral and spider-related words. Results indicated that spider phobics were slower to name the color of the phobic-related words than were nonphobic controls; there were no differences between the groups on neutral words. Although Stroop interference is generally not considered to be a good measure of attentional bias by itself (e.g., Kahneman & Chajczyk, 1983; Mathews, in press), these results are also consistent with findings from studies using other information-processing paradigms that may provide somewhat better evidence of attentional bias.

For example, Burgess, Jones, Robertson, Radcliffe, and Emerson (1981) assessed analogue phobic and clinical phobic subjects using a dichotic listening paradigm in which subjects were asked to shadow the message presented to one ear and to indicate the occurrence of selected neutral or phobic (fear-relevant) words from either the attended or the rejected channels. Recognition of the target words on the attended channel was comparable in phobic and control groups. However, both analogue and clinical phobic subjects showed heightened sensitivity to the fear-relevant words relative to the neutral words that were presented in the rejected channel. These results are consistent with the idea that phobics may have an attentional bias that results in the diversion of attention to cues relevant to their fears. It should be noted, however, that this study had distinct methodological limitations precluding any conclusions regarding whether this diversion of attention occurred automatically or at a preconscious level. In particular, because subjects were explicitly asked to detect the fear-relevant words in the unattended channel, it is quite possible that phobic subjects showed a "guessing bias" (MacLeod & Mathews, 1991) involving interpretation of partial or ambiguous information in a threatening manner. That is, the results might really reflect more of an interpretive bias (see below) than an attentional bias or enhanced perceptual sensitivity. (See MacLeod, Mathews, & Tata, 1986; Mathews & MacLeod, 1986, for more conclusive evidence that such biases are indeed preconscious and automatic with generalized anxiety). Thus, further work in the area of attentional biases associated with fears and phobias is clearly needed.

B. MEMORY BIAS

Surprisingly little work has been done examining whether fears and phobias are associated with a memory bias for fear-relevant material. In one relevant study, Watts, Trezise and Sharrock (1986, Experiment 1) found that spider phobics showed relatively poor recall and recognition memory for large spiders (but not for small spiders) in an incidental learning paradigm. If corroborated by further experiments, this pattern of increased attention and vigilance to fear-relevant stimuli, accompanied by relatively poor memory for such stimuli, would parallel the similar pattern which has been noted with generalized anxiety (see below). That is, both fear and anxiety may be associated with an attentional vigilance for potentially threatening cues that occurs automatically. However, subsequent elaborative processing that is necessary for good retention appears to be avoided (MacLeod & Mathews, 1991; Mogg, Mathews, & Weinman, 1987; Zinbarg, Barlow, Brown and Hertz, 1992). As noted by Zinbarg et al. (1992), this pattern of hypervigilance for threat combined with an avoidance of further processing may serve to maintain or promote fear. In particular, the attentional vigilance may increase the likelihood that phobic subjects identify mildly threatening stimuli, but "subsequent efforts to avoid further processing would prevent more accurate evaluation of those events" (Zinbarg et al., 1992, p. 243). Without a more accurate evaluation of those events, "these threat cues would then retain their anxiety-provoking properties" (Zinbarg et al., 1992, p. 243).

C. JUDGMENTAL BIAS

Certain forms of judgmental biases also appear to be prominent with fears and phobias. Indeed, that phobic subjects overestimate the danger or risk posed by their phobic object or situation is almost a definitional aspect of phobias in the DSM-III-R (American Psychiatric Association, 1987), which requires that the "person recognizes that his or her fear is excessive or unreasonable" (p. 243). This aspect of phobias has been brought into the laboratory and studied in recent years in our work directed toward understanding how phobic fears seem to induce biased judgments of the covariation between feared stimuli and aversive outcomes. These biased judgments associated with phobic fears may well have the effect of serving to promote the maintainance or enhancement of fear.

1. Experiments on Covariation Bias with Snakes or Spiders as the Fear-relevant Stimuli

When Tomarken and I began this work in 1985, we were interested in exploring two questions. First, given increasing evidence for similarities in the processes mediating classical conditioning and judgments of covariation (e.g., see Alloy & Tabachnik, 1984, for a review), we were interested in exploring whether the enhanced conditioning seen by Öhman and his colleagues to fear-relevant stimuli such as snakes and spiders might be only one manifestation of a more general covariation bias. If this were the case, then selective associations should also be evidenced on tasks where subjects are asked explicitly to judge the covariation, or association between fear-relevant stimuli and aversive outcomes. To assess covariation bias an illusory correlation paradigm was used that shares several features in common with Öhman's prepared conditioning paradigm. Illusory correlation paradigms (first developed by Chapman and Chapman, 1967, 1969, in their studies of biased clinical judgment) involve exposure to

different categories of events that, across trials, are veridically uncorrelated. In our series of experiments, categories of stimuli were slides of
fear-relevant objects (snakes or spiders) and fear-irrelevant objects
(flowers and mushrooms), which were randomly paired with aversive and
nonaversive outcomes. That is, each category of slides was followed by
each outcome type an equal number of times. Following exposure to the
series of slides and outcomes (a total of 72 trials), subjects were asked to
judge the probability that each of the three slide categories had been
followed by each of the three outcome types. In reality all conditional
probabilities were identical and equal to .33. Our first hypothesis was that
subjects would overestimate the cooccurrence of fear-relevant stimuli and
aversive outcomes, that is, the covariation between snakes or spiders and
shock.

Second, because of the growing literature on the effects that emotions
have on cognitive processes (e.g., Williams et al., 1988), we were interested in exploring whether individual differences in fear would moderate
any covariation bias that might be seen. In particular, it seemed likely that
subjects with intense fears or phobias of the fear relevant stimuli used
might show enhanced covariation bias relative to that seen in low-fear
subjects. Therefore, in these experiments subjects were preselected for
being high or low in snake or spider fear before being exposed to the
different categories of fear-relevant and fear-irrelevant objects, randomly
paired with aversive and nonaversive outcomes. Our second hypothesis
was that subjects preselected for fear of the fear-relevant objects would
show enhanced covariation bias relative to low fear subjects.

In each of the first three experiments in this series (Tomarken, 1988;
Tomarken et al., 1989), high fear subjects dramatically overestimated the
percentage of trials on which the fear-relevant or phobic stimulus (snake or
spider) had been followed by shock. Their estimates of the other conditional probabilities were fairly accurate. Low fear subjects consistently
showed a similar but less dramatic bias that has only occasionally been
significant. Moreover, the bias seen in high fear subjects is typically significantly greater than that seen in low fear subjects. For example, Fig. 4
illustrates the estimates of covariation for each of the relevant slide/
outcome combinations for both high and low fear subjects. As can be seen,
the bias shown by high fear subjects is rather dramatic, with subjects
estimating that shocks followed the phobic slides (snakes or spiders) on
about 52% of the trials, significantly higher than the veridical probability of
.33. None of the other estimates differed significantly from the veridical .33
probability.

The second experiment in this series (Tomarken et al., 1989, Experiment 2) explored whether the covariation bias seen in high fear subjects

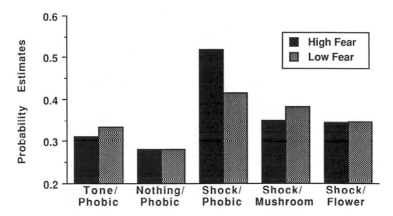

Fig. 4.   Mean estimates of conditional probability of outcomes given the different slide categories for the five pertinent estimates (tone/phobic, nothing/phobic, shock/phobic, shock/mushroom, shock/flower) for high and low snake or spider fear subjects. (From Tomarken et al., 1989).

with snakes and aversive outcomes was simply a consequence of the *salience* of the shock relative to the other two outcomes (tones and nothing), or whether the aversiveness of the shock was important in generating the illusory correlation. This question was of importance because previous research on illusory correlations had demonstrated that subjects sometimes overestimate the covariation between highly salient stimuli (e.g., Chapman, 1967). In this experiment the neutral tone outcome was replaced with a compound audiovisual stimulus outcome which pilot work had determined was rated by subjects as being equally salient and attention-getting as the shock, but which was not rated as aversive. This audiovisual stimulus outcome consisted of four colored flashing lights and a very distinctive chime. Thus, the three categories of slides remained the same, but the three possible outcomes were now shock, nothing, and the chime/flashing light stimulus. Once again, high fear subjects significantly overestimated the percentage of trials on which snakes had been followed by shock (the mean estimate was 58%) but did not overestimate the cooccurrence of snakes and the chime–light outcome, even though the latter outcome was rated as equally salient as the shock. Thus, it appears that the illusory correlation effect seen in high fear subjects is not simply a function of the salience of the shock outcome, but rather of its aversiveness.

   In each of at least six replications of this procedure, some with minor variations, high fear subjects have consistently and dramatically overestimated the proportion of trials on which slides of feared stimuli were followed by shock, but they have generally been quite accurate in all their other covariation estimates. Tomarken et al. (1989) argued that the major implication of these findings for understanding the effects of fear on cognitive processes is that fear appears to lead individuals to process information in a manner that would logically serve to maintain or enhance fear. That is, even though feared objects did not differentially predict the occurrence of aversive outcomes, they were perceived as if they did (Tomarken, 1988).

2. Experiments on the Affective Determinants of Covariation Bias

Several more recent experiments have further explored the affective or emotional basis of these illusory correlations (Sutton, Tomarken, & Mineka, submitted; Sutton & Mineka, in preparation). The first suggestion that they have an affective basis obviously came from the initial observations of a significantly greater bias in high fear subjects than in low fear subjects. Moreover, showing that it was the aversiveness of the shock rather than its salience that was important in generating illusory correlations provided an additional suggestion that the affect generated by the fear-relevant slides and the shock may play an important role in their generation (Tomarken et al., 1989, Experiment 2).

a. Damaged Electric Outlet Experiments.   More recent experiments have examined the importance of the salience of the slides, including their potential for eliciting fear or negative affect. In exploring the importance of the type of fear-relevant stimulus used, the choice of fear-relevant stimulus was guided by previous work on covariation bias showing that strong semantic associations between items may be sufficient to generate illusory correlations (e.g., Chapman, 1967). It was also guided by previous work on classical conditioning which assessed the relative effects of phylogenetically fear-relevant CSs (such as snakes and spiders) and ontogenetically fear-relevant CSs (such as damaged electric outlets) (cf. Hugdahl & Kärker, 1981).[3] Thus, in one experiment on this topic, slides of damaged

---

[3] As noted earlier, in human research on selective associations one cannot make a strong case that the selective associability of putatively phylogenetically fear-relevant CSs actually derives from phylogenetic influences, because all subjects do also have ontogenetically based associations to the fear-relevant stimuli (cf. Delprato, 1980). Nevertheless, a distinction has been made between fear-relevant stimuli where the fear-relevance is likely to have derived from phylogenetic influences (e.g., snakes) vs. where the fear-relevance could not possibly have been derived in this way because the stimuli were not even present in our early evolutionary history (e.g., damaged electric outlets).

electrical outlets were used as the ontogenetically fear-relevant stimuli in our illusory correlation paradigm (Sutton et al., submitted, Experiment 1). The fear-irrelevant stimuli continued to be flowers and mushrooms. Damaged electrical outlets not only can be seen as ontogenetically fear-relevant stimuli, but they also appear to have a strong semantic relationship to the shock used as the aversive outcome in this paradigm. The results of this experiment indicated that subjects did not show even marginally significant covariation bias when slides of damaged electric outlets were the fear-relevant stimuli (the average electric outlet–shock estimate was .34, which was very similar to the average of the other pertinent estimates). A subsequent replication and extension of this experiment confirmed these results. It is interesting to note that these results paralleled those of Hughdahl and Kärker (1981), who also failed to find the superior conditioning with damaged electric outlets as the ontogenetically fear-relevant CSs that they found with snakes as the phylogenetically fear-relevant CSs.

Nevertheless, given other work showing that the use of highly salient stimuli and/or stimuli with strong semantic associability can be sufficient to generate illusory correlations (e.g., Chapman, 1967), at first glance one might well have expected damaged electric outlets and shock to generate illusory correlations. Both are quite salient stimuli, and they would appear to be strongly related to one another at a semantic or conceptual level. In particular, damaged electric outlets and shock are both likely to be perceived as potentially threatening, and both are also strongly associated with electric current. On the other hand, damaged electric outlets probably do not elicit much of an affective response such as slides of snakes do for high snake fear subjects. Thus, it may be that it is the similarity of the affective responses elicited by fear-relevant stimuli and shock which is important in generating illusory correlations with this paradigm, and that strong semantic or conceptual (but nonaffective) associations are not sufficient to do so with this paradigm. However, this conclusion would be much stronger if there were an independent assessment of the semantic associability of electric outlets and shock (relative to snakes and shock), as well as an independent assessment of the affective responses elicited by the various stimuli and outcomes used in these experiments.

Therefore, a follow-up experiment attempted to test in a preliminary way the relative importance of semantic relatedness or belongingness with the importance of affective response matching in generating illusory correlations (Sutton et al., submitted, Experiment 2). To get at the issue of semantic relatedness, we adapted a procedure used by Hamm, Veitl, and Lang (1989) for rating the degree of belongingness of various stimulus–outcome pairs. Subjects were asked to compare two stimulus–outcome pairs and to choose which one "goes together better." Then they were asked to rate on a 0–6 scale how well the pair that they chose actually went together. Specifically, in the first part of this experiment, high and low snake fear subjects were asked to rate the degree of belongingness of each of the three slide stimuli used in the previous experiment (snakes, electric outlets, and flowers) when each was paired with each of the two outcomes used (tones and shocks). Both high and low snake fear subjects rated electric outlets and shocks as belonging better together than did snakes and shock, and in paired comparisons 83% of the subjects chose the electric outlets and shock most often as the pair that belonged together better. Yet two previous experiments had failed to find any evidence of covariation bias when the same slides of damaged electric outlets were used in the illusory correlation paradigm. To the extent the belongingness ratings provide a good measure of "cold" semantic associability, these results suggest at a minimum that such cold semantic associability is not sufficient to generate illusory correlations.

In the second part of the experiment, which occurred several weeks later (to minimize carryover effects), the same subjects were asked to rate their affective responses to these same stimuli (Sutton et al., submitted, Experiment 2). As expected, for high (but not low) fear subjects, slides of snakes did elicit self-reports of fear and negative affect, as did the shock for both high and low fear subjects. By contrast, damaged electric outlets did not elicit fear or other signs of negative affect in either high or low snake fear subjects. Thus, there was some degree of affective response matching for the snakes and shock in high (but not low) fear subjects, but not for outlets and shock. Thus, it seems possible that it is this pattern of affective response matching between the snakes and shock for the high fear subjects that is the mediating factor generating the illusory correlations or biased judgments of covariation. Further confirmation of this hypothesis is obviously necessary, including an experiment which assesses the value of subjects' rating of belongingness and affective responses to the slides and outcomes in predicting the same subject's tendency to show covariation bias.

b. Knife Experiments.   The high levels of snake fear exhibited by the subjects in these studies have probably been with them for many years because most small animal phobias start in childhood (e.g., see Marks, 1987; Öhman et al., 1985, for reviews). It is also of interest to examine whether more temporary activation of fear and danger schemata would also serve as the basis for covariation bias. Another series of experiments originally designed for other purposes does indeed suggest that temporary activation of danger schemata can have this effect (Sutton & Mineka, in preparation). These experiments were originally designed to examine whether subjects would show covariation bias when the fear-relevant stimuli were knives presented in a somewhat threatening context (i.e., in the hand of a male dressed in a black leather jacket). The fear-irrelevant stimuli used continued to be flowers and mushrooms.

The first time this experiment was run, the results indicated that subjects dramatically overestimated the contingency between knives and electric shock (the mean knife/shock estimates was .52, whereas the average estimate for the other pertinent comparisons was .32). This finding was contrary to our original hypothesis (based on the ontogenetic/phylogenetic distinction) that the results with knives would parallel those seen with damaged electric outlets. Two related explanations seemed plausible. First, it was possible that there was something important about the active threatening fashion in which the knives were presented that was crucial to obtaining the effect. In other words, if knives had been presented in a more passive and less threatening context the results might have paralleled those seen with damaged electric outlets as the fear-relevant stimulus. Second, it came to our attention that there had been two fatal stabbing in the recent past that had been prominent in the news media in Austin, Texas, where the experiment had been run. One of the stabbings was of a female university student (and all the subjects in these experiments were female). Thus, it seemed possible that these stabbings had had the effect of priming the idea that knives can be dangerous—particularly when seen in the context of being in the hand of a male dressed in a black leather jacket

The following year at Northwestern University in Evanston, Illinois, an experiment was designed to test out the second hypothesis by attempting to determine if a laboratory priming task could reproduce the results seen in Austin following the fatal stabbing. Subjects were run consecutively in two presumably unrelated experiments in two different laboratories in the same building. The first experiment ostensibly involved a test of comprehension for a variety of pieces of text, and the second experiment was the standard illusory correlation task with knives as the fear-relevant stimuli. In the first task, one group (experimental priming) read one story about a fatal stabbing near the end of a series of other unrelated texts; the other group of subjects (control priming) instead read a passage about mushrooms (one of the other stimuli used in the illusory correlation task). The results of this experiment indicated that neither the experimental priming nor the control priming group showed significant covariation bias with knives and shocks (see Sutton & Mineka, in preparation, for details). At this point it was not possible to determine whether the results obtained in Austin had been an aberration and would not replicate, or whether the experimental priming manipulation that had been used at Northwestern was simply not powerful enough to reproduce the effects that the fatal stabbing may have produced in Austin.

About 6 months later another attempt was made to reproduce the effects seen in Austin by using a slightly different (hopefully more powerful) experimental priming manipulation. However, 1 week before the experiment was set to run, a Northwestern female student (from the Introductory Psychology class that constituted the subject pool for these experiments) was fatally stabbed by her boyfriend. This unfortunate event received intense media coverage and created quite a stir on Northwestern's quiet and peaceful suburban campus. It also created a unique opportunity to replicate the study that had been run in Austin because of the similarity of the powerful naturalistic priming events (which were not under experimenter control). The experiment was run within 1–3 weeks of the stabbing, and the results indicated a very large and significant tendency to overestimate the knife/shock contingency. Indeed, the findings were very similar to those seen in Austin after the stabbings there, with knife/shock estimates averaging .51, and the other pertinent comparison estimates averaging .31. The experimental priming manipulation did not have a significant effect (see Sutton & Mineka, in preparation, for details).

Given that the stabbing incidents occuring near the time and place that these two experiments were conducted received intense media coverage and that they occurred in university communities not accustomed to such violence, it seems reasonable to hypothesize that there had been in each case some powerful priming or activation of danger schemata regarding knives in the hands of a male who could possibly be an assailant. Unfortunately, the various experimental priming manipulations through which we attempted to mimic this effect repeatedly failed to potentiate any covariation bias for knives and shock. However, another way to get at this possibility that priming or activation of danger schemata mediated the bias seen following a stabbing was to assume that the prominence of the fatal stabbing in people's mind would diminish over a matter of months. This led us to then replicate the experiment at Northwestern two more times later in the same year. As illustrated in Fig. 5, the magnitude of the covariation bias showed a linear decline with the passage of time since the stabbing. Indeed, by plotting all five replications not in the sequence in which they were conducted, but rather as a function of time since a fatal student stabbing that was prominent in the local news media, one can see a very clear and statistically significant relationship between the size of the illusory correlation effect and time since the fatal stabbing (see Sutton & Mineka, in preparation, for details).

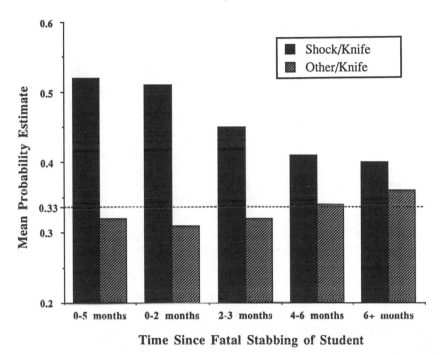

Fig. 5. Mean estimates of conditional probability of outcomes for shock/knife and other/ knife (average of tone/knife and nothing/knife) estimates for the five different replications of this experiment. Approximate times since a fatal stabbing that each replication was run are noted on the abcissa. (From Sutton & Mineka, in preparation).

c. Summary. These findings nicely complement the findings with snakes and spiders because in those experiments subjects only showed strong evidence of covariation bias if they were high in snake or spider fear and hence probably possessed danger schemata about snakes or spiders. In the series of experiments with knives as the fear-relevant stimuli, significant covariation bias was only seen when it can be hypothesized that there had been some activation—in this case by a naturalistic priming incident—of danger schemata regarding knives in the hands of a male who could possibly be an assailant. Thus it may be that stimuli which activate fear or danger schemata are linked to a style of confirmatory processing that may serve to maintain or enhance fear. That is, once fears are acquired, or danger schemata are temporarily activated, a style of confirmatory processing often comes into play which may promote the persistence or even exacerbation of the fear.

3. Important Questions for Future Research

What serves to distinguish situations in which such confirmatory processing is associated with relatively stable and enduring fears and phobias (as
seen with snake fear) from situations in which the confirmatory processing
is associated with only relatively transient activation of danger schemata
(as seen with the stabbing incidents)? Too little is known at this point to
provide a clear-cut answer. However, one possibility is that there is a
differential strength or salience of the fear or danger schemata associated
with phylogenetically versus ontogenetically fear-relevant stimuli. As
noted earlier, Hugdahl and Kärker (1981) did not find the enhanced
resistance to extinction usually seen with snakes as the fear-relevant
stimuli when they used damaged electric outlets as ontogenetically fear-
relevant stimuli. Thus, the idea that phylogenetically fear-relevant stimuli
are associated with enhanced resistance to extinction in conditioning experiments is consistent with the idea that the danger schemata associated
with these fears are more enduring and permanent than are those associations with ontogenetically fear-relevant stimuli such as knives or electric
outlets. Moreover, some of Öhman's recent work suggests that following
conditioning, phylogenetically fear-relevant stimuli such as angry faces
and snakes can elicit conditioned responses even when presented under
conditions that preclude conscious awareness (Öhman, 1986; Öhman,
Dimberg, and Esteves, 1989; Öhman & Soares, in press). By contrast,
when fear-irrelevant stimuli are presented following conditioning under
the same conditions (30 msec followed by a backward mask), conditioned
responses are not elicited. The ability of phylogenetically fear-relevant
stimuli to recruit conditioned emotional responses even under conditions
of preattentive activation may be another indication of the differential
strength or salience of the danger schemata associated with these fears.
However, it should be noted that this conclusion is limited by the fact that
the ability of ontogenetically fear-relevant stimuli (such as knives or electric outlets) to recruit conditioned responses under conditions of preattentive activation has not been tested; the present analysis clearly predicts
that they should be more like fear-irrelevant stimuli than like phylogenetically fear-relevant stimuli in this regard.

It is also important to consider other aspects of the relationship between
these experiments on covariation bias and the experiments discussed
above on selective associations in fear conditioning. In discussing selective associations in fear conditioning, it was noted that human and nonhuman primates seem to have a propensity to selectively associate certain
fear-relevant stimuli with aversive outcomes, as demonstrated in experiments using direct or observational fear conditioning paradigms. In re-

viewing experiments on covariation bias, it has also been apparent that there is a tendency to selectively associate various kinds of fear-relevant stimuli with aversive outcomes in the context of an illusory correlation paradigm. The dependent variables in these two sets of experiments are quite different in that the former involves the occurrence of conditioned responses and the latter involves subjects' estimates of the covariation between different categories of stimuli and different outcomes. Nevertheless, the similarity of the findings suggests that the preparedness or fear-relevance effects seen with classical conditioning paradigms may be one manifestation of a more general covariation bias to selectively associate fear relevant stimuli with aversive outcomes (cf. Tomarken, 1988; Tomarken et al., 1989). These parallels are consistent with accumulating evidence of important parallels between classical conditioning and judgments of contingency (cf. Alloy & Tabachnik, 1984; Dickinson & Shanks, 1985) and with the proposition that the detection of contingency probably underlies the development of conditioned responses (e.g., Mackintosh, 1983).

However, it is also important to note that there are some potentially important differences between these two sets of phenomena. In the work discussed thus far on covariation bias, high levels of fear potentiate the biases that are seen and this is, of course, consistent with the other work on the emotion–cognition interaction that is discussed further below (e.g., MacLeod & Mathews, 1991; Williams et al., 1988). By contrast, in the human research on selective associations in fear conditioning, preselecting subjects for high levels of fear (prior to conditioning) has usually not been shown to have an effect (cf. McNally, 1987; Tomarken, 1988). Whether these differences reflect something fundamentally different about the nature of the mediating mechanisms for these two sets of phenomena is unclear at the present time. Further consideration of this issue will require closer examination of at least two aspects of these experiments on covariation bias. First, some degree of bias is present even in low snake or spider fear subjects. This bias is only sometimes significant within an individual experiment, but its presence in at least mild degrees across many experiments is noteworthy. Moreover, Tomarken et al. (1989, Experiment 3) found at least one condition under which the bias was as strong in low fear subjects as in high fear subjects. In particular, they found comparable bias in high and low fear subjects when the base rate of shock was increased from 33% to 50% (while keeping the relationship between the three stimulus categories and the three outcomes random).

The second relevant issue that requires further exploration in this regard is that significant differences between high and low fear subjects are not seen with some of the other fear-relevant stimuli that have been used in this series of experiments. For example, another set of experiments has examined whether high levels of social anxiety or trait anxiety would potentiate a bias to overestimate the relationship between angry or disgust facial expressions and shocks (Mineka, Sutton, & Luten, in preparation). In these experiments, the angry or disgust facial expressions are used as fear-relevant stimuli for social anxiety (cf. Öhman & Dimberg, 1978; Öhman et al., 1985); happy and neutral facial expressions are the fear-irrelevant stimuli. Although there have been occasional suggestions of such an effect, the differences between high and low anxious subjects have not been found consistently. At present it seems safer to conclude that all subjects show a mild bias to overestimate the relationship between fear-relevant cues for social anxiety (cf. Öhman et al., 1985) and aversive outcomes. In yet another series of experiments, covariation bias has been examined using stimuli which are relevant to blood-injury fear, which is generally considered to be a distinct form of phobic fear (Marks, 1987; Öst, 1992). In this case, the fear-relevant slides were of surgical procedures or of mutilated bodies, and subjects were preselected for being high or low in blood-injury fear (Pury & Mineka, in preparation). The results indicated that both high and low blood-injury fear subjects overestimated the relationship between fear-relevant slides and shocks to a comparable degree (Pury & Mineka, in preparation).

What accounts for these apparent discrepancies in when fear or anxiety does and does not potentiate the covariation bias seen with the different kinds of fear-relevant stimuli that have been used in this series of experiments? At present our favored hypothesis is that a subject's level of fear is most likely to potentiate the bias when the slides of fear-relevant stimuli are particularly good at eliciting high levels of state fear or state anxiety in subjects who have long-standing fears. Although there is, as of yet, no strong evidence to support this hypothesis, there are significant reasons to suspect that it may be correct. First, Öhman et al. (1985) summarized evidence suggesting that subjects high in social anxiety may not show the same pattern of heart rate acceleration to fear-relevant stimuli that small animal phobics show. If this hypothesis is correct, then it seems possible that slides of negative facial affect such as the angry and disgust faces used in our experiments with social anxiety may not be very good in eliciting social anxiety; this is in contrast to the potent effect that slides of snakes or spiders have on eliciting fear and/or disgust in subjects high in snake or spider fear (e.g., Dimberg, 1990; Tomarken, 1988). Thus, although slides of negative facial affect can be conceptualized as fear-relevant when it comes to conditioning of social fears in normal subjects (e.g., Öhman & Dimberg, 1978; see Öhman et al., 1985, for a review), they may not be particularly potent elicitors of social anxiety in subjects with preexisting high levels of social anxiety. Second, informal observations from the Pury and Mineka experiments (in preparation) with slides relevant to blood-injury fear suggest that the slides used in these experiments may have been so prepotent or salient as to elicit comparable levels of fear or disgust in subjects both high and low in mutilation fear. Thus, it seems quite possible that in both cases group differences in the relevant fears did not have an effect on covariation bias because high and low fearful or anxious subjects did not differ in their affective response to the fear-relevant slides. This hypothesis is also in keeping with the emphasis on affective response matching discussed earlier as an important mediator of strong covariation bias. However, further experiments more carefully examining the pattern of affective response to these different categories of slides are required in order to more fully evaluate this hypothesis.

4. Covariation Bias and Selective Associations: A Summary

In summary, this series of experiments on biased judgments of covariation between feared stimuli and aversive outcomes suggests that there are some important parallels, and perhaps some important distinctions, between this phenomenon and the phenomenon of selective associations in fear conditioning discussed earlier. The primate research on selective associations in fear conditioning suggests that natural selection has played a role in determining which objects or situations are most likely to become the sources of fears and phobias. Human research on selective associations using paradigms for classical conditioning of electrodermal responses (e.g., Öhman et al., 1985; Öhman, 1986) is also consistent with this proposition. Given that a number of important similarities and parallels between classical conditioning and judgments of covariation have been noted in recent years (e.g., Alloy & Tabachnik, 1984; Dickinson & Shanks, 1985), it is of interest that selective associability of fear-relevant objects and aversive outcomes can be added to this list of similarities and parallels. In other words, the mild levels of covariation bias for fear-relevant stimuli and aversive outcomes seen in human subjects even low in fear in the series of experiments using an illusory correlation paradigm can be taken as another instance of selective associations, thereby illustrating one more parallel between classical conditioning and judgments of contingency (e.g., Alloy & Tabachnik, 1984; Dickinson & Shanks, 1985). That preexisting fears can potentiate this covariation bias suggests that, once acquired, fears appear to induce a style of confirmatory processing that may serve to maintain or enhance the fear. This is, of course, consistent with the adaptive conservatism hypothesis of Tomarken (1988) that fear is associated with "a 'conservative' perceptual and cognitive bias" (p. 77).

V. Cognitive Biases Associated with Anxiety and Depression

If the adaptive conservatism hypothesis has any relevance for understanding fears and phobias, are there any parallel principles that have relevance for understanding other emotions and emotional disorders? Fear is generally considered to be a basic emotion that has clear adaptive value in that it activates the fight/flight response of the sympathetic nervous system, preparing the animal for dealing with danger or threat (e.g., Barlow, 1988; Beck & Emery, 1985; Izard, 1977; Öhman et al., 1989, 1985). Anxiety and depression, by contrast, are more diffuse emotional states, generally thought to involve a blend of basic emotions (e.g., Barlow, 1988; Izard, 1977; Lazarus, 1991). They share many symptoms and often co-occur, but they also have some distinguishing features (e.g., Alloy, Kelly, Mineka, & Clements, 1990; Barlow, 1988; Clark & Watson, 1991; Tellegen, 1985). The adaptive value of anxiety and depression may be less clear-cut than is the adaptive value of fear, but many have argued that the emotional states of anxiety and depression are indeed adaptive. For example, anxiety involves anticipation of real or imagined future threats, helping the organism to prepare for, and ideally to avoid, those threats (e.g., Barlow, 1988; Beck & Emery, 1985; Bowlby, 1973). Depression may have been adaptive in that it promotes withdrawal and conservation of resources in times of stress when coping efforts have all failed (e.g., Engel, 1962; Izard, 1977; Kaufman, 1973; Klinger, 1975). Depression may also serve a social communication function (e.g., Bowlby, 1969, 1973, 1980; Kaufman, 1973; Klerman, 1974), and "may serve to motivate and reinforce maintenance of social order" (Rehm & Naus, 1990, p. 30). These adaptive functions may especially be true for animals and young children (e.g., Klerman, 1974). Admittedly, when these emotional states become severe and chronic, as in cases of clinical anxiety and depression in adults, the adaptive function is no longer clear (e.g., Izard, 1977, p. 105; Klerman, 1974). But what is adaptive in the short term may not be in the long term (e.g., Klerman, 1974), and what is adaptive in mild or moderate degrees may not be when carried to extremes (e.g., Izard, 1977). Moreover, what may have been adaptive in our early evolutionary history may no longer be so in the modern world (e.g., Rehm & Naus, 1990).

If anxiety and depression, like fear, have some adaptive value, are the effects that these emotions have on cognitive processing at all parallel to those reviewed above for fear? The apparent answer is yes. Indeed, in the past decade there has been a great deal of research on the emotion–cognition interaction documenting the prominent effects that anxiety and depression have on cognitive processing (see MacLeod & Mathews, 1991; Williams et al., 1988, for reviews). As with fear, these effects would appear to serve the function of confirming, reinforcing, or enhancing the emotion. Again, the cognitive biases being discussed here are defined as any selective or nonveridical processing of emotion-relevant information (Mineka & Tomarken, 1989; Mineka & Sutton, 1992). The three primary types of cognitive bias that will briefly be reviewed are attentional bias, memory bias, and judgmental or interpretive bias. Although these biases are being discussed separately here, it should be noted that the biases may be more interrelated than this somewhat artificial separation would suggest. Nevertheless, the separations and distinctions made here are largely consistent with those made in the literature.

A. JUDGMENTAL OR INTERPRETIVE BIASES

Several forms of judgmental or interpretive bias are associated with depression and anxiety. For example, both depression and anxiety are associated with biased judgments of the likelihood that negative events will happen to the individual (e.g., Butler & Mathews, 1983; see MacLeod & Mathews, 1991; Williams et al., 1988, for reviews). Anxious subjects also show a greater tendency to interpret ambiguous information in a threatening manner than do nonanxious controls. For example, one study had clinically anxious subjects and nonanxious controls read a series of ambiguous sentences such as "The doctor examined little Emma's growth" or "They discussed the priest's convictions." A later memory test in which the sentences were presented in disambiguated formats revealed that anxious subjects were more likely than were the nonanxious controls to remember the threatening meaning of the sentence ("The doctor looked at little Emma's cancer" or "They talked about the clergyman's criminal record"; Eysenck, Mogg, May, Richards, & Mathews, 1991). Overestimating the likelihood of negative events and having a marked tendency to interpret ambiguous information in a threatening manner can once again be seen as serving to reinforce, confirm, or enhance the anxiety or depression that drives the bias in the first place.

B. ATTENTIONAL BIAS

Clinically, it has long been noted that anxious patients seem to have a tendency toward heightened perception of, and vigilance for, threat and danger cues (e.g., Beck, 1976; Beck & Emery, 1985). Moreover, there is now a substantial amount of empirical work documenting that anxiety appears to have a preconscious, automatic influence on attention, resulting in attention being directed toward potentially threatening stimuli in the environment. The most elegant experimental confirmation of such a bias comes from experiments by Mathews and MacLeod and their colleagues on patients with generalized anxiety disorder (e.g., MacLeod et al., 1986; Mathews et al., 1986; see MacLeod & Mathews, 1991; Mathews, in press, for reviews). Using a number of different kinds of experimental tasks, their results have repeatedly shown that anxious patients show evidence of their attention being diverted, without awareness, toward threatening cues when there is a mixture of threatening and nonthreatening cues in the environment. Nonanxious individuals, if anything, show an opposite bias, directing attention away from threatening stimuli (see MacLeod & Mathews, 1991; Mathews, in press, for reviews).

For example, in one particularly elegant experiment, MacLeod et al. (1986) had subjects read aloud the upper of two words that were presented briefly (500 msec) on a video display screen; some of the words were neutral in content and some were threat-relevant words. On some trials one of the words was followed by a small dot probe and subjects were asked to respond rapidly when they saw the probe. Latency to respond is faster when the probe appears in the attended part of the display. Results indicated that clinically anxious subjects detected the probe fastest when it appeared following threat words, indicating that their attention shifted toward threat stimuli when they appeared on the screen. Nonanxious controls, by contrast, showed a tendency for their attention to be directed away from threat cues (see MacLeod et al., 1986, for details).

A subsequent experiment by MacLeod and Mathews (1988) attempted to tease apart the relative role of trait and state anxiety in mediating this effect by testing medical students high and low in trait anxiety, both at the beginning of the semester when state anxiety was relatively low, and at the end of the semester right before final examinations when state anxiety was relatively high. Neither group showed significant attentional bias at the beginning of the semester. By the end of the semester, when both groups showed comparable increases in state anxiety (although the absolute level of state anxiety differed), both groups showed an attentional bias. However, the direction of the bias was opposite for low and high trait anxious subjects. Specifically, high trait anxious subjects showed the same pattern of bias seen in the earlier MacLeod et al. (1986) study using clinically anxious subjects, with attention being diverted and directed toward threatening stimuli on the screen. By contrast, when low trait anxious subjects had increases in state anxiety, their attention was diverted away from these same threat stimuli.

One theoretical interpretation of these results is that anxious patients have danger schemata which lead to preattentive shifts of information-processing resources toward threat cues. If anxiety leads one to focus more and more on threat and danger cues, it is easy to see how anxiety is likely to be maintained or exacerbated. Although corroborating evidence is not

yet available that such an attentional bias does indeed mediate the maintenance or exacerbation of anxiety, it certainly seems like a strong possibility (e.g., MacLeod & Mathews, 1991). Moreover, it is interesting to note
that nonanxious subjects seem to have an opposite kind of bias which may
serve to protect them from becoming clinically anxious. It is interesting to
speculate that the attentional bias seen in high trait anxious subjects when
their state anxiety is elevated (see also, Broadbent & Broadbent, 1988)
may mediate the increased risk that high trait anxious subjects are thought
to have for developing generalized anxiety disorder (e.g., Eysenck, 1989).
However, prospective longitudinal studies will have to be conducted before this interesting hypothesis can be corroborated.

Although most contemporary theories of emotion and cognition would
predict that depression should also be associated with an attentional bias
for mood-congruent information (e.g., Beck & Clark, 1988; Bower, 1981;
see Williams et al., 1988, for a review), there is in fact little convincing
evidence for a similar attentional bias in depression. Some studies (e.g.,
Gotlib & McCann, 1984) have shown that depression is associated with
Stroop interference (i.e., slower color naming latencies for negative mood-
congruent words). However, as noted earlier, Stroop interference is not
generally considered to be a good measure of attentional bias (cf.
Mathews, in press; MacLeod & Mathews, 1991). Moreover, these studies
of depressed subjects have generally not assessed the role that concomi-
tant anxiety may be playing in the interference, and this is of crucial
importance given the high degree of comorbidity between anxiety and
depression, both at the symptom level and at the diagnostic level (e.g.,
Clark, 1989; Clark & Watson, 1991). Other paradigms which are thought to
provide a better measure of attentional bias such as the dot probe reaction
paradigm described earlier have not produced evidence of an attentional
bias for negative information in depression (e.g., Gotlib, McLachlan, &
Katz, 1988; MacLeod et al., 1986; see MacLeod & Mathews, 1991, for a
review).

C. MEMORY BIAS

If one looks at evidence for memory biases for mood-congruent information, the pattern of findings for anxiety versus depression seems to be
opposite to that seen with attentional biases. That is, there is a good deal of
evidence that depression is associated with a bias to recall mood-
congruent information, but little consistent evidence that anxiety is associated with a similar memory bias (cf., MacLeod & Mathews, 1991;
Mathews, in press, for reviews). The general approach to studying mood-
congruent memory in depression involves comparing individuals who ex-

perience high levels of depression with matched nondepressed controls. Stimulus items for the memory tasks are usually lists of words which vary in affective content, and the encoding task usually needs to be a self-referential one (see MacLeod & Mathews, 1991, for a review). In numerous studies it has been shown that subjects with clinical depression show a strong bias to recall negative, especially self-referential, information. The bias occurs both when the negative material is autobiographical and when it is experimentally presented. The bias appears to be opposite that usually shown by nondepressed subjects who generally show a bias favoring recall of positive material (see MacLeod & Mathews, 1991; Williams et al., 1988, for reviews). The mood-congruent memory biases associated with clinical depression seem to remit following recovery from depression (cf., MacLeod & Mathews, 1991, for a review).

Teasdale (1988) and others have argued that this memory bias for negative self-referential material, in combination with the interpretive and judgmental biases discussed briefly above, can be seen as creating what Teasdale calls a vicious cycle of depression. If someone is already depressed and his memory is strongly biased so that he remembers primarily the bad things that have happened to him and interprets events in a negative way, this is only going to help perpetuate the depression. Consistent with this idea are findings by Dent and Teasdale (1988). In their study, depressed women completed a task similar to that used by Derry and Kuiper (1981) in which they were asked to rate the degree to which each of 26 trait words (some positive, some negative) were descriptive of their personality. This was followed by an incidental recall task for these words. They found that the number of negative trait words that were endorsed as self-descriptive was highly correlated (.8) with the number of such words recalled on the incidental recall task, and that both of these predicted how depressed the subjects would be 5 months later. Indeed, of the many predictor variables used in this study, number of negative trait words endorsed was the only one other than initial level of depression to significantly predict levels of depression 5 months later. Unfortunately, because these two predictor variables were so highly correlated, the authors chose not to examine the predictive validity of the incidental recall measure by itself. Future studies with a similar design should examine this issue more carefully by using a mood-congruent memory bias index to directly predict future depression levels.

An important question also addressed by Teasdale (1988) is why not all individuals who experience a depressed mood get locked into the vicious cycle just described. He has argued that the likelihood of getting into such a vicious cycle is based on a complex interaction of biological, psychological, social, and environmental factors. For example, the severity of mood state is related to the degree of biased recall that is shown (e.g., Clark & Teasdale, 1982). In addition, his theory assumes "that individuals differ in the nature of the representations and interpretative constructs that are accessible in the state of initial depression, and that these differences will determine whether or not experiences will be interpreted as highly aversive and uncontrollable" (p. 254). Moreover, "differences between individuals in the representations and constructs that become accessible in the depressed state are an important aspect of cognitive vulnerability to depression" (p. 255). So, for example, if the negative constructs that become accessible are relatively mild (e.g., thoughtless, inconsiderate, rude), the likelihood of getting locked into the vicious cycle will be much lower than if the negative constructs that become accessible are more global negative traits (e.g., worthless, pathetic). So although much work remains to be done to delineate more precisely the nature of such vicious cycles and the factors determining which individuals are most likely to get locked into them, there are at least some preliminary hypotheses to guide this work.

By contrast to the strong evidence for mood-congruent memory biases in depression, as noted above, the majority of studies examining whether anxiety is also associated with a memory bias for threatening information has not found such an effect (see MacLeod and Mathews, 1991; Mathews, in press, for reviews). When significant findings have been obtained, they have often failed to replicate. For example, Mathews, Mogg, May, and Eysenck (1989) reported results suggesting that anxious patients may show an implicit but not an explicit memory bias for threatening information. However, Mathews (in press) has recently reported a failure to replicate that effect, and two recent studies from my laboratory (Nugent & Mineka, in preparation) have failed to find evidence for an implicit memory bias for threatening information in high trait anxious subjects even though a paradigm very similar to that used by Mathews et al. (1989) was used.

MacLeod and Mathews (1991) and Mathews (in press) have argued that this pattern of results seen with anxious subjects (i.e., an automatic preconscious attentional bias for threat cues, but no memory bias) occurs because of a failure of elaborative rehearsal following the activation of a threatening representation. Thus, although there is vigilance for threat cues occuring at very early stages in the information processing sequence, they argue that there is also avoidance of further elaborative processing. This is a very similar pattern (based on a much stronger data base) to that discussed earlier for fear. As was speculated with fear, the combined effects of these two tendencies would appear to serve particularly well to promote the maintenance or exacerbation of anxiety. This is because avoidance of further processing of activated threat representations prevents a more accurate evaluation of the degree of threat that is posed (Zinbarg et al., 1992).

D.   THEORETICAL APPROACHES TO UNDERSTANDING THE COGNITIVE BIASES ASSOCIATED WITH ANXIETY AND DEPRESSION

To summarize this section, it appears that anxiety and depression have somewhat different effects on cognitive processing (cf. MacLeod & Mathews, 1991; Williams et al., 1988). Anxiety appears to be associated with an attentional bias for danger or threat cues, and depression appears to be associated with a memory bias for negative self-referential information. Theories of cognition and emotion need to address this apparent dissociation between the most prominent biases for these two different disorders (cf. MacLeod & Mathews, 1991; Williams et al., 1988). At present, the two most prominent theories that have been used to account for the relationship between affect and cognition predict that evidence for both memory and attentional biases should be evident in both anxiety and depression. One of these is the semantic associative network model of Bower (e.g., 1981), and the other is Beck's schema model (Beck, 1976; Beck & Emery, 1985; Beck & Clark, 1988). Only in the last few years have investigators such as Mathews, Macleod, Watts, and Williams begun to develop models that may eventually help us to understand these differential effects of anxiety and depression on attention versus memory (e.g., MacLeod & Mathews, 1991; Mathews, in press; Williams et al., 1988). Moreover, much work remains to be done to further understand the degree to which these biases are indeed distinct for depression versus anxiety. For example, none of the studies conducted to date have compared anxious and depressed individuals on both memory and attentional tasks within the same study. In addition, because depression and anxiety so often co-occur and share many features in common (e.g., Alloy et al., 1990; Clark, 1989; Clark & Watson, 1991), it is important to explore whether both attentional and memory biases for mood-congruent material would be exhibited by individuals with high levels of anxiety and depression (see also Mineka & Sutton, 1992).

Nevertheless, although further confirmation of this distinction is needed, at an intuitive level, when considered in an adaptive functional framework, one might well have expected anxiety and depression to have different effects on information processing. For example, Plutchik (1984) has argued that "cognitions have largely evolved in the service of emotions" (p. 209), and the two emotions evolved to meet different environmental needs and pressures. Anxiety, like fear, probably evolved to aid in the anticipation of, and rapid identification of, potentially threatening stimuli (e.g., Beck & Emery, 1985; Tellegen, 1985). Depression, by contrast, involves significant reflective consideration of events that have led to failure and loss (Beck, 1967, 1976; Bowlby, 1980; Rehm & Naus, 1990; Tellegen, 1985).[4] Thus, as Mathews (in press) has argued, it makes some sense that anxiety as a forward-looking emotion leads to attentional biases which will facilitate the rapid detection of threat and its subsequent avoidance. Depression as a more backward-looking emotion leads to memory biases, perhaps because, as Mathews (in press) has argued, "Cognitive processes involved in the recall of past events and reflection on their meaning are more relevant to the function of sadness than are those involved in maintaining vigilance for possible future threat" (pp. 20–21). (See also Rehm & Naus, 1990, for a similar argument.) It is also interesting to note that judgmental or interpretive biases which appear to occur in both depression and anxiety may involve components of both attentional and memory biases (Williams et al., 1988).

VI. Conclusions

This article has reviewed a number of different aspects of contemporary research employing the paradigms and principles of experimental psychology to further understanding of the emotional disorders. Some of this work has been conducted within the framework of contemporary conditioning theory and some has been conducted within the framework on an information processing perspective on the emotion–cognition interaction. Where appropriate, I have tried to suggest some possible links (many of them quite speculative) between some of these different lines of research. A brief summary of the major points may serve to highlight and underscore these links. First, some evidence was reviewed strongly suggesting that human and nonhuman primates may have a phylogenetically based predisposition to acquire fears and phobias to certain fear-relevant stimuli that may once have posed a threat to our early ancestors (see Cook & Mineka, 1989, 1990, 1991; Öhman et al., 1985; Öhman, 1986; Seligman,

---

[4] The depressed person does, of course, also ruminate about imagined future negative consequences that are seen as likely to ensue given past losses and failures (Beck, 1967, 1976). However, this tendency is probably moderated by a different sort of cognitive bias than the attentional bias for anxiety reviewed above. In particular, depressed individuals have been shown to have what has been called a depressive attributional style involving a tendency to attribute negative events to internal, stable, and global causes (e.g., Abramson, Metalsky, & Alloy, 1989). As Abramson et al. (1989) have argued, this style is likely to contribute to the hopelessness about the future often associated with depression.

1971). Although the mechanisms through which these evolutionary memories are represented in the brain are not yet understood, it seems likely that these selective associations are involved in mediating the non-random distribution of fears and phobias that is seen clinically.

If natural selection was involved in determining which objects and situations are likely to become the sources of fears and phobias as the work on selective associations suggests, others have also considered the possibility that it may also have helped to shape the memory processes which appear to promote the maintenance and overgeneralization of fear with the passage of time (e.g., Hendersen, 1985; Tomarken, 1988; Mineka & Tomarken, 1989). In order to illustrate this possibility, animal research on memory for conditioned fears was reviewed which showed the variety of different processes which serve to promote the maintenance and over-generalization of fear with time. These included the loss of memory for specific CS and UCS attributes, leading animals to show fear-motivated behaviors in situations where they would not have soon after conditioning (e.g., Hendersen, 1985; Riccio et al., 1984). Additional examples included the forgetting of fear inhibitors (e.g., Hendersen, 1978) and the context specificity of extinction effects (e.g., Bouton, 1991). Especially when considering the combination of the robustness of conditioned excitatory effects and the fragility of conditioned inhibitory and extinction effects, it seems quite possible that these processes may have evolved along principles of adaptive conservatism. Human research on covariation bias for fear-relevant stimuli and aversive outcomes that is consistent with the adaptive conservatism hypothesis was also reviewed. In particular, it appears that individuals with a variety of different kinds of phobic fears show a marked tendency to overestimate the association between feared stimuli and aversive outcomes. It seems likely that such biases would serve to confirm or enhance fears once they are acquired. Thus, a substantial amount of work conducted with both animal and human subjects, using a variety of different paradigms, is consistent with Tomarken's proposition that fear is "associated with a 'conservative' perceptual and cognitive bias" (1988, p. 77).

Finally, the possibility was considered that parallel principles may also be operating with anxiety and depression. Highlights of research on the emotion–cognition interaction that has been conducted in people with anxiety and depression were reviewed. Anxiety appears to be associated with an attentional bias (but not a memory bias) for threatening material (MacLeod & Mathews, 1991; Mathews, in press). This combined tendency to be hypervigilant for threat cues but to avoid further elaborative process-ing would appear to be particularly effective in promoting the maintenance of anxiety, because without futher elaborative processing it is not possible to evaluate the real threat value of those cues (Mogg et al., 1987; Zinbarg et al., 1992). Depression, by contrast, appears to be associated with a memory bias (but not an attentional bias) for negative self-referential information. Both anxiety and depression appear to be associated with various interpretive or judgmental biases. Although much work remains to be done to establish the real consequences of these cognitive biases, it seems likely that all these biases for emotion-relevant material can be expected to have the effect of reinforcing or confirming the current emotional state. Thus they may play important roles in the maintenance of these disorders. Whether they also play a significant role in the etiology of the disorders is less clear at the present time and will require long-term prospective studies of individuals at risk for the development of the disorders.

Acknowledgments

Much of the research described in this article was generously supported by the following grants to S. Mineka: Grant BNS-8507340 from the National Science Foundation, a grant from the Hogg Foundation for Mental Health, and a grant from Northwestern University Graduate School. The author would like to gratefully acknowledge Michael Cook, Steven Sutton, and Andrew Tomarken for their enormous help over many years in conducting much of the research described here, as well as for their invaluable intellectual input into the various ideas and series of experiments described here. More recently, Alice Luten, Kathy Nugent, and Cindy Pury have also made significant contributions to the research described here. It should be noted, however, that these individuals do not necessarily agree with all the ideas presented here. Doug Medin and Bob Hendersen also made very helpful comments on an earlier version of this chapter.

References

Abramson, L., Metalsky, G., & Alloy, A. (1989). Hopelessness depression: A theory-based subtype of depression. *Psychological Review, 96,* 358–372.

Alloy, L. B., Kelly, K. A., Mineka, S., & Clements, C. M. (1990). Comorbidity in anxiety and depressive disorders: A helplessness/hopelessness perspective. In J. D. Maser & C. R. Cloninger (Eds.), *Comorbidity in anxiety and mood disorders* (pp. 499–544). Washington, DC: American Psychiatric Press.

Alloy, L. B., & Tabachnik, N. (1984). Assessment of covariation in humans and animals: The joint influence of prior expectancy and current situational information. *Psychological Review, 91,* 112–149.

American Psychiatric Association. (1987). *Diagnostic and statistical manual of mental disorders* (3rd ed. revised). Washington, DC: Author.

Bandura, A. (1991). Social cognitive theory and social referencing. In S. Feinman (Ed.), *Social referencing and social construction of reality.* New York: Plenum Press.

Barlow, D. H. (1988). *Anxiety and its disorders: The nature and treatment of anxiety and panic.* New York: Guilford.

Beck, A. T. (1967). *Depression: Clinical, experimental and theoretical aspects*. New York: Harper & Row.

Beck, A. T. (1976). *Cognitive therapy and the emotional disorders*. New York: International Universities Press.

Beck, A. T., & Clark, D. A. (1988). Anxiety and depression: An information processing perspective. *Anxiety Research, 1*, 23–36.

Beck, A. T., & Emery, G. (1985). *Anxiety disorders and phobias: A cognitive perspective*. New York: Basic Books.

Bennett-Levy, J., & Marteau, T. (1984). Fear of animals: What is prepared? *British Journal of Psychology, 75*, 37–42.

Bouton, M. E. (1991). A contextual analysis of fear extinction. In P. Martin (Ed.), *Handbook of behavior therapy and psychological science: An integrative approach* (pp. 435–453). New York: Pergamon.

Bouton, M. E., & Bolles, R. C. (1979). Contextual control of the extinction of conditioned fear. *Learning and Motivation, 10*, 445–466.

Bouton, M., & Bolles, R. (1985). Contexts, event-memories, and extinction. In P. D. Balsam & A. Tomie (Eds.), *Context and Learning* (pp. 133–166). Hillsdale, NJ: Erlbaum.

Bouton, M. E., & Swartzentruber, D. (1991). Sources of relapse after extinction in Pavlovian and instrumental learning. *Clinical Psychology Review, 11*, 123–140.

Bower, G. H. (1981). Mood and memory. *American Psychologist, 36*, 129–148.

Bowlby, J. (1969). *Attachment and loss, Vol. 1: Attachment*. New York: Basic Books.

Bowlby, J. (1973). *Attachment and loss, Vol. 2: Separation: Anxiety and anger*. New York: Basic Books.

Bowlby, J. (1980). *Attachment and loss, Vol. 3: Loss: Sadness and depression*. New York: Basic Books.

Broadbent, D., & Broadbent, M. (1988). Anxiety and attentional bias: State and trait. *Cognition and Emotion, 2*, 165–183.

Burgess, I. S., Jones, L. M., Robertson, S. A., Radcliffe, W. N., & Emerson, E. (1981). The degree of control exerted by phobic and non-phobic verbal stimuli over the recognition behaviour of phobic and non-phobic subjects. *Behaviour Research and Therapy, 19*, 233–243.

Butler, G., & Mathews, A. (1983). Cognitive processes in anxiety. *Advances in Behaviour Research and Therapy, 5*, 51–62.

Chapman, L. J. (1967). Illusory correlation in observational report. *Journal of Verbal Learning and Verbal Behavior, 6*, 151–155.

Chapman, L. J., & Chapman, J. P. (1967). Genesis of popular but erroneous psychodiagnostic observations. *Journal of Abnormal Psychology, 72*, 193–204.

Chapman, L. J., & Chapman, J. P. (1969). Illusory correlation as an obstacle to the use of valid diagnostic signs. *Journal of Abnormal Psychology, 74*, 271–280.

Clark, D. M., & Teasdale, J. D. (1982). Diurnal variation in clinical depression and accessibility of memories of positive and negative experiences. *Journal of Abnormal Psychology, 91*, 87–95.

Clark, L. (1989). The anxiety and depressive disorders: Descriptive psychopathology and differential diagnosis. In P. C. Kendall & D. Watson (Eds.), *Anxiety and depression: Distinctive and overlapping features* (pp. 83–129). New York: Academic Press.

Clark, L., & Watson, D. (1991). Theoretical and empirical issues differentiating depression from anxiety. In J. Becker & A. Kleinman (Eds.), *Advances in mood disorders, Vol. 1: Psychological aspects* (pp. 39–65) Hillsdale, NJ: Erlbaum.

Cook, E., Hodes, R., & Lang, P. (1986). Preparedness and phobia: Effects of stimulus content on human visceral conditioning. *Journal of Abnormal Psychology, 95*, 195–207.

Cook, M., & Mineka, S. (1987). Second-order conditioning and overshadowing in the observational conditioning of fear in monkeys. *Behaviour Research and Therapy, 25,* 349–364.

Cook, M., & Mineka, S. (1989). Observational conditioning of fear to fear-relevant versus fear-irrelevant stimuli in rhesus monkeys. *Journal of Abnormal Psychology, 98,* 448–459.

Cook, M., & Mineka, S. (1990). Selective associations in the observational conditioning of fear in monkeys. *Journal of Experimental Psychology: Animal Behavior Processes, 16,* 372–389.

Cook, M., & Mineka, S. (1991). Selective associations in the origins of phobic fears and their implications for behavior therapy. In P. Martin (Ed.), *Handbook of behavior therapy and psychological science: An integrative approach* (pp. 413–434). New York: Pergamon.

Cook, M., Mineka, S., Wolkenstein, B., & Laitsch, K. (1985). Observational conditioning of snake fear in unrelated rhesus monkeys. *Journal of Abnormal Psychology, 94,* 591–610.

Delprato, D. (1980). Hereditary determinants of fears and phobias. *Behavior Therapy, 11,* 79–103.

Dent, J., & Teasdale, J. (1988). Negative cognition and the persistence of depression. *Journal of Abnormal Psychology, 97,* 29–34.

Derry, P., & Kuiper, N. (1981). Schematic processing and self-reference in depression. *Journal of Abnormal Psychology, 90,* 286–297.

Dickinson, A., & Shanks, D. (1985). Animal conditioning and human causality judgment. In L.-G. Nilsson & T. Archer (Eds.), *Perspectives on learning and memory* (pp. 167–191). London: Erlbaum.

Dimberg, U. (1990). Facial reactions to fear-relevant stimuli for subjects high and low in specific fear. *Scandanavian Journal of Psychology, 31,* 65–69.

Domjan, M., & Galef, B. (1983). Biological constraints on instrumental and classical conditioning: Retrospect and prospect. *Animal Learning and Behavior, 11,* 151–161.

Engel, G. (1962). Anxiety and depression withdrawal: The primary affects of unpleasure. *International Journal of Psychoanalysis, 43,* 89–97.

Eysenck, M. W. (1989). Anxiety and cognition: Theory and research. In T. Archer & L.-G. Nilsson (Eds.), *Aversion, avoidance and anxiety: Perspectives on aversively motivated behavior.* (pp. 323–337). Hillsdale NJ: Erlbaum.

Eysenck, M. W., Mogg, K., May, J., Richards, A., & Mathews, A. (1991). Bias in interpretation of ambiguous sentences related to threat in anxiety. *Journal of Abnormal Psychology, 100,* 144–150.

Gotlib, I. H., & McCann, C. D. (1984). Construct accessibility and depression: An examination of cognitive and affective factors. *Journal of Personality and Social Psychology, 47,* 427–439.

Gotlib, I. H., McLachlan, A. L., & Katz, A. N. (1988). Biases in visual attention in depressed and nondepressed individuals. *Cognition and Emotion, 2,* 185–200.

Grey, S., Sartory, G., & Rachman, S. (1979). Synchronous and desynchronous changes during fear reduction. *Behaviour Research and Therapy, 17,* 137–147.

Hailman, J. (1976). Uses of the comparative study of behavior. In R. Masterton, W. Hodos, & H. Jerison (Eds.), *Evolution, brain, and behavior: Persistent problems* (pp. 13–22). Hillsdale, NJ: Erlbaum.

Hamm, A. O., Veitl, D., & Lang, P. J. (1989). Fear conditioning, meaning, and belongingness: A selective association analysis. *Journal of Abnormal Psychology, 98,* 395–406.

Hendersen, R. (1978). Forgetting of conditioned fear inhibition. *Learning and Motivation, 8,* 16–30.

Hendersen, R. (1985). Fearful memories: The motivational significance of forgetting. In F. R. Brush & J. B. Overmier (Eds.), *Affect, conditioning, and cognition: Essays in the determinants of behavior* (pp. 43–53). Hillsdale, NJ: Erlbaum.

Hendersen, R., Patterson, J., & Jackson, R. (1980). Acquisition and retention of control of instrumental behavior by a cue-signalling air blast: How specific are conditioned anticipations? *Learning and Motivation, 11*, 407–426.

Hugdahl, K., & Kärker, A.-C. (1981). Biological versus experiential factors in phobic conditioning. *Behaviour Research and Therapy, 16*, 315–321.

Izard, C. (1977). *Human Emotions*. New York: Plenum.

Johnston, T. (1981). Contrasting approaches to a theory of learning. *Behavioral and Brain Sciences, 4*, 125–173.

Kahneman, D., & Chajczyk, D. (1983). Tests of the automaticity of reading: Dilution of Stroop effects by color-irrelevant stimuli. *Journal of Experimental Psychology: Human Perception and Performance, 9*, 497–509.

Kaufman, C. (1973). Mother–infant separation in monkeys: An experimental model. In J. P. Scott & E. Senay (Eds.), *Separation and Depression: Clinical and Research Aspects* (pp. 33–52). Washington, DC: AAAS.

Klerman, G. (1974). Depression and adaptation. In R. Friedman & M. Katz (Eds.), *The psychology of depression: Contemporary theory and research* (pp. 127–145). New York: Winston/Wiley.

Klinger, E. (1975). Consequences of commitment to and disengagement from incentives. *Psychological Review, 82*, 1–25.

Lazarus, R. (1991). *Emotion and adaptation*. New York: Oxford University Press.

LoLordo, V. (1979a). Constraints on learning. In Bitterman, M., LoLordo, V., Overmier, J. B., & Rashotte, M. (Eds.), *Animal learning: Survey and analysis* (pp. 473–504). New York: Plenum.

LoLordo, V. (1979b). Selective associations. In A. Dickinson & R. Boakes (Eds.), *Mechanisms of learning and motivation: A memorial to Jerzy Konorski* (pp. 367–398). Hillsdale, NJ: Erlbaum.

LoLordo, V., & Droungas, A. (1989). Selective associations and adaptive specializations: Food aversion and phobias. In S. Klein & R. Mowrer (Eds.), *Contemporary learning theories: Instrumental conditioning theory and the impact of biological constraints on learning* (pp. 145–179). Hillsdale, NJ: Erlbaum.

Mackintosh, N. (1974). *The psychology of animal learning*. London: Academic Press.

Mackintosh, N. (1983). *Conditioning and associative learning*. New York: Oxford University Press.

MacLeod, C., & Mathews, A. M. (1988). Anxiety and the allocation of attention to threat. *Quarterly Journal of Experimental Psychology: Human Experimental Psychology, 38*, 659–670.

MacLeod, C., & Mathews, A. M. (1991). Cognitive-experimental approaches to the emotional disorders. In P. Martin (Ed.), *Handbook of behavior therapy and psychological science: An integrative approach* (pp. 116–150). New York: Pergamon Press.

MacLeod, C., Mathews, A., & Tata, P. (1986). Attentional bias in emotional disorders. *Journal of Abnormal Psychology, 95*, 15–20.

Marks, I. (1969). *Fears and phobias*. New York: Academic Press.

Marks, I. (1987). *Fears, phobias, and rituals: Panic, anxiety, and their disorders*. New York: Oxford University Press.

Mathews, A. (in press). Anxiety and the processing of emotional information. In L. Chapman & D. Fowles (Eds.), *Progress in experimental personality and psychopathology research*.

Mathews, A., & MacLeod, C. (1986). Discrimination of threat cues without awareness in anxiety states. *Journal of Abnormal Psychology, 95,* 131–138.

Mathews, A., Mogg, K., May, I., & Eysenck, M. (1989). Implicit and explicit memory bias in anxiety. *Journal of Abnormal Psychology, 98,* 236–240.

McNally, R. (1987). Preparedness and phobias: A review. *Psychological Bulletin, 101,* 283–303.

Mercklebach, H., van den Hout, M., & van der Molen. (1987). Fear of animals: Correlations between fear ratings and perceived characteristics. *Psychological Reports, 60,* 1203–1209.

Mineka, S. (1985). Animal models of anxiety-based disorders: Their usefulness and limitations. In J. Maser & A. Tuma (Eds.), *Anxiety and the anxiety disorders* (pp. 199–244). Hillsdale, NJ: Erlbaum.

Mineka, S., & Cook, M. (in press). Mechanisms involved in the observational conditioning of fear. *Journal of Experimental Psychology: General.*

Mineka, S., Davidson, M., Cook, M., & Keir, R. (1984). Observational conditioning of snake fear in rhesus monkeys. *Journal of Abnormal Psychology, 93,* 355–372.

Mineka, S., Keir, R., & Price, V. (1980). Fear of snakes in wild- and lab-reared rhesus monkeys. *Animal Learning and Behavior, 8,* 653–663.

Mineka, S., & Sutton, S. K. (1992). Cognitive biases and the emotional disorders. *Psychological Science, 3,* 65–69.

Mineka, S., Sutton, S. K., & Luten, A. G. (in preparation). *Social anxiety and covariation bias for fear-relevant stimuli and aversive outcomes.*

Mineka, S., & Tomarken, A. J. (1989). The role of cognitive biases in the origins and maintenance of fear and anxiety disorders. In T. Archer & L.-G. Nilsson (Eds.), *Aversion, avoidance, and anxiety: Perspectives on aversively motivated behavior* (pp. 195–221). Hillsdale, NJ: Erlbaum.

Mogg, K., Mathews, A., & Weinman, J. (1987). Memory bias in clinical anxiety. *Journal of Abnormal Psychology, 96,* 94–98.

Nugent, K., & Mineka, S. (in preparation). *The effect of high and low trait anxiety on implicit and explicit mood-congruent memory tasks.*

Öhman, A. (1986). Face the beast and fear the face: Animal and social fears as prototypes for evolutionary analyses of emotion. *Psychophysiology, 23,* 123–145.

Öhman, A., & Dimberg, U. (1978). Facial expressions as conditioned stimuli for electrodermal responses: A case of "preparedness"? *Journal of Personality and Social Psychology, 36,* 1251–1258.

Öhman, A., Dimberg, U., & Esteves, F. (1989). Preattentive activation of aversive emotions. In T. Archer & L.-G. Nilsson (Eds.), *Aversion, avoidance, and anxiety: Perspectives on aversively motivated behavior* (pp. 169–199). Hillsdale, NJ: Erlbaum.

Öhman, A., Dimberg, U., & Öst, L.-G. (1985). Animal and social phobias: Biological constraints on learned fear responses. In S. Reiss & R. Bootzin (Eds.), *Theoretical issues in behavior therapy* (pp. 123–175). New York: Academic Press.

Öhman, A., Fredrikson, M., Hugdahl, K., & Rimmö, P.-A. (1976). The premise of equipotentiality in human classical conditioning: Conditioned electrodermal responses to potentially phobic stimuli. *Journal of Experimental Psychology: General, 105,* 313–337.

Öhman, A., & Soares, J. (in press). On the automatic nature of phobic fear: Conditioned electrodermal responses to masked fear-relevant stimuli. *Journal of Abnormal Psychology.*

Öst, L.-G. (1992). Blood and injection phobia: Background cognitive physiological, and behavioral variables. *Journal of Abnormal Psychology, 101,* 68–74.

Pavlov, I. (1927). *Conditioned Reflexes*. London: Oxford University Press.

Plutchik, R. (1984). Emotions: A general psychoevolutionary theory. In K. Scherer & P. Ekman (Eds.), *Approaches to emotion* (pp. 197–219). Hillsdale, NJ: Erlbaum.

Pury, C. L., & Mineka, S. (in preparation). *Blood-injury fear and covariation bias for fear-relevant stimuli and aversive outcomes*.

Rachman, S., & Lopatka, C. (1988). Return of fear: Underlearning and overlearning. *Behaviour Research and Therapy, 26,* 99–104.

Rehm, L., & Naus, M. (1990). A memory model of emotion. In R. Ingram (Ed.), *Contemporary psychological approaches to depression* (pp. 23–35). New York: Plenum Press.

Riccio, D., Richardson, R., & Ebner, D. (1984). Memory retrieval deficits based upon altered contextual cues: A paradox. *Psychological Bulletin, 96,* 152–165.

Seligman, M. (1971). Phobias and preparedness. *Behavior Therapy, 2,* 307–320.

Sutton, S. K., & Mineka, S. (in preparation). *Naturalistic priming of covariation bias between knives and shock*.

Sutton, S. K., Tomarken, A. J., & Mineka, S. (submitted). *Affective determinants of fear-relevant covariation bias*.

Teasdale, J. B. (1983). Negative thinking in depression: Cause, effect, or reciprocal relationship? *Advances in Behaviour Research and Therapy, 5,* 3–25.

Teasdale, J. D. (1988). Cognitive vulnerability to persistent depression. *Cognition and Emotion, 2,* 247–274.

Tellegen, A. (1985). Structures of mood and personality and their relevance to assessing anxiety, with an emphasis on self-report. In A. H. Tuma & J. D. Maser (Eds.), *Anxiety and the anxiety disorders* (pp. 681–706). Hillsdale, NJ: Erlbaum.

Thomas, D. (1979). Retention of conditioned inhibition in a bar-press suppression paradigm. *Learning and Motivation, 10,* 161–177.

Tomarken, A. J. (1988). *Fear-relevant selective associations and covariation bias*. Unpublished doctoral dissertation. University of Wisconsin-Madison.

Tomarken, A. J., Mineka, S., & Cook, M. (1989). Fear-relevant selective associations and covariation bias. *Journal of Abnormal Psychology, 98,* 381–394.

Watts, F. N., McKenna, F. P., Sharrock, R., & Trezise, L. (1986). Colour naming of phobia-related words. *British Journal of Psychology, 77,* 97–108.

Watts, F. N., Trezise, L., & Sharrock, R. (1986). Processing of phobic stimuli. *British Journal of Clinical Psychology, 25,* 253–259.

Williams, J. M. G., Watts, F. N., MacLeod, C., & Mathews, A. (1988). *Cognitive psychology and emotional disorders*. Chichester, England: Wiley.

Zinbarg, R., Barlow, D., Brown, T., & Hertz, R. (1992). Cognitive-behavioral approaches to the nature and treatment of anxiety disorders. *Annual Review of Psychology, 43,* 235–267.

INVESTIGATIONS OF AN EXEMPLAR-BASED CONNECTIONIST MODEL OF CATEGORY LEARNING

Robert M. Nosofsky
John K. Kruschke

I. Introduction

Learning to categorize objects stands among the most fundamental cognitive processes. Categorizing brings order and organization to our mental lives and is a building block of more complex cognitive processes such as reasoning, problem solving, and thinking. Central issues in the study of categorization include how categories are represented in memory, and what decision processes are involved when people make categorization judgments. Furthermore, how are these category representations learned? Researchers often pursue these questions by developing formal models of categorization and testing these models in experiments in which subjects learn new, artificial categories in laboratory settings.

For over a decade, one of the leading formal models of categorization has been the context model of classification proposed by Medin and Schaffer (1978) and elaborated by Estes (1986) and Nosofsky (1984, 1986). According to the context model, people represent categories by storing individual exemplars in memory and make classification decisions on the basis of similarity comparisons with the stored exemplars. The context model has proved to be successful at predicting quantitative details of classification performance in a wide variety of experimental paradigms and

207

has compared favorably with a variety of competing models including prototype, simple rule-based, and feature frequency models. It accounts for numerous fundamental categorization phenomena, such as prototype effects and effects of specific exemplars, sensitivity to correlated dimensions, the importance of individual item frequency and old–new similarity relations, category size and frequency effects, performance on both linearly separable and non–linearly separable structures, "rule-described" categorization, probability matching behavior, and so forth. In addition, the model has provided excellent accounts of relations between categorization and other fundamental cognitive processes, such as identification and old–new recognition. (For reviews, see Medin & Florian, in press; Nosofsky, 1992, in press-a, in press-b.)

Most of the context model's successes to date, however, have occurred in categorization *transfer* situations, in which subjects classify both old and new objects following the completion of a category learning phase. A major shortcoming of the model is that it was not formalized to account for the processes of category *learning*. In other words, the context model is static in nature, designed to account for performance at given stages of the learning process, but does not account for dynamic changes in categorization as a function of learning experience.[1]

Recently, Kruschke (1990, 1992) elaborated the context model by incorporating key elements of it within the framework of a multilayered connectionist network (for closely related ideas, see Estes, 1988, in press; Hurwitz, 1990). Kruschke's model, which we refer to as ALEX in this chapter, can be characterized as an exemplar-based network model. The hidden nodes in this multilayered network correspond to individual exemplars, and they are activated by using the same similarity rules as are used in the context model. Unlike the context model, however, ALEX is intended to account for category *learning* phenomena.

The purpose of the present article is to provide an overview of ALEX, discuss its relation to the context model, and illustrate applications of the model in a variety of category learning situations. In Section II we compare and contrast the context model and ALEX. In Section III we apply ALEX to several previously published data sets that have been fitted accurately by the context model. The main goal is to provide some quantitative tests of ALEX and demonstrate that it performs well in situations in which the context model has performed well. In Sections IV and V we

---

[1] The original application of the context model was in the domain of discrimination learning (Medin, 1975), and this application included a learning algorithm. However, this version of the context model has not been tested in the domain of complex, human classification learning.

illustrate advantages that are yielded by elaborating the context model as an exemplar-based network. In particular, we demonstrate a variety of phenomena that are characterized well by ALEX but not by the context model. Finally, in Section VI we discuss limitations of the exemplar-based network, consider how the model might be further extended, and summarize and evaluate the model's applications.

II. Overview of the Context Model and ALEX

A. THE CONTEXT MODEL

According to the context model, people represent categories by storing individual exemplars in memory and classify items based on the degree to which they activate these stored exemplars. In the generalized context model (GCM) proposed by Nosofsky (1984, 1986), exemplars are represented as points in a multidimensional psychological space, and similarity between exemplars is assumed to be a decreasing function of their distance in the space (e.g., Shepard, 1958a, 1987). It is assumed in the model that because of factors such as frequency of presentation, stimulus "salience," and so forth, exemplars may reside in memory with differential strength. The degree to which exemplar j is activated when presented with item i is determined jointly by the exemplar's strength in memory and its similarity to the presented item i.

Formally, the psychological evidence for Category J given presentation of item i is found by summing the activations of all the Category J exemplars, and then multiplying by the response bias for Category J. This evidence is then divided by the sum of evidences for all categories to predict the conditional probability with which item i is classified in Category J:

$$R(R_J|i) = b_J \sum_{j \in C_J} M_J s_{ij} \bigg/ \sum_K b_K \sum_{k \in C_K} M_k s_{ik}, \qquad (1)$$

where s_{ij} is the similarity between item i and exemplar j; M_j is the strength with which exemplar j is stored in memory; and b_J is the Category J response bias.

A critical assumption in the model is that similarities between exemplars may not be invariant across different experimental situations. Rather, because of selective attention processes, similarities between exemplars may be modified in systematic ways. Selective attention is formalized in the model in terms of a set of attention-weight parameters that serve to stretch and shrink the psychological space in which the exemplars are embedded.

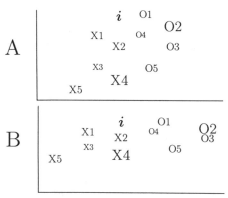

Fig. 1. Schematic category structure for illustrating the predictions of the GCM. There are five exemplars in each of two categories, X and O. (The differing sizes of the letters reflect the fact that the exemplars can reside in memory with differing strengths.) In A, item i is roughly equally similar to the exemplars of Categories X and O, so it would be classified in each category with roughly equal probability. B illustrates the category structures after selective attention to the relevant horizontal dimension. Item i now becomes far more similar to the exemplars of Category X, so it would be classified in that category with high probability.

The selective attention process can dramatically influence the patterns of generalization that are predicted by the GCM. For example, Fig. 1 illustrates two categories consisting of five exemplars each. Without selective attention operating (Fig. 1A), item i is roughly equally similar to the exemplars of Categories X and O, so it would be classified in Categories X and O with roughly equal probability. Suppose, however, that subjects attended selectively to the horizontal dimension. This process is represented in the model in terms of stretching of distances along the horizontal dimension, and shrinking of distances along the vertical dimension, as shown in Fig. 1B. (Note that such a selective attention process would benefit classification performance for the structure illustrated in Fig. 1, because it would increase subjects' ability to discriminate between the members of contrasting categories.) With selective attention to the horizontal dimension, item i becomes far more similar to the exemplars of Category X than to the exemplars of Category O, so the GCM predicts that item i would be classified in Category X with high probability.

These ideas are formalized in the model as follows. Each exemplar is represented as a point in an M-dimensional space. The distance d_{ij} between exemplars i and j is computed by using the (weighted) Minkowski power model (cf. Carroll & Wish, 1974),

$$d_{ij} = \left[\sum_m \alpha_m \mid x_{im} - x_{jm} \mid^r \right]^{1/r}, \tag{2}$$

where x_{im} is the psychological value of exemplar i on dimension m, and α_m $(0 \leq \alpha_m, \Sigma\alpha_m = 1)$ is the "attention weight" given to dimension m. This distance is transformed to a similarity measure by using the function

$$s_{ij} = \exp(-c \cdot d_{ij}{}^p), \tag{3}$$

where c is a sensitivity parameter reflecting overall discriminability in the space. The value of r in Eq. (2) and the value of p in Eq. (3) determine the form of distance metric and similarity gradient respectively. Common distance metrics are the city block $(r = 1)$ and Euclidean $(r = 2)$, and common similarity gradients are the exponential $(p = 1)$ and Gaussian $(p = 2)$ (e.g., Nosofsky, 1985; Shepard, 1958a, 1987). The particular distance metric and similarity gradient that operate depend systematically on experimental conditions, as we discuss in more detail later in this article.

In general, to apply the GCM to predict categorization, one first derives a psychological scaling solution for the exemplars. As illustrated in Section III, this scaling solution can be derived from direct similarity judgments among exemplars, or from matrices of identification confusions among exemplars. Once the scaling solution is derived, the GCM [Eq. (1–3)] can be used to predict categorization by estimating relatively few free parameters. The critical parameters tend to be the weights in Eq. (2), which describe how similarities among exemplars are modified because of selective attention processes.

B. ALEX

Kruschke's (1990, 1992) exemplar-based network is illustrated in Fig. 2. The model consists of a set of input nodes that code the values on the psychological dimensions composing a given input item; a set of hidden nodes that code locations in the multidimensional space in which the exemplars are embedded; and a set of category output nodes that code the degree to which the alternative categories are activated.

Each hidden node in ALEX corresponds to an exemplar.[2] When presented with an input pattern, each exemplar node is activated according to

[2] Kruschke (1990, 1992) called this model ALCOVE, which stands for Attention Learning COVEring map, because the original conception of the model included a hidden layer in which numerous nodes were randomly scattered over the stimulus space, thereby forming a covering map of the input space. The motive for the covering map assumption was that the model could not know in advance just which particular exemplars would subsequently appear during training, so it should initially be receptive to the entire potential stimulus space. Kruschke (1990) showed empirically that the covering map and exemplar-based versions behaved similarly in most situations. For that reason, the computationally less demanding exemplar-based version has been used in later applications (Kruschke, 1991a, 1992; Nosofsky, Kruschke, & McKinley, 1992). The present article also assumes the exemplar-based version, and to emphasize that fact, changes the name to ALEX: Attention/Association Learning EXemplar model.

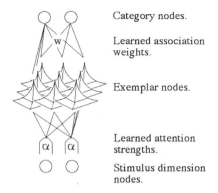

Category nodes.

Learned association weights.

Exemplar nodes.

Learned attention strengths.

Stimulus dimension nodes.

Fig. 2.   Illustration of Kruschke's (1990, 1992) ALEX model. Input nodes code values on the respective stimulus dimensions. These values are gated by the attention weights α_m. Hidden nodes code locations in the multidimensional space in which the exemplars are embedded. Each hidden exemplar node is activated according to its similarity to the input pattern. The pyramids show the activation profile of a hidden node using a city block metric with exponential decay. The hidden exemplar nodes are connected to category output nodes by the association weights W_{Kj}. Learning of the attention weights and the association weights takes place by using the generalized delta rule.

its similarity to the input pattern, where similarity is computed as in the GCM. Note in particular that the input nodes in ALEX are gated by dimensional attention weights. These weights enter into the similarity function for computing the exemplar node activations in the same manner as described previously for the GCM. Thus, when presented with item i, the degree to which each exemplar node j is activated is given by Eqs. (2) and (3).

It is assumed in ALEX that associations are learned between the exemplars and the categories. These associations, which are allowed to be positive or negative, are modeled by the association weights W_{Kj} that link each exemplar node j to each category output node K (see Fig. 2). Upon presentation of item i, the output to category node K is found by summing the similarity of i to all exemplar nodes j, weighted by their associations to Category node K:

$$O_K(i) = \sum s_{ij} \cdot W_{kj} \qquad (4)$$

Thus, if item i is highly similar to a group of exemplars that are strongly associated to Category K, then when item i is presented, the Category K node would be strongly activated. A variety of response-mapping functions for converting these output activations to response probabilities are possible. For simplicity in this article, we use the same response rule as in the GCM,

$$P(R_J \mid i) = b_J \cdot O_J(i) \Big/ \sum b_k \cdot O_K(i). \qquad (5)$$

The major conceptual difference between the GCM and ALEX concerns how the association weights between exemplars and categories are learned. The GCM can be conceptualized as a multilayered network (Fig. 2) in the same manner as ALEX, except the rules for learning the association weights are exceedingly simple. In the GCM, each time exemplar j is presented and feedback for Category K is provided, the association weight between exemplar node j and category output node K is incremented by one. No other association weights are affected on that trial. Thus, learning of association weights from different exemplars is noninteractive, and increments are constant throughout training, regardless of the performance of the system.

By contrast, learning of the association weights in ALEX is accomplished by an interactive error-correction procedure. This learning procedure is based on gradient descent on sum-squared error, as in standard back propagation models (Rumelhart, Hinton, & Williams, 1986). Although the learning principles are the same, the architecture of ALEX is quite different from that of standard back propagation models, a point that we discuss in the Appendix (Section VII).

The specific learning procedure that we use in this article is as follows. All association weights in the system are initialized at zero. When presented with item i and feedback for Category J, output node J receives a teaching signal of $t_j = 1$, and all other output nodes receive teaching signals of zero. (The teaching signals correspond to the desired outputs that should be produced by the system.) The error at each output node K is then defined as[3]

$$\delta_K = t_K - O_K(i). \qquad (6)$$

Following feedback and computation of the error signals at the output nodes, all association weights are changed by a small amount to decrease the error. Specifically, the change in association weight from exemplar node j to Category output node K is given by

$$\Delta W_{Kj} = \lambda_W \cdot \delta_K \cdot s_{ij}, \qquad (7)$$

[3] Depending on the experimental situation, a superior learning rule may result by assigning zero error when the category outputs are more extreme than the teaching signals. Kruschke (1990, 1992) argues for the psychological plausibility of such "humble teachers" in a variety of learning situations. All modeling in the present chapter used strict rather than humble teachers, but the results do not depend on which type of teacher is used.

where $\lambda_W > 0$ is the association-weight *learning rate*. This learning rule is the same as in the network models of Gluck and Bower (1988a, 1988b), although the architecture of ALEX is quite different from that of Gluck and Bower's network models (see Kruschke, 1992, and Nosofsky, Kruschke, & McKinley, 1992, for extensive discussions).

The learning rule in ALEX is error-driven because the association weights are changed in proportion to the error produced [Eqs. (6) and (7)]. If there is no error produced at output node K, then associations between the exemplars and Category K remain unchanged. The learning rule is also interactive, because when item i is presented, it activates not only exemplar node i, but *all* exemplar nodes in the system (according to how similar item i is to each exemplar node). Thus, the error produced at output node K depends not only on the association weight from exemplar node i to output node K, but simultaneously on the degree to which all other exemplar nodes are activated *and* on the association weights between each exemplar node and the output node. This highly interactive, error-driven system provides ALEX with a learning mechanism that may model human learning more closely than the simple mechanism found in the GCM. In particular, there is good evidence that much learning in both animals and humans operates according to error-driven principles (e.g., Chapman & Robbins, 1990; Gluck & Bower, 1988a; Rescorla & Wagner, 1972; Schank, 1982; Shanks, 1991). We demonstrate advantages of ALEX's learning mechanism in Section IV.

ALEX stands for Attention/Association-Learning Exemplar Model. In addition to providing a mechanism for how associations between exemplars and categories are learned, ALEX also provides mechanisms for how the attention weights and sensitivity parameter can be learned [Eqs. (2) and (3)]. In past applications of the GCM, Nosofsky (e.g., 1984, 1989, 1991) provided evidence that subjects adjust their attention weights during the course of learning so as to nearly optimize their categorization performance. He also provided evidence of changes in sensitivity (perceptual differentiation) as a function of learning (Nosofsky, 1987). However, actual mechanisms were not specified for how the attention weights and sensitivity were updated. In ALEX, the attention weights and sensitivity can be learned by using the same error correction principles as are used for learning the association weights. The error produced at the output nodes is back-propagated through the network in a manner analogous to that described by Rumelhart et al. (1986). The precise learning rules for updating the attention weights and the sensitivity parameter are derived and presented by Kruschke (1990, 1992). Depending on the application, we will sometimes take advantage of these other learning mechanisms.

III. Quantitative Tests of ALEX

In this section we illustrate applications in which ALEX is used to predict quantitative details of classification performance in a variety of experimental settings. Although the GCM has already fared well in these domains, it is important to demonstrate that modifying the GCM by incorporating interactive, error-driven learning will not adversely affect its previous successes. This section also serves to introduce the range of phenomena to which ALEX is applicable.

A. Relations between Identification and Categorization Performance

A central theme of research that has been motivated by the testing of the exemplar-based GCM is to account for relations between identification and categorization performance. By identification, we mean a choice experiment in which each object is assigned a unique response; whereas in categorization, objects are grouped into classes. A reasonable idea is that when subjects learn to identify stimuli, unique representations of the objects are stored in memory. Furthermore, the extent to which individual objects are confused during identification depends on similarities among the objects. If category learning also involves the storage of individual object or exemplar information, then there ought to be systematic relations between performance in identification and categorization tasks involving the same sets of exemplars.

In one experiment for testing these ideas, Nosofsky (1987) followed up on some classic studies conducted by Shepard (1958b) and Shepard and Chang (1963) by having subjects learn to either identify or categorize a set of 12 Munsell colors. As shown in Fig. 3, according to the Munsell system the colors were of a constant red hue but varied in their saturation and brightness. In the identification condition, subjects were required to learn a unique response label for each color (the numbers 1–12, randomly assigned for each subject). On each trial, a color was presented, the subject attempted to identify it, and corrective feedback was provided. There were three blocks of learning trials, with each color presented nine times per block. During the early trials the subjects were merely guessing because they needed to learn the stimulus–response assignments. By the end of the training sequence, identification performance was extremely accurate. Importantly, throughout the training sequence, colors that were similar to one another (e.g., Colors 2 and 4 in Fig. 3) were confused more often than those that were dissimilar (e.g., Colors 1 and 12 in Fig. 3). The

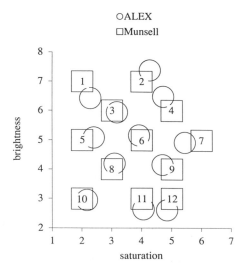

Fig. 3. Saturation–brightness coordinates for the 12 Munsell colors used in Nosofsky's (1987) identification and categorization learning studies. Squares denote the Munsell coordinates for the colors, and circles denote the psychological coordinates for the colors that were derived by fitting ALEX to the identification learning data. (For reasons discussed by Nosofsky, 1987, the Munsell saturation values are scaled by a factor of $\frac{1}{2}$.)

learning data were summarized in three 12×12 identification confusion matrices, one matrix for each block (Nosofsky, 1987, Table 1). Each cell (i,j) of a matrix gave the frequency with which color i was identified as color j during that block.

Can ALEX characterize in quantitative fashion the course of identification learning for these 12 Munsell colors? To apply the model, we built a network with 2 input nodes, one coding the psychological value of saturation and the other the value of brightness; 12 exemplar nodes corresponding to the 12 Munsell colors presented during training; and 12 category output nodes corresponding to the 12 unique identification responses. Following Shepard (1987), we assumed a Euclidean metric for modeling distances among these integral dimension stimuli, and an exponential decay function for transforming these distances to similarities. We then conducted a computer search to find the parameter values that maximized the likelihood of the data with respect to the model. Note that the model is being used to predict simultaneously the frequency with which each color was confused with every other color in each of the three learning blocks, so the data set is quite challenging.

The parameters in the model are the set of 24 (psychological) saturation–brightness coordinates for the 12 colors; 12 identification response bias parameters; separate learning rate constants for the association weights and sensitivity parameter (attentional learning was not used); and a guessing parameter that was used to model the identification responses in the very early trials of the learning sequence (cf. Nosofsky, 1987, pp. 94–96). Note that the 24 saturation–brightness coordinates constitute a psychological scaling solution for the colors. Thus we are deriving a psychological scaling solution by fitting a cognitive process model to the identification learning data (cf. Nosofsky, 1992).

Figure 4 shows the fit of ALEX to the three blocks of identification learning data. Each panel of Fig. 4 shows a scatterplot of the observed against predicted identification confusion probabilities for that block of trials. The root mean squared deviation (RMSD) between predicted and observed confusion probabilities was .0212, .0125, and .0138 in Blocks 1, 2, and 3 respectively. Clearly, the model does an impressive job of characterizing the course of identification learning.

The psychological scaling solution for the colors that was derived by fitting ALEX to these data is shown with the Munsell solution in Fig. 3. (The scaling solution was rotated so as to bring it into maximal correspondence with the Munsell solution.) As can be seen in the figure, the derived solution is quite similar to the Munsell solution.

The critical question now is whether in addition to predicting these identification learning data, ALEX can also predict category learning involving this same set of stimuli. As will be seen, because the psychological scaling solution for the exemplars has already been derived, ALEX can be applied to predict category learning by estimating only a few free parameters.

Using the same set of 12 Munsell colors, Nosofsky (1987) tested the six category structures illustrated in Fig. 5. In each structure, colors enclosed by circles denote exemplars of Category 1, colors enclosed by triangles

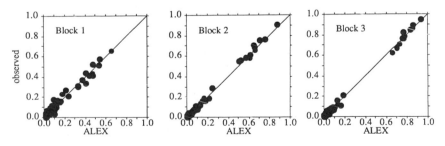

Fig. 4. Observed confusion probabilities plotted against predicted confusion probabilities (ALEX) for each of the three blocks of identification learning in Nosofsky's (1987) experiment.

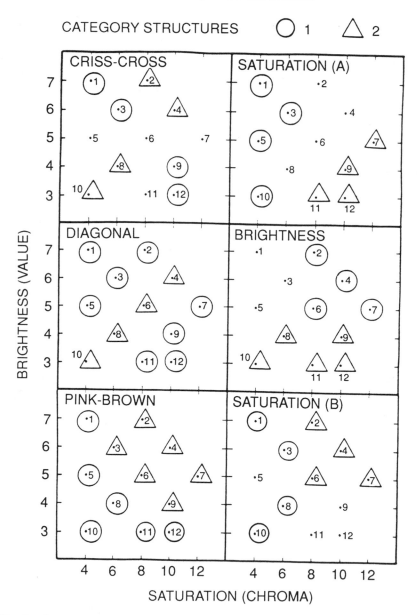

Fig. 5.   Structures tested in Nosofsky's (1987) color categorization learning experiment. (Circles = Category 1 stimuli. Triangles = Category 2 stimuli. Stimuli not enclosed by a circle or triangle were unassigned transfer stimuli.)

denote exemplars of Category 2, and unenclosed colors denote unassigned transfer stimuli. As in the identification condition, on each trial a color was presented, subjects attempted to categorize it, and corrective feedback was then provided. (Feedback was simply withheld on those trials in which unassigned transfer stimuli were presented.) Nosofsky (1987, Table 4) reported the category learning data from the second block of training in terms of the probability with which each color was classified into Category 1, and it is these data that we now attempt to fit.

To apply ALEX, the architecture of the network is the same as described previously, except instead of having 12 output nodes corresponding to the 12 identification response, there are now 2 output nodes corresponding to the 2 categories. The learning rate parameters for adjusting the association weights and overall sensitivity were held fixed at those values that best fit the identification learning data. Fitting the model to each category learning problem required searching for three free parameters: an overall starting sensitivity value c, an attention weight α_1 for Dimension 1 (with $\alpha_2 = 1 - \alpha_1$), and a Category 1 response bias parameter b_1 (with $b_2 = 1 - b_1$).

The fit of ALEX to the category learning data is shown graphically in Fig. 6, where we plot the observed Category 1 response probabilities for each color in each condition against the predicted probabilities. For all six

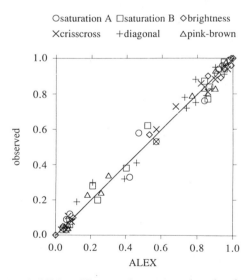

Fig. 6. Observed probabilities of Category 1 responses plotted against predicted probabilities (ALEX) for each of the 12 colors in each of the 6 conditions in Nosofsky's (1987) category learning experiment.

problems, ALEX characterizes the category learning data quite well (average RMSD = .0422), and we were unable to detect any systematic discrepancies.

Note that in three of the conditions (saturation A, saturation B, brightness) the categories have essentially unidimensional structures. For these structures, the attention weight parameter was critical in allowing ALEX to predict the data, particularly patterns of generalization for some of the transfer stimuli (e.g., see Fig. 1B). Note also that two of the category structures (diagonal and crisscross) are non–linearly separable. By non–linearly separable, we mean that the objects cannot be partitioned into the two categories by drawing a straight line through the stimulus space. ALEX predicts learning performance on both linearly separable and non–linearly separable categories in the same manner. Simple prototype models and independent feature frequency models are unable, of course, to predict accurate performance on nonlinearly separable categories (e.g., see Reed, 1972).

B. Prototype Effects

A classic phenomenon is that category prototypes, even if not presented during training, are often classified as well or better than the old exemplars and are classified far better than other new patterns (e.g., Posner & Keele, 1968, 1970; Reed, 1972). ALEX predicts such effects because the prototypes are often quite similar to many of the training exemplars. Thus they strongly activate numerous exemplar nodes that are associated to the correct category.

A simple illustration comes from an experiment by Nosofsky (1991, Experiment 1A) in which subjects learned to classify a set of schematic faces varying along the dimensions of eye height, eye separation, nose length, and mouth height (a replication and extension of an earlier study conducted by Reed, 1972). There were five training faces for each of two categories, and subjects cycled through 12 blocks of learning. Following the training phase there was a transfer phase in which the 10 old faces plus 24 new faces were presented. Among these new faces were the prototypes of the two categories, defined as those faces with dimension values that were the category averages.

A separate group of subjects provided similarity judgments for all pairs of faces in the set. A traditional nonmetric multidimensional scaling (MDS) procedure was then used to derive a psychological scaling solution for the faces. A four-dimensional solution, with psychological dimensions that corresponded closely to the four physically manipulated dimensions, provided an excellent account of these similarity judgments. (For details of the scaling, see Nosofsky, 1991, pp. 5–6.)

We used ALEX to predict the category learning data by building a network with 4 input nodes, with each node coding one of the psychological dimensions; 10 exemplar nodes corresponding to the 10 training faces; and 2 category output nodes. The coordinates of the various input stimuli and the locations of the exemplar nodes were given by the derived MDS solution for the faces. We used a Euclidean distance metric and an exponential decay similarity function for computing similarities between the input stimuli and the exemplar nodes. The free parameters in the model were separate learning rates for the association weights and sensitivity; an initial sensitivity value; three freely varying dimensional attention weights; and a category response bias parameter.

Figure 7 plots the observed against predicted Category 1 response probabilities for each of the 34 transfer faces. (The data are from a subset of subjects that Nosofsky, 1991, referred to as "learners," namely those subjects who performed well during the initial learning phase.) As is evident from inspection, ALEX provides an excellent account of the categorization transfer data (RMSD = .0370). Note in particular that the exemplar-based network predicts the excellent performance observed for the two category prototypes, labeled P1 and P2 in Fig. 7.

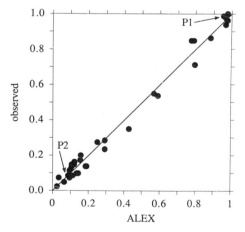

Fig. 7. Observed probabilities of Category 1 responses plotted against predicted probabilities (ALEX) for each of the 34 schematic faces in Nosofsky's (1991) face categorization experiment.

C. THE DOT PATTERN PROTOTYPE DISTORTION PARADIGM

A classic experimental paradigm for testing models of classification is the dot pattern prototype distortion paradigm made famous by Posner and Keele (1968, 1970), Homa (1984), and others. In this paradigm, the experimenter constructs random dot pattern prototypes that define each category; generates various distortions of these prototypes by using a statistical distortion algorithm; trains subjects to classify these old distortions into their appropriate categories; and then tests subjects in a transfer phase by presenting the old distortions, the prototypes, and various new distortions of the prototypes.

Quantitative modeling of performance in this paradigm poses an interesting challenge, because the underlying psychological dimensions that compose the dot patterns are not known and are probably fairly complex. Nevertheless, as illustrated by Shin and Nosofsky (in press), by deriving multidimensional scaling solutions for the dot patterns, a variety of models can be tested in quantitative fashion. In particular, here we demonstrate that ALEX does a good job of predicting classification performance in the dot pattern prototype distortion paradigm.

We apply ALEX to predict the classification data in Experiment 1 of Shin and Nosofsky (in press). In this experiment there were three categories, each composed of six old distortions. Following a training phase, there was a transfer phase in which the old distortions, the prototypes, and new distortions were presented (a total of 30 transfer patterns). By collecting similarity ratings for all pairs of these 30 stimuli, Shin and Nosofsky (in press) derived a six-dimensional scaling solution for the dot patterns.

ALEX is applied to predict the classification transfer data by defining 6 input nodes, one for each dimension of the MDS solution; 18 exemplar nodes corresponding to the locations of the old distortions in the MDS solution; and 3 output nodes, one for each category. Fitting the model required estimating only three free parameters—an association weight learning rate, a sensitivity learning rate, and an initial sensitivity value. (In the present application, the attention weights turned out not to be critical for predicting the data.) The results are shown in Fig. 8, where we plot the observed against predicted probabilities that each of the 30 patterns was classified into each of the 3 categories. Given that we are predicting 90 classification probabilities with only 3 free parameters, and given that the dot pattern stimuli are relatively complex, we consider these results to be quite good. The RMSD between predicted and observed classification probabilities was .0632. By comparison, Shin and Nosofsky (in press) found that a prototype model with eight free parameters yielded an RMSD of .1323.

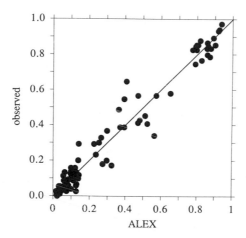

Fig. 8. Observed probability with which each dot pattern was classified in each category plotted against the predicted categorization probabilities (ALEX). The data are from Shin and Nosofsky's (in press, Experiment 1) dot pattern classification study.

D. CATEGORY SIZE, ITEM FREQUENCY, AND OLD–NEW SIMILARITY

A variety of fundamental variables are known to have effects on classification performance in the dot pattern paradigm. Category size is defined as the number of unique old distortions defining a category. In general, as category size increases, ability to correctly classify patterns improves, especially for the prototypes and new distortions. Effects of individual item frequency are also well documented. In general, as one increases the frequency with which a training exemplar is presented, classification accuracy for that item improves. In addition, objects that are similar to the high frequency item also tend to be classified in that item's category, whereas objects that are dissimilar to the high frequency item are not much affected.

ALEX predicts category size effects for several reasons. In general, as category size increases, there is an increased likelihood that a given new distortion will be highly similar to one of the old distortions from its own category (cf. Hintzman, 1986). Also, assuming a fixed number of training blocks (with each category member presented once per block), stronger association weights will be built up as category size increases. The reason is that old distortions presented during training will tend to activate the hidden nodes corresponding to other old distortions from the same category; thus, the greater the number of old distortions, the more association weight learning that will take place.

ALEX predicts effects of individual item frequency because the more frequently an item is presented, the stronger will be the association weight between that item's hidden node and the category output node. In addition, because objects that are similar to the high frequency item will activate its hidden node, they too will be influenced by the strong association weight.[4]

These points are illustrated in Experiment 3 of Shin and Nosofsky (in press), who partially replicated and extended an earlier study conducted by Homa, Dunbar, and Nohre (1991). In one condition, each of two categories was defined by 3 old distortions, whereas in a second condition each category was defined by 10 old distortions. Within each category size condition, there were an equal frequency and an unequal frequency condition. In the equal frequency condition, all exemplars were presented with the same frequency, whereas in the unequal frequency condition, a single exemplar from each category was presented five times as often as the other training exemplars. We refer to these high frequency items as HF–Olds. Transfer items were constructed that had specific old–new similarity relations to these HF–Olds. Within each category, there was one related–new–1 (RN1) pattern, one related–new–4 (RN4) pattern, and two unrelated–new (URN) patterns. RN1 was highly similar to the high frequency item, RN4 was slightly less similar, and the URNs were relatively dissimilar to this item.

The main results are shown in Fig. 9 (top panels). There was a large category size effect: The prototypes and URNs were classified much more accurately in the Size-10 condition than in the Size-3 condition. There was also a large effect of individual item frequency: The HF–Olds were classified much more accurately in the unequal frequency conditions than in the equal frequency conditions. This frequency effect also extended to the related new patterns (RN1 and RN4). There was little if any effect of the frequency manipulation on the remaining patterns, which were not highly similar to the HF–Olds (i.e., the prototypes, other old exemplars, and URNs).

We fit ALEX to the complete matrix of classification transfer data obtained in each of the four main conditions (Size-3 equal frequency, Size-3 unequal frequency, Size-10 equal frequency, and Size-10 unequal

---

[4] Our arguments about the importance of category size and individual item frequency in influencing the strength of the association weights do not hold if learning is continued to an errorless criterion. The association weights will no longer be updated once there is errorless performance. This may help explain why after extensive training, individual item frequency may play less of a role than early in training (e.g., Homa, Dunbar, & Nohre, 1991).

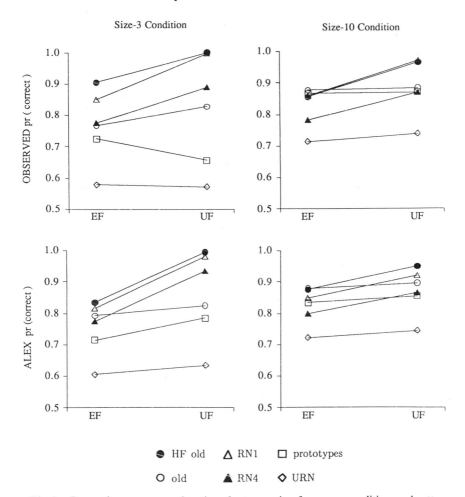

Fig. 9. Proportion correct as a function of category size, frequency condition, and pattern type in Shin and Nosofsky's (in press) Experiment 3. (Top panels = observed proportions. Bottom panels = predicted proportions from ALEX.)

frequency). The average RMSD across the four conditions was .0418. The summary results are shown in the bottom panels of Fig. 9. As can be seen, ALEX predicts all the main qualitative effects, and does a fairly good job of quantitatively predicting the data.

E. OLD–NEW RECOGNITION MEMORY

To gain converging evidence about the nature of category representations, researchers often collect old–new recognition judgments following the completion of a category learning phase. The exemplar-based GCM has been applied successfully to model old–new recognition memory data collected in classification learning situations (e.g., Nosofsky, 1988a, 1991; Nosofsky, Clark, & Shin, 1989; Shin & Nosofsky, in press). The key assumption is that recognition judgments are based on the absolute summed similarity of an item to all the exemplars stored in memory. This summed similarity gives a measure of overall "familiarity," with higher familiarity values leading to higher recognition probabilities.

ALEX can be used to model old–new recognition judgments by incorporating a decision rule that is analogous to the summed similarity rule in the GCM. The familiarity for item i (F_i) is given by the summed output of all the category output nodes:

$$F_i = \sum_K O_k(i), \tag{8}$$

where the category outputs are computed as before. Note in general that items that are similar to numerous of the old exemplars would tend to produce large summed outputs, so would be recognized as old.

We illustrate an application of ALEX by fitting it to some old–new recognition data collected by Nosofsky (1991). The data are from the same face classification study that we discussed earlier in this section. Following the classification learning phase, Nosofsky collected old–new recognition judgments for all 34 faces in the set (10 trained and 24 novel faces). To use ALEX to predict these recognition judgments, the network was trained on the 10 old exemplars in the same manner as described previously. The probability of making an "old" recognition judgment at time of transfer was then given by:

$$P(\text{old}|i) = F_i^p/[F_i^p + k], \tag{9}$$

where p is a parameter for scaling the familiarities, and k reflects a criterion for making old versus new judgments. Figure 10 shows a scatterplot of the observed against predicted recognition probabilities. ALEX predicts these recognition data very well (RMSD = .0449).

F. SUMMARY

In summary, in this section we provided an overview of ALEX's ability to quantitatively predict classification performance in a variety of experimental paradigms, with stimuli that included colors, schematic faces, and complex dot patterns generated from prototypes. ALEX was able to ac-

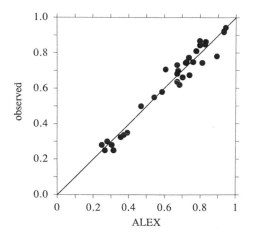

Fig. 10.   Observed probability with which each face was recognized as "old" plotted against predicted probabilities (ALEX) for Nosofsky's (1991, Experiment 1) face recognition study.

count for relations between categorization and identification performance, to predict performance involving both linearly separable and non–linearly separable structures, and to predict prototype effects and effects of specific exemplars. It also accounted for effects of category size, individual item frequency, and old–new similarity relations, and gave a good account of old–new recognition performance.

IV.   Association Weight Learning in ALEX

In Section III we demonstrated successful quantitative applications of ALEX to a variety of categorization phenomena and related cognitive processes. In all cases, however, the GCM has successfully modeled these same phenomena. In the present section, we illustrate advantages that ALEX has over the GCM due its use of an interactive, error-driven learning rule for adjusting the association weights.

A.   BASE RATE NEGLECT

Gluck and Bower (1988a) demonstrated an important base rate neglect phenomenon in a probabilistic classification paradigm. Because their study is very well known and their results have been discussed, modeled, replicated, or extended in numerous recent papers (e.g., Anderson, 1990; Estes, Campbell, Hatsopoulos, & Hurwitz, 1989; Kruschke, 1992; Nosofsky et al., 1992; Shanks, 1990), we only briefly summarize it here. Subjects learned to classify objects varying along four binary-valued dimensions into two probabilistically defined categories. A common category occurred with prior probability .75, and a rare category with prior probability .25. Category feature probabilities and category base rates were defined such that the probability of each category given the presence of a particular target feature was .50. The critical empirical result was that when subjects were tested with this feature alone, without knowledge of the values of the remaining features, they tended to classify it in the rare category. It was as if subjects were not taking full account of the differential base rates of the categories when making their probability judgments.

As documented by Nosofsky et al. (1992), this result poses problems for the GCM. Because of its strictly incremental mechanism for adjusting the strength of the association weights, the GCM predicts that subjects should have been sensitive to the differential base rates and classified the target feature into the common category with probability at least .50. Nosofsky et al. (1992) demonstrated further that a simple response bias explanation of the results was not tenable.

As demonstrated by Kruschke (1992) and Nosofsky et al. (1992), however, ALEX is able to predict this base rate neglect phenomenon by virtue of its error-driven learning and similarity-activated exemplar representation. Consider, for sake of exposition, the two-dimensional example illustrated in Fig. 11, where a and a^* represent the two alternative features

rare / common
(total)

	a	a*	
b	10 / 1 (11)	5 / 14 (19)	15 / 15 (30)
b*	5 / 14 (19)	5 / 50 (55)	10 / 64 (74)
	15 / 15 (30)	10 / 64 (74)	

Fig. 11. Structure for illustrating ALEX's ability to predict base rate neglect phenomena in category learning. Each cell shows the frequency with which the corresponding stimulus is in each category: rare freq./common freq. (total freq.) The marginal frequencies of individual features are also shown.

on Dimension 1, and *b* and *b** represent the two alternative features on Dimension 2. Figure 11 shows the frequency of each stimulus as a member of the rare or common category. Note that the marginal probability of the rare category given feature *a* is 15/30, or .50, so a Bayesian classifier would not favor either the rare or common category given *a* alone.

Figure 11 can be viewed as a geometric analogue of a two-dimensional stimulus space. According to ALEX, there would be four exemplar nodes representing each of the locations (cells) of the figure. Consider the two neighboring cells in the lower row, *ab** and *a*b**. Both are more likely given the common category (14 of 19 cases and 50 of 55 cases respectively). Feature pair *a*b** is the more frequent pair of the two (55 cases vs. 19), so the exemplar node centered on it will develop a strong positive connection to the common category node (and a negative connection to the rare category node). When the neighboring feature pair *ab** occurs, the exemplar node over *a*b** is partially activated, in turn activating the common category node. As a result, relatively little error is produced, and the connection from the *ab** node becomes only weakly weighted to the common category node. On the other hand, the node centered on the top left cell, *ab,* must develop a moderately strong positive weight to the rare category node, forced to be even stronger by the presence of conflicting neighbors *ab** and *a*b*.

When the single feature *a* is input to ALEX, the exemplar nodes centered over the left column, *ab* and *ab**, are maximally activated, and the nodes centered over the right column are only partially activated. Because the connection weights from *ab* strongly favor the rare category, and the connection weights from *ab** only weakly favor the common category, the result is that the rare category node is more strongly activated than the common category node, and ALEX appears to exhibit base rate neglect.

In summary, it is the dual effect of error-driven learning and similarity-based exemplar node activations that lets ALEX exhibit base rate neglect. If the learning rule were not error driven, as in the GCM, or if similar exemplar nodes were not co-activated, as could happen in ALEX with extremely high sensitivity values [*c* in Eq. (3)], then exemplars would have no influence on each other's learning, and base rates would not be neglected.

Our discussion of Gluck and Bower's (1988a) base rate neglect phenomenon has been qualitative in nature, but it is important to remember that ALEX has achieved quantitative accuracy in its predictions of probabilistic classification learning and transfer. For example, in the Nosofsky et al. (1992) study, the design of the probabilistic category structures was the same as the one used by Gluck and Bower (1988a), except all subjects experienced the same sequence of training exemplars (cf. Estes et al.,

1989). This experimental method allowed ALEX to be fit to the classification learning data on a trial-by-trial basis. The results, reported as
averages over 10-trial blocks, are shown in Fig. 12. ALEX does a fine job
of quantitatively predicting the sequence of probabilistic classification
learning data. Following the learning phase, Nosofsky et al. (1992) tested
subjects in a transfer phase in which not only the single features were
presented (as in Gluck and Bower, 1988a), but also all pairs, triples, and
quadruples of features, plus the null pattern (a total of 81 patterns in all). In
addition to accounting for the base rate neglect phenomenon observed for
the single feature tests, ALEX accounted for 94.9% of the variance in this
large set of transfer data (see Nosofsky et al., 1992, for details of the
theoretical analysis.

B. EARLY VERSUS LATE SHIFTS DURING CATEGORY LEARNING

Consider a category learning paradigm in which, at some point during the
learning sequence, the prevailing assignments of exemplars to categories
are changed. For example, items that were initially assigned to Category *A*
might be switched to Category *B*. Because of the purely incremental nature
of its learning rule, the GCM makes the prediction that the greater the
amount of initial training on the exemplars, the longer it should take to
learn the new category assignments. According to the learning rule in the
GCM, association strengths between exemplars and categories should

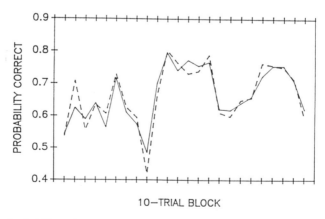

Fig. 12. Probability of correct classifications as a function of 10-trial blocks in the
probabilistic classification learning experiment conducted by Nosofsky et al. (1992, Experiment 1, Categorization Group). (Solid curve = observed probabilities. Dashed curve = predicted probabilities from ALEX.)

keep building without limit as learning progresses. Thus, the greater the amount of initial training, the more work that is needed to undo the original associations.

Estes (1989) provides a brief report of an experiment in which the above prediction was tested. Subjects learned to assign artificial words to three grammatical categories (call them A, B, and C). There was a 240-trial learning sequence. Assignments for Category A were held constant throughout the sequence. For an early shift group, assignments for Categories B and C were switched after trial 60. That is, all exemplars that would have been assigned to Category B before the switch were now assigned to Category C, and vice versa. For a late shift group, the same switch occurred after trial 180.

The critical result observed by Estes (1989) was that the learning curves following the shift were extremely similar for the early and late shift groups. There was no evidence that it took the late shift group any longer than the early shift group to relearn the category assignments, in direct contrast to the predictions of the GCM.

Because of its error-driven learning rule, ALEX is not forced into the same prediction as the GCM. In ALEX, the association weights between exemplars and categories will not continue to grow without limit as training progresses. Once a point is reached at which there is relatively little error, further changes in the association weights will be negligible. Thus, if there is a shift in category assignments during the learning sequence, new associations can be learned just as rapidly if this shift occurs late or early.

To verify these arguments, we conducted simulations of ALEX under conditions similar to those described in the Estes (1989) experiment. To create a stimulus set, three random prototype vectors were chosen to define each of three categories (A, B, and C), and eight random distortions of each prototype vector were then constructed to serve as training instances. There were 10 blocks of learning trials, with each of the 24 training instances presented once in a random order in each block. Assignments for Category A were constant throughout, but assignments were switched for Categories B and C during the sequence. In an early shift set of simulations, the switch occurred following the third block of training, whereas in a late shift set of simulations, the switch occurred following the sixth block of training. All parameters were held constant across the two sets of simulations.

The results of these simulations of ALEX are shown in the left panel of Fig. 13. For both the early shift and late shift simulations, performance drops down to very low levels immediately following the shift, but relearning of the new associations then occurs rapidly and at the same rate for both groups. The right panel of Fig. 13 shows the results of analogous

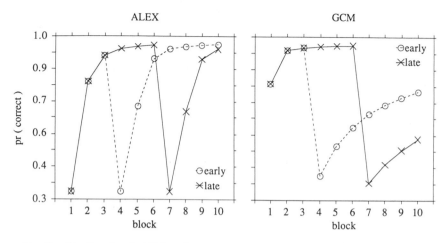

Fig. 13. Predicted probabilities of correct responses in Estes' (1989) category shift experiments. (Left panel gives the predictions from ALEX, and right panel gives the predictions from the GCM. Dashed curve with circles = early shift condition. Solid curve with X's = late shift condition.)

simulations that were conducted for the GCM. After the shift, performance stays at low levels even after substantial retraining, and relearning occurs less rapidly for the late shift group than for the early shift group.

V. Attentional Learning in ALEX

Whereas in the previous section we emphasized ALEX's mechanism for learning the association weights, in the present section we emphasize its attention weight learning mechanism. As discussed previously, differential weighting of dimensions has been a critical assumption of the GCM. However, in most applications, the attention weights have been free parameters estimated from the data. Nosofsky (1984, 1986) proposed an attention optimization hypothesis, according to which subjects will distribute attention among component dimensions so as to optimize their categorization performance. Indeed, in numerous tests of the GCM, the best-fitting attention weights are close to the theoretically optimal ones (e.g., Nosofsky, 1986, 1987, 1989, 1991). However, there is no mechanism in the GCM for how these weights are learned. Such a weight-learning mechanism is provided by ALEX.

A. DIMENSIONAL RELEVANCE AND CLASSIFICATION PROBLEM SOLVING

In this section we apply ALEX to account for the classic results reported by Shepard, Hovland, and Jenkins (1961), who studied the difficulty of learning different categorization problems. A key theme of Shepard et al.'s (1961) work was to demonstrate the importance of selective attention phenomena in classification learning. Thus, their results provide an ideal testing ground for the attention-learning mechanism found in ALEX.

In the Shepard et al. (1961) study, subjects were tested on six different categorization problems. In each problem, there were eight stimuli constructed from three binary-valued dimensions. Four of the stimuli were assigned to one category, and the remaining four stimuli to a second category. Under these constraints, there are six main structural types of categories. These category types are shown in Fig. 14, with the exemplars represented as the vertices of a cube. Assignment of exemplars to each category is indicated by solid or open vertices. Each face of the cube represents a value along one of the binary-valued dimensions. For ease of description, we imagine that the dimensions correspond to shape (square vs. triangle), color (black vs. white), and size (large vs. small), as is illustrated in the bottom part of the figure. Any assignment of exemplars to

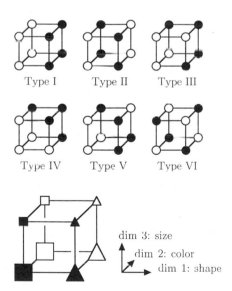

Fig. 14. The six types of category structures tested in the classification learning experiments of Shepard et al. (1961).

categories, with four exemplars in each category, can be rotated or reflected into one of the structures shown in the figure.

The simplest structure is Type I, because only information about Dimension 1 (shape) is relevant to solving the problem. For Type II, exactly two dimensions are relevant: black triangles and white squares are assigned to one category, the reverse for the other category. (The size dimension is irrelevant.) Note that the Type II problem is the exclusive-or problem in its two relevant dimensions. The Type VI problem is the most complex category structure, with all three dimensions being equally relevant. Finally, Types III–V are intermediate in complexity between Type II and Type VI. All three dimensions are relevant, but to differing extents. These types can be characterized as rule-plus-exception structures. For example, for Type V, the rule is that triangles are assigned to one category and squares to the other, except the small white triangle is switched with the small white square.

Shepard et al. (1961) measured the difficulty of learning these categorization problems in terms of the number of errors that subjects made until they reached a criterion. Shepard et al. found that Type I was the easiest to learn, followed by Type II, followed by Types III, IV, and V, which were about equal in difficulty, and finally Type VI. To the extent that difficulty of learning a categorization problem is determined by how many dimensions must be attended, these results seem very sensible. Importantly, Shepard et al. demonstrated that the ordering of difficulty could not be predicted by a pure stimulus generalization hypothesis. In modern-day language, this means that exemplar-based category-learning models that do not incorporate some form of selective attention cannot predict these results (cf. Nosofsky, 1984).

Kruschke (1992) demonstrated that ALEX, which is an exemplar-based model that does incorporate selective attention, correctly predicts the ordering of difficulty for the category-learning problems tested by Shepard et al. In his simulations there were three input nodes coding the three binary-valued dimensions, eight exemplar nodes, and two category output nodes. As in the illustration in Fig. 14, the coordinates of the exemplar nodes were the vertices of a (unit) three-dimensional cube. A city block metric was used for computing distance, and an exponential decay function was used to transform the distances to similarities. The initial distribution of attention weights was uniform.

The results of simulations of ALEX that incorporated the attention-learning process are shown in the top panel of Fig. 15, and the results without attentional learning are shown in the bottom panel. With attention learning, ALEX predicts perfectly the ordering of difficulty for the six problem types. Without attention learning, the model predicts incorrectly

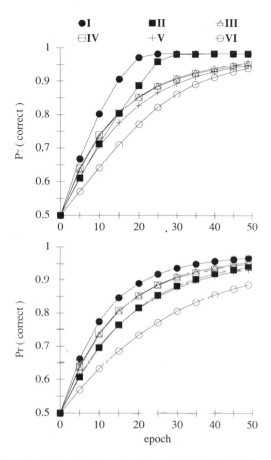

Fig. 15. Results of applying ALEX to the Shepard et al. (1961) category types. Top panel shows the predictions with moderate attention learning, and bottom panel shows the predictions with zero attention learning. With moderate attention learning, ALEX predicts perfectly the ordering of difficulty for the six types. Without attention learning, ALEX predicts incorrectly that Type II will be learned as slowly as Type V.

that the Type II structure will be more difficult to learn than Types III–V. These results corroborate Shepard et al.'s arguments about the importance of attention learning in determining the difficulty of solving these problems.

By the end of learning, the dimensional attention weights in ALEX were redistributed as expected. For the Type I problem, the attention weight given to Dimension 1 was increased, and the attention weight given to the irrelevant Dimensions 2 and 3 dropped nearly to zero. For Type II, attention to the two relevant dimensions increased, and attention to the third dimension dropped nearly to zero. For the remaining problem types, all three dimensions retained large attention weights.

In a previous theoretical analysis of Shepard et al.'s results, Nosofsky (1984) showed that the GCM could predict the ordering of difficulty for the problems, as long as it was assumed that subjects came to distribute their attention weights among the component dimensions so as to optimize their categorization performance. The present analysis goes beyond Nosofsky's demonstrations by providing a mechanism that *learns* a set of weights that, in general, will be close to the performance-optimizing ones.

B. LEARNING TO ATTEND TO CORRELATED DIMENSIONS

Medin, Altom, Edelson, and Freko (1982) demonstrated subjects' sensitivity to correlated dimensions in learning artifical categories. The category structure that they used is shown in Table I. A critical aspect of the structure is that the values on Dimensions 3 and 4 are perfectly correlated in the training set, such that their combination serves as a perfect predictor of category membership. However, the values on Dimensions 3 and 4 are not individually diagnostic, each being associated with the alternative categories 50% of the time. By contrast, the values on Dimensions 1 and 2 are individually diagnostic. For both Dimensions 1 and 2, the probability of Category A given value 1 is .75, and the probability of Category B given value 2 is .75.

Thus, the Medin et al. (1982) structure pits individual dimension diagnosticity against correlated dimensions diagnosticity. To the extent that subjects attend to Dimensions 3 and 4 in making their categorization decisions, then when tested with novel patterns they should tend to choose Category A when the values on Dimensions 3 and 4 agree, and choose Category B when these values disagree. On the other hand, if subjects attend primarily to Dimensions 1 and 2, then they should choose Category A more often when these dimensions have value 1.

In the Medin et al. experiment, subjects freely inspected the eight training exemplars during a 10 min period to learn their category assignments. Following this inspection period, they classified both the training exemplars and the transfer patterns. The classification data suggested that subjects were quite sensitive to the correlations, because novel patterns that preserved the correlation (i.e., for which the values on Dimensions 3 and 4 agreed) were classified primarily in Category A, and novel patterns that broke the correlation were classified primarily in Category B. Some sensitivity to the individual dimension diagnosticities was also evident, however, because patterns N3 and N4 were classified in Category A more

TABLE I

CATEGORY A TRANSFER PROBABILILITIES FOR EACH STIMULUS IN
MEDIN ET AL.'S (1982) EXPERIMENT AND IN BLOCKS 1 AND 6 OF
MCKINLEY AND NOSOFSKY'S (IN PREPARATION) EXPERIMENT

Stimulus	Coding	Medin et al. (1982)	McKinley & Nosofsky (in preparation)	
			Block 1	Block 6
Category A				
A1	1111	.88	.64	.96
A2	2111	.89	.64	.93
A3	1122	.73	.66	1.00
A4	1222	.77	.55	.96
Category B				
B1	1212	.12	.57	.02
B2	2212	.17	.43	.00
B3	2121	.25	.46	.05
B4	2221	.33	.34	.00
New				
N1	2222	.53	.46	.66
N2	2211	.53	.41	.64
N3	2122	.75	.52	.64
N4	1211	.67	.50	.66
N5	1112	.45	.73	.36
N6	1121	.38	.59	.36
N7	2112	.36	.39	.27
N8	1221	.28	.46	.30

often than patterns N1 and N2, and patterns N5 and N6 were classified in
Category A more often than patterns N7 and N8 (see Table I).

McKinley and Nosofsky (in preparation) extended the Medin et al.
(1982) experiment by presenting the training exemplars in a fixed sequence
to all subjects. There were 12 blocks of training trials, with each exemplar
presented twice in each block. After every two training blocks, transfer
tests were given in which subjects classified the novel patterns as well as
the training exemplars. No feedback was provided during the transfer
blocks. McKinley and Nosofsky's (in preparation) goal was to use ALEX
to predict the evolution of transfer performance over blocks.[5]

ALEX predicts that subjects should increase their attention to the correlated dimensions during the course of learning. If the original distribution

---

[5] Kruschke (1992) demonstrated that ALEX could predict the original Medin et al. (1982)
transfer data but did not study the model's ability to characterize changing patterns of
generalization as a function of learning.

of attention is uniform, and attention is redistributed toward the correlated dimensions as learning progresses, then different patterns of generalization should be observed early and late in transfer. McKinley and Nosofsky's (in preparation) observed classification data for the first transfer block and the final transfer block are shown in Table I, and they conform to the above-stated prediction. By the final transfer block, patterns N1–N4 tend to be classified in Category A, and patterns N5–N8 in Category B, providing evidence of attention to the correlated dimensions. But in the first transfer block, the overall tendency is for patterns N5 and N6 to be classified in Category A, and patterns N1 and N2 in Category B, indicating a strong influence of the individual dimension diagnosticities.

McKinley and Nosofsky (in preparation) used ALEX to predict the probability that each item was classified in Category A or B during each of the six transfer blocks. The free parameters in the model were an association weight learning rate, an attention weight learning rate, an overall sensitivity value, and a background noise constant (cf. Nosofsky et al., 1992). This 4-parameter model was used to predict the 96 classification probabilities (16 stimuli × 6 blocks) observed during the evolution of transfer. The model accounted for 95.3% of the variance across the six blocks of classification transfer. It also predicted accurately the changing patterns of generalization (described above) that were observed as a function of learning. Not surprisingly, by the end of learning, the attention weights in ALEX were redistributed such that there was increased attention to the correlated dimensions and decreased attention to the individually diagnostic dimensions. This analysis provides support for the dynamic attention-learning mechanism found in ALEX.

C. FILTRATION VERSUS CONDENSATION TASKS

Another categorization phenomenon commonly attributed to selective attention is the ease of filtration relative to condensation. The term *filtration* applies to categorization tasks in which some stimulus dimensions are irrelevant and can be filtered out of consideration. The term *condensation* refers to tasks in which more than one dimension is relevant, and information from multiple dimensions must be condensed into a single response (Garner 1974; Posner 1964). It is well established that filtration is easier than condensation (e.g., Garner 1974; Gottwald & Garner, 1975; Posner 1964). In this section we show that ALEX exhibits filtration advantage because of its attention-learning mechanism, whereas other connectionist models without attention learning do not show this advantage.

Kruschke (1991a) obtained trial-by-trial learning data from filtration and condensation tasks. The stimuli were rectangles that could have one of four heights, with an interior vertical segment that could have one of four lateral positions. Thus the stimuli had two psychological dimensions of variation, height (of rectangle) and position (of interior segment). Four different categorization conditions were tested; their structures are shown in Fig. 16. In each condition, the same eight stimuli were used; all that varied between conditions was the assignment of exemplars to categories. The top panel shows two filtration conditions: Height can be filtered away without loss of classification accuracy in the top left structure; position can be filtered away in the top right structure. The bottom panel shows two condensation conditions in which information from both dimensions is needed for accurate classification.

Separate groups of subjects were tested on each of the four categorizations. Each subject in each group saw the same sequence of stimuli; all that varied between groups was the feedback (category assignments). Results are shown in Fig. 17, top panel. As expected, the filtration tasks were much easier to learn than the condensation tasks.

To fit ALEX to these data, the stimuli must first be described in terms of their psychological coordinates. By collecting similarity judgments, Kruschke (1991a) derived a psychological scaling solution for the stimuli. The solution was very similar to the physical structure illustrated in Fig. 16, but the middle interval on the position dimension was notably bigger than the middle interval on the height dimension.

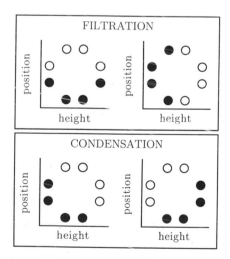

Fig. 16.   The four category structures used in Kruschke's (1991a) category learning study (Experiment 2). Horizontal axes correspond to rectangle height and vertical axes correspond to position of the interior segment. Top two structures show filtration tasks; bottom two show condensation tasks.

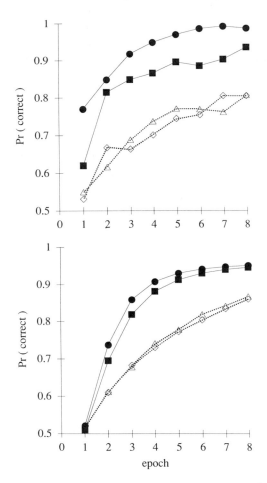

Fig. 17.   Top panel shows the learning data from Kruschke's (1991a) filtration and condensation learning conditions. Each datum indicates the mean percent correct for the preceding 8
trials (one "epoch"). Filled circles = filtration, position relevant. Filled squares = filtration,
height relevant. Open triangles = condensation, category boundary along the left diagonal in
Fig. 16. Open diamonds = condensation, right diagonal boundary in Fig. 16. Bottom panel
shows the best fit of ALEX to the learning data.

ALEX was fitted to the learning data of the four groups simultaneously,
so that the same set of parameter values had to predict performance in all
four groups. The best fit is shown in Fig. 17, bottom panel. ALEX shows
pronounced filtration advantage. The reason is that in the filtration task,
attention to the irrelevant dimension rapidly decreases, and attention to
the relevant dimension increases, but in the condensation task, differential

attention to dimensions is of no benefit. The top panel of Fig. 18 shows how attention shifts in ALEX can benefit learning in the filtration condition. Increasing attention to the horizontal dimension makes the two categories more discriminable, and decreasing attention to the vertical dimension makes exemplars within categories psychologically more similar. The lower panel indicates that the analogous benefits cannot occur in the condensation condition. ALEX can shift attention along only the psychological stimulus dimensions and cannot shift attention along "diagonal" dimensions.

ALEX also predicts correctly that the position-relevant filtration is learned more easily than the height-relevant filtration. ALEX makes this prediction because its hidden nodes encode the psychological coordinates of the exemplars and thereby reflect the larger middle interval on the position dimension relative to the height dimension.

Kruschke (1991a) also fit the learning data with two other connectionist models, standard back propagation and the configural cue model of Gluck and Bower (1988b), and found that these models made essentially no distinction among the four category conditions. In the case of backprop, the reason is that linear logistic hidden nodes are insensitive to the orientation of category boundaries in stimulus space (see the Appendix), because they pay no special attention to the dimensions on which the input is encoded. Hidden nodes in backprop treat the input space isotropically. In

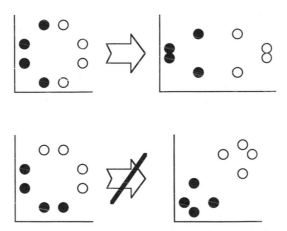

Fig. 18. Top panel shows that increasing attention to the horizontal dimension and decreasing attention to the vertical dimension causes exemplars of the two categories (denoted by filled and open circles) to have greater between-category dissimilarity and greater within-category similarity. Bottom panel shows that ALEX cannot differentially attend to diagonal axes.

the case of the configural cue model, the stimuli are encoded in such a way that there is no information about which values come from same or different dimensions, so that dimensional information is largely lost from the representation. Of course, if dimensional information is absent, it cannot be differentially attended. (See Kruschke, 1991a, for more details and discussion of extended versions of these models.)

The main point of this discussion of filtration versus condensation is similar to the point made previously in the discussion of the six category types of Shepard et al. (1961). Indeed, inspection of Fig. 14 reveals that Type I is a filtration task, whereas Type IV is a (linearly separable) condensation task. As we discussed earlier, the learning data from Shepard et al.'s research indicated that Type IV was much more difficult than Type I, as would be predicted by consideration of filtration versus condensation alone. However, an advantage of Type I over Type IV can also be predicted on the basis of overall similarity alone, without any dimensional attention learning. (That is, exemplar similarity models without attention also predict the Type I advantage.) The stimulus configuration used by Kruschke (1991a) actually gives the overall similarity advantage to the condensation tasks.

VI.   Limitations, Extensions, and Evaluations

In this final section, we briefly discuss a variety of limitations of ALEX that will require further research, discuss ways in which the model might be extended, and summarize and evaluate our applications of the model.

A.   THE INVERSE BASE RATE EFFECT

In its current form, ALEX fails to explain the inverse base rate effect reported by Medin and Edelson (1988). The essential features of Medin and Edelson's experimental design were as follows. Subjects were trained that a pair of symptoms ab predicted Disease 1 and a second pair of symptoms ac predicted Disease 2. During training, the ab pair occurred three times as often as the ac pair. In a transfer phase, Medin and Edelson presented subjects with individual symptoms (a, b, and c), conflicting symptoms (bc), and all three symptoms combined (abc). As expected, subjects classified the individual perfect predictors (b and c) into their appropriate category and tended to classify the individual imperfect predictor (a) into the high base rate category (Disease 1). The critical result was that subjects tended to classify the *conflicting* pair (bc) into the *low* base rate category (Disease 2), yet when all three symptoms were combined (abc), they again went to the *high* base rate category.

As explained by Medin and Edelson (1988), the standard context model fails to predict the inverse base rate effect involving the conflicting pair bc. Because the ab exemplar was presented more frequently than the ac exemplar, and the conflicting pair bc is equally similar to these exemplars, the context model and ALEX predict that bc should tend to be classified in the category of exemplar ab.

To account for the surprising results, Medin and Edelson suggested that an exemplar-specific form of selective attention may have been operating during category learning. The key idea was that subjects gave greater attention to symptom c (in exemplar ac) than to symptom b (in exemplar ab), so when bc was presented, c was more influential than b.

This idea that selective attention to dimensions may be *exemplar specific* differs from the previous proposals of Medin and Schaffer (1978) and Nosofsky (1984), in which selective attention was presumed to operate globally on entire dimensions. In addition to the idea of exemplar-specific selective attention, we should also note that versions of the context model (and ALEX) can also predict Medin and Edelson's results if *exemplar-specific sensitivity* is allowed. In all tests to date, the GCM and ALEX have assumed a global sensitivity [a single value of c in Eq. (3)] that applies to all exemplars. A straightforward generalization is to allow separate sensitivity values for each exemplar (e.g., Kruschke, 1990, 1992). Indeed, because recent research suggests that high frequency exemplars may become differentiated from other objects in the set (e.g., Nosofsky, 1988b, 1991; Shiffrin, Ratcliff, & Clark, 1990), allowing for exemplar-specific sensitivity may be quite important.

The main problem with allowing exemplar-specific selective attention and exemplar-specific sensitivity is that it adds numerous free parameters to the models. A possible remedy for this problem, at least within the framework of ALEX, is to have the model *learn* the parameters, rather than estimating them post hoc. Exemplar-specific selective attention and sensitivity can be incorporated into ALEX without adding any free parameters. The idea would be to update these parameters on a trial-by-trial basis by using the same principles of back propagation as are used in the present version of the model.

B. ALL-OR-NONE LEARNING AND HYPOTHESIS-TESTING BEHAVIOR

Another limitation of ALEX is that in its present form it predicts gradual adjustment of both the association and attention weights. This gradual adjustment seems inconsistent with the variety of all-or-none learning phenomena that were observed in early studies of concept identification (e.g., Trabasso & Bower, 1968). Some evidence that ALEX may indeed predict learning performance that changes too gradually was reported by Kruschke (1991a) in his experimental studies of filtration and condensation. Although ALEX predicted correctly the much faster learning that occurred on the filtration tasks than on the condensation tasks, it severely underpredicted performance on the filtration task during the very early learning blocks. It may be that we need alternative functions for mapping activations of the category output nodes onto responses. For example, instead of using a choice rule for predicting response probabilities [Eq. (4)], noise could be introduced into the actual activation process, and a deterministic response rule could be used for making categorization choices (cf. Ashby & Gott, 1988; McClelland, 1991; Nosofsky, 1991).

The gradual adjustment of the attention weights in ALEX seems inconsistent with hypothesis-testing forms of behavior in which subjects shift attention abruptly from one dimension to another (e.g., Levine, 1975). Kruschke (1990, 1992) suggested that attentional learning in ALEX might serve to steer a higher order process of rule generation. The idea is that when people engage in hypothesis-testing behavior, they might sample rules based on those dimensions that currently have the highest attention weights. In ALEX, attention weight learning is based on gradient descent on error. Alternative mechanisms of attention weight learning might also be considered. Nosofsky and Gluck (1989) discussed a version of the GCM in which the attention weights were adjusted in accord with a hill-climbing algorithm of resource allocation proposed by Busemeyer and Myung (1987) and showed that such a model predicted accurately the ordering of difficulty of the Shepard et al. (1961) classification problem types. A virtue of this hill-climbing model of attention weight learning is that if the step size is large, it can predict abrupt shifts in attention to dimensions.

C. TASK-SPECIFIC CONNECTION WEIGHTS

A potential problem for numerous connectionist models is that the weights that the system learns are task specific. The weights are updated so as to minimize an error function defined with respect to the task at hand. The human learner, however, is often able to display knowledge that appears to go beyond these task-specific connection weights.

For example, in learning categories, ALEX learns those attention weights and association weights that minimize the error produced at the category output nodes. Although these weights are useful (and are often close to optimal) for purposes of categorizing, they may not be very useful if it becomes the subject's task to make old–new recognition judgments or frequency judgments for individual items. To take an extreme example, suppose that during a category learning phase all the training instances were colored various shades of blue, and that during transfer all new items were colored red. Assuming that color is an irrelevant attribute for purposes of categorizing, the network would learn to give it zero weight. But color provides a perfect cue for discriminating old versus new items, and subjects would undoubtedly give it a great deal of weight in making their recognition decisions.

Indeed, earlier in this chapter we discussed a classification experiment conducted by Nosofsky (1991) in which subjects were required to categorize and recognize a set of schematic faces. We illustrated ALEX's ability to predict both the classification and recognition data in this experiment. A point that we did not emphasize, however, is that different sets of attention weights were needed for quantitatively predicting the data. The best fitting weights for classification were close to the ones that would optimize subjects' ability to discriminate the two categories of faces. But for recognition, the best fitting weights were redistributed in a manner that would facilitate subjects' ability to discriminate old from new items. The critical question is, How can new weights be applied when the goal of the task is changed, and from where in the network can knowledge of these more useful weights be obtained?

D. EVALUATION

The issues we raised in this final section indicate that we are still a good way from a fully adequate model of category learning. Nevertheless, as demonstrated throughout our chapter, ALEX has achieved some impressive successes. It accounts for detailed quantitative relations between identification and classification learning; for prototype effects and effects of specific exemplars; effects of category size, individual item frequency, and new–old similarity relations; and for relations between categorization and old–new recognition judgments. Its error-driven mechanism for learning association weights allows it to account for apparent base rate neglect and for the detailed course of probabilistic classification learning. Furthermore, this mechanism allows ALEX to adapt fairly quickly to changed category assignments during the course of learning, as people appear to do. ALEX's attention-learning mechanism allows it to model the difficulty of learning alternative classification problems with differing numbers of relevant dimensions. This attention-learning mechanism also allows ALEX to model changing patterns of generalization based on individual versus correlated dimension diagnosticities. Finally, ALEX is sensitive, in the same way as people are, to the orientation of category boundaries in psychological space.

ALEX's success in modeling these diverse phenomena should not be considered surprising, because it is a composite model that synthesizes previously successful ideas and theoretical approaches. It incorporates classic ideas about stimulus generalization and the metric structure of the stimulus space (e.g., Shepard, 1987), exemplar-based category representations and selective attention (e.g., Estes, 1986; Medin & Schaffer, 1978; Nosofsky, 1986), and error-driven learning principles (e.g., Gluck & Bower, 1988a; Rumelhart et al., 1986), all of which appear to be fundamental components of category learning and representation. In our view, this composite model represents some significant, cumulative progress in theorizing about categorization.

VII. Appendix: Comparisons with Standard Back Propagation Models

Although ALEX and standard back propagation (Rumelhart et al., 1986) share the properties of being feed-forward networks that learn by gradient descent on error, they behave very differently in several important situations. To compare the models, the input and output layers of standard backprop can be defined to be the same as in ALEX, so that the only difference between the models is the activation function of the hidden nodes. In standard backprop, the activation of hidden node j is given by a linear-sigmoid function:

$$a_j(i) = 1/[1 + \exp(-\Sigma \, w_{jm}x_{im})], \qquad (A1)$$

where x_{im} is the value of stimulus i on dimension m, and w_{jm} is the (learned) connection weight from input node m to hidden node j.

A comparison between Eqs. (3) and (A1) reveals two key differences between the hidden node activations in ALEX and backprop. First, there are no dimensional attention weights in backprop, so the input dimensions are not privileged axes as they are in ALEX. Consequently, backprop is insensitive to the orientation of category boundaries relative to the psychological dimensions—a diagonal boundary is learned just as quickly as a boundary orthogonal to a stimulus dimension. In Section V we demonstrate that humans are indeed sensitive to boundary orientation.

A second difference between the hidden node activations in ALEX and backprop is the shape of their receptive fields, that is, the region of input space that leads to a fairly strong activation of the hidden node. As illustrated for a two-dimensional example in Fig. 19A, the receptive fields in ALEX are diamond-shaped, with maximal activation at the center that

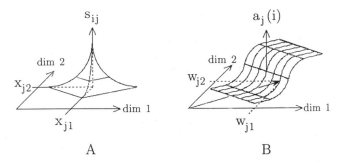

Fig. 19. Illustration of the hidden-node receptive fields in ALEX (A) and standard back propagation (B).

decays exponentially with distance from the center. (This activation profile follows from the assumption that similarity is an exponential decay function of city block distance in psychological space. The precise shape of the profile will vary with the metric structure of the similarity space.) The critical point is that in ALEX a given hidden node responds strongly to only a limited, local region of the input space.

We also illustrate in Fig. 19B the activation profile for a hidden node in standard backprop (again, a two-dimensional example). The receptive field is an entire half space with a linear boundary. Two consequences are that backprop is overly sensitive to linear category boundaries (e.g., Gluck, 1991), and it suffers catastrophic interference (e.g., Ratcliff, 1990). By contrast, ALEX learns linearly separable and nonlinearly separable category boundaries in the same manner and is immune to catastrophic interference (Kruschke, 1992).

These differences between ALEX and standard backprop are described at greater length by Kruschke (1990, 1991a, 1991b, 1992). The important point is that despite incorporating similar learning principles, the different hidden node activation functions of ALEX and standard backprop result in vastly differing behaviors for the two models.

ACKNOWLEDGMENTS

This work was supported by Grants PHS R01 MH48494-01 from the National Institute of Mental Health and BNS 87-19938 from the National Science Foundation to Robert M. Nosofsky, and by BRSG Grant RR 7031-25 from the Biomedical Research Support Grant Program, Division of Research Resources, National Institutes of Health, to John K. Kruschke.

REFERENCES

Anderson, J. R. (1990). *The adaptive character of thought*. Hillsdale, NJ: Erlbaum.

Ashby, F. G., & Gott, R. E. (1988). Decision rules in the perception and categorization of multidimensional stimuli. *Journal of Experimental Psychology: Learning, Memory, and Cognition, 14*, 33–53.

Busemeyer, J. R., & Myung, I. J. (1987). Resource allocation decision making in an uncertain environment. *Acta Psychologica, 66*, 1–19.

Carroll, J. D., & Wish, M. (1974). Models and methods for three-way multidimensional scaling. In D. H. Krantz, R. C. Atkinson, R. D. Luce, & P. Suppes (Eds.), *Contemporary developments in mathematical psychology* (Vol. 2, pp. 54–105). San Francisco: W. H. Freeman.

Chapman, G. B., & Robbins, S. J. (1990). Cue interaction in human contingency judgment. *Memory & Cognition, 18*, 537–545.

Estes, W. K. (1986). Array models for category learning. *Cognitive Psychology, 18*, 500–549.

Estes, W. K. (1988). Toward a framework for combining connectionist and symbol-processing models. *Journal of Memory and Language, 27*, 196–212.

Estes, W. K. (1989). Early and late memory processing in models for category learning. In C. Izawa (Ed.), *Current Issues in Cognitive Processes: The Tulane Symposium on Cognition* (pp. 11–24). Hillsdale, NJ: Erlbaum.

Estes, W. K. (in press). *Classification and cognition*. Oxford University Press.

Estes, W. K., Campbell, J. A. Hatsopoulos, N., & Hurwitz, J. B. (1989). Base-rate effects in category learning: A comparison of parallel network and memory storage-retrieval models. *Journal of Experimental Psychology: Learning, Memory, and Cognition, 15*, 556–571.

Garner, W. R. (1974). *The processing of information and structure*. New York: Wiley.

Gluck, M. A. (1991). Stimulus generalization and representation in adaptive network models of category learning. *Psychological Science, 2*, 50–55.

Gluck, M. A., & Bower, G. H. (1988a). From conditioning to category learning: An adaptive network model. *Journal of Experimental Psychology: General, 117*, 227–247.

Gluck, M. A., & Bower, G. H. (1988b). Evaluating an adaptive network model of human learning. *Journal of Memory and Language, 27*, 166–195.

Gottwald, R. L., & Garner, W. R. (1975). Filtering and condensation tasks with integral and separable dimensions. *Perception & Psychophysics, 18*, 26–28.

Hintzman, D. L. (1986). ''Schema abstraction'' in a multiple-trace memory model. *Psychological Review, 93*, 411–428.

Homa, D. (1984). On the nature of categories. *The Psychology of Learning and Motivation, 18*, 49–94.

Homa, D., Dunbar, S., & Nohre, L. (1991). Instance frequency, categorization, and the modulating effect of experience. *Journal of Experimental Psychology: Learning, Memory, and Cognition, 17*, 444–458.

Hurwitz, J. B. (1990). *A hidden-pattern unit network model of category learning*. Unpublished doctoral dissertation, Harvard University, Cambridge, MA.

Kruschke, J. K. (1990). *A connectionist model of category learning*. Doctoral dissertation, University of California, Berkeley. (University Microfilms)

Kruschke, J. K. (1991a). Dimensional attention learning in connectionist models of human categorization. *Cognitive Science Research Report 50*. Bloomington, IN. (Submitted for publication.)

Kruschke, J. K. (1991b). *Three reasons that back propagation is a poor model of human category learning*. Paper presented at the Twenty-Fourth Annual Mathematical Psychology Meetings, Bloomington, IN.

Kruschke, J. K. (1992). ALCOVE: An exemplar-based connectionist model of category learning. *Psychological Review, 99,* 22–44.

Levine, M. (1975). *A cognitive theory of learning: Research on hypothesis testing.* Hillsdale, NJ: Erlbaum.

McClelland, J. L. (1991). Stochastic interactive processes and the effect of context on perception. *Cognitive Psychology, 23,* 1–24.

McKinley, S. C., & Nosofsky, R. M. (in preparation). *Attention learning in models of classification.*

Medin, D. L. (1975). A theory of context in discrimination learning. In G. H. Bower (Ed.), *The psychology of learning and motivation* (Vol. 9). New York: Academic Press.

Medin, D. L., Altom, M. W., Edelson, S. M., & Freko, D. (1982). Correlated symptoms and simulated medical classification. *Journal of Experimental Psychology: Learning, Memory, and Cognition, 8,* 37–50.

Medin, D. L., & Edelson, S. M. (1988). Problem structure and the use of base-rate information from experience. *Journal of Experimental Psychology: General, 117,* 68–85.

Medin, D. L., & Florian, J. E. (in press). Abstraction and selective coding in exemplar-based models of categorization. In A. Healy, S. Kosslyn, & R. Shiffrin (Eds.), *From Learning Processes to Cognitive Processes: Essays in Honor of William K. Estes* (Vol. 2). Hillsdale, NJ: Erlbaum.

Medin, D. L., & Schaffer, M. M. (1978). Context theory of classification learning. *Psychological Review, 85,* 207–238.

Nosofsky, R. M. (1984). Choice, similarity, and the context theory of classification. *Journal of Experimental Psychology: Learning, Memory and Cognition, 10,* 104–114.

Nosofsky, R. M. (1985). Overall similarity and the identification of separable-dimension stimuli: A choice model analysis. *Perception & Psychophysics, 38,* 415–432.

Nosofsky, R. M. (1986). Attention, similarity, and the identification–categorization relationship. *Journal of Experimental Psychology: General, 115,* 39–57.

Nosofsky, R. M. (1987). Attention and learning processes in the identification and categorization of integral stimuli. *Journal of Experimental Psychology: Learning, Memory, & Cognition, 13,* 87–109.

Nosofsky, R. M. (1988a). Exemplar-based accounts of relations between classification, recognition, and typicality. *Journal of Experimental Psychology: Learning, Memory, and Cognition, 14,* 700–708.

Nosofsky, R. M. (1988b). Similarity, frequency, and category representations. *Journal of Experimental Psychology: Learning, Memory and Cognition, 14,* 54–65.

Nosofsky, R. M. (1989). Further tests of an exemplar-similarity approach to relating identification and categorization. *Perception & Psychophysics, 45,* 279–290.

Nosofsky, R. M. (1991). Tests of an exemplar model for relating perceptual classification and recognition memory. *Journal of Experimental Psychology: Human Perception and Performance, 17,* 3–27.

Nosofsky, R. M. (1992). Similarity scaling and cognitive process models. *Annual Review of Psychology, 43,* 25–53.

Nosofsky, R. M. (in press-a). Exemplars, prototypes, and similarity rules. In A. Healy, S. Kosslyn, & R. Shiffrin (Eds.), *From Learning Theory to Connectionist Theory: Essays in Honor of William K. Estes* (Vol. 1). Hillsdale, NJ: Erlbaum.

Nosofsky, R. M. (in press-b). Exemplar-based approach to relating categorization, identification, and recognition. In F. G. Ashby (Ed.), *Multidimensional models of perception and cognition.*

Nosofsky, R. M., Clark, S. E., & Shin, H. J. (1989). Rules and exemplars in categorization, identification, and recognition. *Journal of Experimental Psychology: Learning, Memory, and Cognition, 15,* 282–304.

Nosofsky, R. M., & Gluck, M. A. (1989). *Adaptive networks, exemplars, and classification rule learning*. Paper presented at Thirtieth Annual Meeting of the Psychonomic Society, Atlanta, GA.

Nosofsky, R. M., Kruschke, J. K., & McKinley, S. C. (1992). Combining exemplar-based category representations and connectionist learning rules. *Journal of Experimental Psychology: Learning, Memory, and Cognition, 18*, 211–233.

Posner, M. I. (1964). Information reduction in the analysis of sequential tasks. *Psychological Review, 71*, 491–504.

Posner, M. I., & Keele, S. W. (1968). On the genesis of abstract ideas. *Journal of Experimental Psychology, 77*, 353–363.

Posner, M. I., & Keele, S. W. (1970). Retention of abstract ideas. *Journal of Experimental Psychology, 83*, 304–308.

Ratcliff, R. (1990). Connectionist models of recognition memory: Constraints imposed by learning and forgetting functions. *Psychological Review, 95*, 285–308.

Reed, S. K. (1972). Pattern recognition and categorization. *Cognitive Psychology, 3*, 382–407.

Rescorla, R. A., & Wagner, A. R. (1972). A theory of Pavlovian conditioning: Variations in the effectiveness of reinforcement and nonreinforcement. In A. Black & W. Prokasy (Eds.), *Classical conditioning II* (pp. 64–99). New York: Appleton-Century-Crofts.

Rumelhart, D. E., Hinton, G. E., & Williams, R. J. (1986). Learning internal representations by error propagation. In D. E. Rumelhart & J. L. McClelland (Eds.), *Parallel distributed processing: Explorations in the microstructure of cognition: Vol 1. Foundations* (pp. 318–362). Cambridge, MA: Bradford Books/MIT Press.

Schank, R. C. (1982). *Dynamic memory: A theory of reminding and learning in computers and people*. Cambridge: Cambridge University Press.

Shanks, D. R. (1990). Connectionism and the learning of probabilistic concepts. *Quarterly Journal of Experimental Psychology, 42A*, 209–237.

Shanks, D. R. (1991). Categorization by a connectionist network. *Journal of Experimental Psychology: Learning, Memory, and Cognition, 17*, 433–443.

Shepard, R. N. (1958a). Deduction of the generalization gradient from a trace model. *Psychological Review, 65*, 242–256.

Shepard, R. N. (1958b). Stimulus and response generalization: Tests of a model relating generalization to distance in psychological space. *Journal of Experimental Psychology, 55*, 509–523.

Shepard, R. N. (1987). Toward a universal law of generalization for psychological science. *Science, 237*, 1317–1323.

Shepard, R. N., & Chang, J. J. (1963). Stimulus generalization in the learning of classifications. *Journal of Experimental Psychology, 65*, 94–102.

Shepard, R. N., Hovland, C. I., & Jenkins, H. M. (1961). Learning and memorization of classifications. *Psychological Monographs, 75* (13, Whole No. 517).

Shiffrin, R. M., Ratcliff, R., & Clark, S. E. (1990). List-strength effect: II. Theoretical mechanisms. *Journal of Experimental Psychology: Learning, Memory, and Cognition, 16*, 179–195.

Shin, H. J., & Nosofsky, R. M. (in press). Similarity scaling studies of "dot pattern" classification and recognition. *Journal of Experimental Psychology: General*.

Trabasso, T., & Bower, G. H. (1968). *Attention in learning: Theory and research*. New York: Wiley.

RECONSTRUCTING THE PAST: CATEGORY EFFECTS IN ESTIMATION

Janellen Huttenlocher
Larry V. Hedges

I. Introduction

This article is concerned with people's reconstructions of the past in cases where their memories are inexact. When people are unsure about what actually happened on some occasion, their reconstructions tend to be biased in that they are influenced by categorical or schematic information (e.g., Bartlett, 1932; Brewer & Nakamura, 1984). For example, a person who spent the summer in Sweden and saw a car accident on September 10 may recall the car as shaped more like a recent Saab and the date as more central to the summer season than was actually the case. In our recent work, we have shown that bias may arise in reconstructing particular past episodes even if memory itself is unbiased, but is inexact. We proposed that people may combine inexact but unbiased information about a particular episode with category information in estimating what actually happened. We suggested that it may be "rational" to use category information in reconstructing inexactly remembered past episodes. That is, while the use of category information introduces bias, it may, on average, improve accuracy.

We have developed a formal model that makes precise predictions about the ways category information is used in estimation (Huttenlocher, Hedges, & Prohaska, 1988; Huttenlocher, Hedges, & Duncan, 1991). The model has been tested for certain limited aspects of memory. One purpose of the present article is to review our earlier work, describing the model as developed thus far and showing how it explains the biases we have observed. The other and major purpose is to consider the possibility of extending the model to make it applicable to other aspects of memory.

People remember, more or less completely, many different aspects of the situations they encounter; their setting (time and place), the objects and persons present, including their physical characteristics (and, for persons, their intentions, emotions), the actions that occurred, and so on. They may seek to recover from memory more information about a particular episode than they are able to retrieve. The general assumptions underlying our model of the estimation processes involved in reconstructing past episodes are the following. We assume that the information about a situation is organized at more than one level of detail; it includes both categorical information and *individuating* information particular to that situation. Further, we assume that what people recover from memory may include various fragments of information. These fragments may pertain to any aspect of the episode and may vary in level of detail. Finally, we assume that people's certainty about the fragments they recover also may vary.

If the fragments of information pertaining to an episode that are recovered from memory are unrelated, they may be combined to provide an overall account of that episode. If the fragments recovered are mutually constraining, they may be combined to yield a *blend* (e.g., Belli, 1988). In such blends, greater weight may be given to those fragments of information about which a person is more certain. One case examined in the literature arises when people recover contradictory pieces of information. For example, consider a situation, used in experiments by Loftus (e.g., Loftus, Miller, & Burns, 1978), where a subject sees an object or event and later hears an alternative description of that object or event. The model we have proposed, and which we develop further in the present article, concerns another case of mutual constraint that may lead to blends. It is a constraint that may arise when people recover fragments of information at different levels of detail; for example, inexact information that the date of an event was in late March or early April, and category information that the event occurred in the spring academic quarter (that began April 1).

Thus far, we have examined category effects in estimating time and location. We observed large biases that could be fully explained by positing that people used category information to adjust memories for particular episodes that were inexact, but unbiased. Further, we showed that using this adjustment process led to greater overall accuracy than the use of unadjusted memories alone. To see why the use of category information might improve overall accuracy in the temporal and spatial domains, consider a remembered value near a category boundary; e.g., a date near the start of spring academic quarter. A range of true dates might have given rise to that remembered value. Since most of those true dates lie further into the quarter, it would be reasonable to adjust a sampled value in that direction, toward the center of the quarter. We begin by reviewing the model as it applies to the temporal and spatial domains and reporting the findings we have obtained.

II.   The Model Thus Far

A.   Fine Grain Values

We refer to the most detailed level of information in memory as a *fine grain value*. Fine grain values may vary in degree of precision. For example, the length of an object may be represented to the nearest inch or the nearest foot. Relative to the information a person seeks to recover, this fine grain memory may be inexact. The model was developed to test the possibility that, while fine grain coding may be inexact, it is unbiased. An unbiased (but inexact) memory can be thought of as a distribution that is centered at the true stimulus value; that is, the actual length of the object, the actual time an event occurred. This is illustrated in Fig. 1A, in which the memory

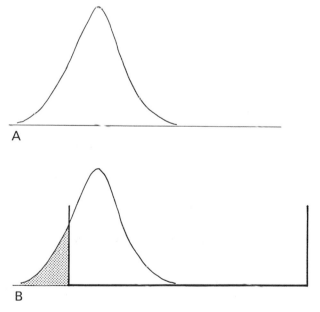

Fig. 1.   Memory for a one-dimensional stimulus as a distribution centered at the true value. A, with no boundary effects; B, with truncation due to a category boundary.

for a particular stimulus value is shown as a distribution centered at the true value; for instance, memory for the length of an object, for the time an event occurred, and so on. The less exact the memory, the greater the dispersion around the true value.

According to the model, recovery of a fine grain value on a given occasion is obtained by sampling from this distribution. A sense of the inexactness of a memory can be obtained by sampling a few values from this distribution and examining their dispersion. Note that, while the recovered sampled values will vary, the mean for a sufficiently large sample will lie at the true value.

B. CATEGORIES

A *category* is a region consisting of a range of fine grain values. Category information includes *boundaries* that specify the region included. A fine grain value that falls within that range is a category member. However, boundaries are to some extent inexact, and, very near a boundary, it may be unclear if a stimulus falls in the category. A category also includes a presumed pattern of values across the bounded region encompassed; those values may be thought to form a relatively normal distribution (with most instances in the middle), a uniform distribution (with instances spread out across the range), and so on. This presumed pattern is captured by a central value (the mean or median of observed instances), or *prototype,* and an inexactness of the prototype (the dispersion of values in the category).

C. ESTIMATION

The model posits two procedures by which category information may be used in estimating a stimulus value along a dimension. These are procedures that may be applied in adjusting an inexact fine grain stimulus value given that a category has been recovered. They include truncation due to boundaries and weighting with a prototype. First, consider truncation due to category boundaries. Suppose a person remembers inexactly a stimulus value as in Fig. 1A (which shows a true value with a particular distribution of inexactness around it). Suppose the person also remembers a category into which the stimulus falls. Figure 1B shows this category information superimposed on the fine grain representation. Note that the distribution of fine grain values extends past the category boundary. A person who has coded the event as being in the category will not report a value outside its boundary. Thus the distribution of uncertainty will be truncated by the boundary.

Adjustment of values due to truncation can be thought of as a process in which a person draws a value from the underlying unbiased distribution of potential values and, if it falls outside the category, discards it and draws another. The overall effect of truncation is to move the mean of estimated values inward from the true value, away from the category boundary. This process leads to bias but decreases variance. The bias is most marked for true values very near the boundaries, where a sizable portion of the distribution of potential values lies outside the boundary. The bias due to truncation is greater when fine grain values are more inexact. The reason is that, if two objects are equally far from boundaries, a greater proportion of the distribution of uncertainty will be eliminated by truncation for a value which is more inexactly represented.

The second estimation procedure is weighting with a category prototype. A prototype with an associated inexactness captures the presumed pattern of instances across a category. As in Bayesian procedures, people may use assumptions about the distribution of instances to adjust recollected fine grain values. If particular values were remembered exactly, no weight would be given to the prototype; if particular values were entirely forgotten, the prototype itself would be reported. When a fine grain value is remembered, but inexactly, recollected fine grain and prototype values may be combined, using weights corresponding to their associated inexactness. The optimal weight of the prototype maximizes the decrease in variability in relation to the increase in bias. The extent to which variability can be reduced depends on the inexactness of the fine grain value and the prototype. If the inexactness of fine grain values is equal across a category, the optimal prototype weight will be constant, leading to a linear pattern of bias toward the prototype. Where inexactness differs over a dimension, the optimal weight of the prototype will be greater for more inexact values, leading to a nonlinear pattern of bias, with more inexact values showing greater "pull" to the prototype.

D. APPLICATION IN TEMPORAL ESTIMATION

Even though time is a single dimension, people use a variety of schemes to keep track of time. There are cyclic schemes of varying scope—hour of the day, day of the week, month of the year, the seasons, the academic year, etc. Each keeps track of time over a bounded period—24 hours, 7 days, 12 months—up to the length of the cycle. That is, to say an event happened "on Wednesday" keeps track of time over a 7-day period. In addition, there are noncyclic schemes which keep track of time over unbounded periods. Two such schemes are the calendar year (e.g., 1815, 1921) and elapsed time (days ago, weeks ago, etc.). Information from different schemes may be independent (e.g., the day of the week indicates nothing about time of day, month, or year), or mutually constraining (e.g., the season constrains the month and the month specifies the season).

Below we provide evidence that temporal memory consists of a set of separate entries, as opposed to a time line. In a time line, different temporal schemes are coordinated (e.g., that an event occurred at 2 P.M., January 21, 1980), so that information at one level of detail entails preservation of more coarse grain information; for instance, knowing (or not knowing) the time of the day of an event would imply knowing (or not knowing) the day of the week, the month, and the year. We do not find such coordination among independent schemes in people's temporal reports. Before turning to the data, consider why different schemes might be separately represented in memory. The time of an event might be specified in terms of its place in an event sequence; that is, its relation to fixed events such as breakfast time (e.g., 8 A.M.) to days off work (e.g., Sunday), holidays (e.g., Christmas), and so on. The time of a target event could be reconstructed from its relation to such events. If there are different fixed events for the different temporal schemes, temporal information for these different schemes would be specified separately.

1. Independent Information

There are some data in the existing literature to suggest that temporal memory may consist of several separate pieces of information (e.g., Friedman and Wilkins, 1985, Friedman, 1987). The evidence is that when the temporal features are themselves independent, memory for those features is independent. We have obtained systematic data about the relation among different temporal schemes in memory from a large number of people (Huttenlocher, Hedges, & Prohaska, in press). They were asked about the time of occurrence of a unique target event consisting of an interview in subjects' homes lasting about 2 hr. The data were obtained in a telephone call between 4 and 75 days after the home interview. Subjects reported the time of day, day of the week, and number of elapsed days since the interview.

We looked at two cases involving memory for independent temporal features. First, we considered errors in reports of day of the week for interviews that occurred at different times of day. Given a time line representation, a person should misremember morning interviews as occurring on the preceding day and evening interviews as occurring on the following day. Given separate representation of information in different schemes, memory for day of the week should not be affected by the time of day of the interview. We found that the direction of errors did not differ significantly at different times of day.

Second, we considered the relation between reports of day of the week and reports of the number of elapsed days since the interview. In a time line representation, knowing the day of the week entails knowing the number of elapsed days. In a multiple entry representation, these pieces of information are separate. Note, however, that if subjects know exactly when the event occurred, reports of all facets of time will match (i.e., be correct) even if they are unrelated to each other in memory; that is, correct reports are necessarily coordinated. Reports of day of the week and reports of number of elapsed days were not coordinated after 2 weeks, nor even for the first 2 weeks, if we consider just reports where there were errors either in reports of elapsed time or of day of the week. In short, the data support the view that temporal memory involves a set of separate entries.

2. Mutually Constraining Information

Consider now two cases where, we would argue, separate but mutually constraining pieces of temporal information are recovered from memory. The first case concerns memory for the day of the week of a target event. Suppose people remember the day by relating it to events with fixed times of occurrence within the week. Suppose also that the week is organized into different multiday categories; notably, that the weekday period is associated with work activities. Consider a person who recovers the day of the week (but is uncertain about it) and also that the event occurred during the weekday period. In this case, we should find category effects; for instance, if an event occurred on Tuesday (with the distribution of uncertainty centered at Tuesday), recall of category information (i.e., that it occurred on a weekday) would constrain the day to lie within the weekday period. Thus the distribution of uncertainty will be truncated (the event could not have been on Sunday). This will lead to inward misplacement from the true day toward the center of the weekday period.

We obtained data on memory for day of the week in the study described above. There was strong evidence of hierarchical organization of the weekday period. Few reports were misplaced out of the weekday period onto a weekend day; further, reports were misplaced away from weekend boundaries toward Wednesday. The observed bias was totally explained by positing truncation by weekend boundaries.

Not just cyclic schemes like the week, but also schemes that preserve historic (unbounded) time, may be hierarchically organized; for instance, the date. For historic time, hierarchical organization should lead to greater misplacement of the time of events with increases in the amount of elapsed time. This is because memory becomes less exact over time. Hence the forward bias due to truncation at the beginning boundaries of temporal periods or categories should be greater than the backward bias due to truncation at the ending boundaries. Potentially, then, our model might account for a well-known phenomenon in temporal reporting—*forward telescoping*. The data from another study (Huttenlocher, Hedges, & Prohaska, 1988) demonstrate both hierarchical organization and forward telescoping. In that study, people reported the dates of movies presented at the University of Chicago during an academic year, which is organized into academic quarters. Figure 2 shows the bias we found in reporting dates. Along the horizontal axis are actual dates, along the vertical axis is bias. If the mean of people's reports is the same as the true date, bias is zero. Points above the line show forward movement. Points below the line show backward movement. Bias can be seen, consisting of misplacement away from quarter boundaries. The data thus indicate that dates are hierarchically organized into academic quarters. In addition, forward misplacement was greater than backward misplacement, reflecting greater uncertainty in memory for events further in the past. The bias was totally explained by positing truncation of the distribution of uncertainty for dates by the quarter boundaries.

E. APPLICATION IN SPATIAL ESTIMATION

Space, like time, is a continuous domain. The locations of objects in a plane can be objectively measured using the dimensions of distance and/or angle, measured from landmarks. Yet there is evidence of bias in people's distance judgments; that is, the distance between two items is reported as

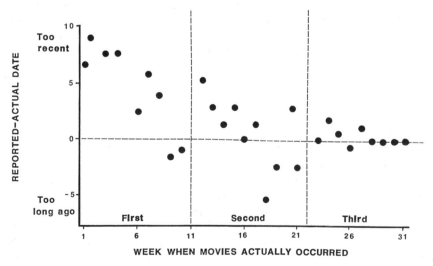

Fig. 2.   Bias in reports of dates as a function of time of occurrence.

greater when the items are in different subsections of a space (actual or only implicit) than when they are in the same subsection. Such findings have been interpreted as indicating that people's representation of space is biased (e.g., Hirtle and Jonides, 1985; MacNamara, in press). Clearly, the bias is related to hierarchical organization in the representation of spatial location; for instance, an object that is in a particular city is in a particular country. It is not clear, however, that the bias reflects a distortion in representation itself. Our model suggests an alternative interpretation of the bias. That is, reporting bias would occur if the location of an item is represented at two levels of detail—a particular (fine grain) location and a region (category)—which are mutually constraining, and the information at different levels is combined in estimation.

Our studies thus far have been concerned with reports of the location of a point in a small bounded space (Huttenlocher et al., 1991). We have obtained evidence of category effects in the estimation of particular locations in such spaces. Subjects reported the location of a dot in a homogeneous circle. We presented subjects a series of trials in which they were shown a dot in different locations in the circle. Afte a dot was shown, the display was removed and they placed a dot on a comparable circle. There was systematic bias in their responses. The bias is shown schematically in Fig. 3. Dots were misplaced angularly away from the horizontal and vertical axes, and radially away from the center and circumference line.

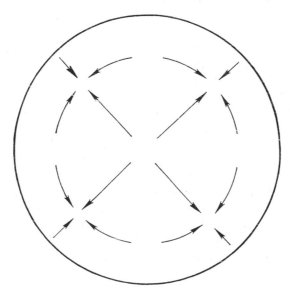

Fig. 3.   Directions of systematic bias in reports of item location in a circle.

We have argued that subjects divide the circle into quadrants along the horizontal and vertical axes, and that they code the location of a dot at two levels. The fine grain location consists of an angular and a radial value. The category location consists of a particular quadrant. A prototype is formed lying at the center of mass of each quadrant. Inexact fine grain values are weighted with the prototypic angular and radial values. We also obtained evidence in another experiment that bias due to a prototype increases with the inexactness of representation of fine grain values. We interposed an interference task after showing each dot and before allowing subjects to respond by placing a dot. Both angular bias and radial bias were considerably greater than in the absence of an interference task.

For these spatial location experiments, we obtained evidence that weighting of inexactly remembered fine grain values with a prototype increased the overall accuracy of reporting despite the introduction of bias. We estimated the inaccuracy that would have resulted from the use of inexact fine grain values alone and demonstrated that reports of these values alone would have been less accurate, on average, than the adjusted values. Thus weighting with the prototype is a "rational" process in these experiments.

F.   APPLICATION TO OTHER BIASES

In addition to explaining the biases described above, our model may, potentially, explain other biases described in the literature. These biases too have been interpreted as showing that memory itself is biased. Our explanation for bias in reporting is quite different. It is that memory for fine grain stimulus values is unbiased (in the sense that the memory consists of a distribution of fine grain values centered at the true value). However, people also have category information and may use it to adjust inexactly remembered fine grain values. Let us briefly consider one of these biases in reporting. In consists of an asymmetry in reports of the distance between two spatial locations. When people are asked the distance between two points, they may give different answers, depending on the direction of comparison (from A to B or from B to A). While it seems to certain investigators that this finding provides incontrovertible evidence of bias in representation (e.g., MacNamara, Hardy, & Hirtle, 1989), such asymmetries clearly would follow if inexact fine grain representations are adjusted using category information.

Consider two items in a category, one near the center and the other near a boundary (e.g., two dots in the same quadrant of a circle). After seeing each of these items in succession, subjects are given a task where one of the items is fixed, and they must locate the other item (or estimate its distance from the fixed item). First consider the case where the center item is fixed at its true location. Since the location of the item near the boundary (which the subject places) is "shrunk" toward the prototype, its distance from that fixed center item will be underestimated. Next consider the case where the item near the boundary is fixed at its true location. Since the location of the central object (which the subject places) is relatively unaffected by the prototype, its distance from a fixed item near the boundary will not show a corresponding underestimation of distance. Hence our model predicts asymmetries in judgments of distance (similarity) depending on which object is fixed without positing distorted representations. (We are currently investigating this issue in collaboration with Nora Newcombe.)

III. Extension of the Model

We have presented a model which holds that, when people seek more detailed information about a past episode than they can retrieve from memory, they may make an estimate using the pieces of information they *can* recover. According to the model, people may recover mutually constraining pieces of information at different levels of detail. In such cases, category information (boundaries and the presumed pattern of values) may be used in adjusting inexactly remembered (but unbiased) fine grain values. We showed that, even though the use of category information introduces bias, it can increase overall accuracy. Thus far the model has been constructed to deal with temporal and spatial categories that are, in many ways, unlike the categories generally discussed in the literature. First, the items in these categories are similar because they occur in a common temporal or spatial unit, not because the items themselves have similar characteristics; that is, commonalities in appearance, internal structure, function, and so on. Second, these categories are units in imposed measurement scales (weeks, quadrants, etc.) rather than *inductively based* (that is, derived directly or indirectly from situations encountered).

In the remainder of this article we discuss extending the model to stimuli that are grouped on the basis of similar characteristics, forming inductively based categories. Such categories capture environmental regularities, permitting inferences about aspects of situations not observed in given encounters, predictions about what may happen next, and so on. It is not that observed regularities simply exist in the world and give rise to categories. As Goodman (1972) and others point out, the number of ways to group stimuli is virtually unlimited. Thus stimuli that are highly similar when evaluated in terms of one set of dimensions may be highly dissimilar when evaluated in terms of other dimensions. Categories capture regularities that matter for human purposes. However, such categories, even those that serve a role in general theories (cf. Murphy & Medin, 1985), derive from environmental regularities; they are embedded in knowledge structures that codify and explain them. As Anderson (1991) puts it, category formation is a rational process that captures statistical regularities among stimuli, including such factors as differential frequencies of certain stimulus values, and so on (as studied, e.g., by Homa: Homa & Cultice, 1984; Homa & Vosburgh, 1976).

It should be noted that our model, which posits that the use of category information may improve accuracy in estimating inexactly remembered fine grain stimulus values, is most obviously applicable to categories that are rational in Anderson's sense. Such categories provide "on average" information derived from whole sets of encounters. The use of information about environmental regularities, as summarized through categories, stabilizes estimates involving inexact information about particular cases by setting them in the context of prior encounters—in effect, information about what to expect. A category provides a type of information about a stimulus that is distinct from its particular value. It defines (by virtue of the category boundaries) a region where an arbitrary stimulus is located and suggests (via patterns of values) where it is most likely to be.

In extending the present version of the model, several issues must be considered. Thus far, we have examined only one-dimensional categories (the two spatial dimensions in a plane were treated separately in our studies). In contrast, inductively based categories are usually multidimensional, and the constituent dimensions may be correlated; for instance, objects may vary in size, texture, color, and so on. The boundaries of such categories define a region in a multidimensional space whose shape is determined by an observed distribution of stimulus values. The shape of the bounded region that forms a category is critical to our model because it determines the effect of truncation in adjusting inexact stimulus values.

Thus far, we have dealt with categories that consist of imposed measurement units. For such categories (e.g., months, quadrants), there is no reason to suppose that some stimulus values (dates or locations) are more likely than others. Hence, we simply assumed that the pattern of values that characterizes such categories is uniform. In contrast, for inductively based categories the pattern of values that characterizes a category (i.e., the location of the prototype and its inexactness) derives from an observed distribution of values. Further, for the one-dimensional categories we have examined thus far, adjustment of fine grain values due to the prototype occurs in one direction, whereas in a multidimensional category this adjustment may occur in more than one direction depending on the location of the stimulus relative to the prototype.

Thus far, we have been concerned with uncertainty of fine grain stimulus values given a category, not with uncertainty of the category itself (except for uncertainty as to the exact location of a boundary or prototype). Category uncertainty is important in dealing with inductively based categories. These categories tend to be embedded in larger knowledge structures. Such structures may have major effects on the likelihood that a stimulus if from a certain category; for instance, the probability that the animal I saw was a wolf or a dog depends on whether I was in the jungle or on the street in Chicago. These "base rate" differences will, in turn, affect the use of categories in adjusting fine grain stimulus values. Further, for inductively based categories, the amount of data is a central aspect of category information, as Anderson (1991) has noted. Provisional categories can be constructed from minimal information (e.g., two cases). Each encounter contributes new information. That is, revisions occur as additional instances accumulate, resulting in updated summary representations. A new instance has more impact on summaries when these are based on only a few observed values. Category information may be used in estimating particulars at various points during this data collection process but may be given less weight in estimation early on since that information is more inexact.

In the discussion below, we focus on stimuli whose essential characteristics can be captured by specifying objectively measurable values on a set of continuous dimensions; for instance, object length or weight. For these, the actual stimulus values can be determined objectively (i.e., the actual length or weight can be obtained), so it is possible to establish whether fine grain values are unbiased. The notions of inexactness for fine grain values and category information are well defined, and estimation processes, including boundary adjustment and weighting with a prototype, are justifiable. Hence it is possible to determine whether observed bias is attributable to the use of category information to adjust inexact but unbiased fine grain values. At the end of the chapter, we will examine the possibility of extending the model to an even broader range of stimuli.

A. FINE GRAIN VALUES

The treatment of fine grain values and their inexactness for multidimensional stimuli is a straightforward extension from the one-dimensional case. A dimension constitutes an ordered set of numbers corresponding to a set of stimulus values. The coding of a stimulus as having a value on that dimension can be thought of abstractly as assigning a number to that stimulus. The coding of an n-dimensional stimulus can be thought of abstractly as a process of assigning an ordered n-tuple of numbers (one for each dimension) to the stimulus. The inexactness of the memory for a fine grain value, as we deal with it here, consists of the degree of dispersion of values on each of the dimensions. Thus a fine grain value in memory constitutes a symmetric distribution around the true value in multidimensional space. Figure 4A shows a normal frequency distribution for an inexactly remembered two-dimensional stimulus (with frequency shown on the third dimension), comparable to Fig. 1A, which showed a one-dimensional stimulus (with frequency shown on the second dimension). Recovery of a fine grain value, according to the model, involves sampling a value (i.e., an ordered pair) from this distribution.

B. CATEGORIES

In one sense the treatment of categories also is a straightforward extension from the one-dimensional case. That is, a category can be formally described as a mapping from a set of fine grain values onto a coarse grain value. This coarse grain value or category forms a bounded region contain-

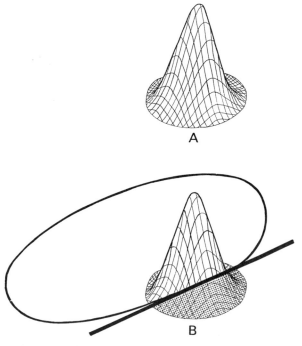

Fig. 4. Memory for a two-dimensional stimulus as a distribution centered at the true value. A, with no boundary effects; B, with truncation due to an elliptically shaped category boundary.

ing some presumed pattern of values.[1] However, as noted above, we must consider how observed stimulus distributions give rise to categories of particular shapes characterized by certain patterns of values.

1. Category Boundaries

Consider first how an observed pattern of values along a single dimension may give rise to an inductively based category with particular boundaries. Boundaries may be formed at junctures in the distribution of values. That is, if the stimulus values observed form clusters, that is, areas of high and low frequency (density), boundaries may be formed in regions of low density. For example, a set of rods of variable length might form clumps centered around 4 inches (10 cm), 12 inches (30 cm), and 36 inches (1 m), with a sparsity of values at intermediate lengths. Given such a distribution of lengths, people might form three categories—short, medium, and long sticks.

For multidimensional stimuli, junctures in the distribution of values in a multidimensional space also may give rise to boundaries. In thinking about the joint distribution of values in a multidimensional space, imagine a two-dimensional category. Each stimulus value consists of an ordered pair of values corresponding to a point on a plane. The frequency of each value is represented by a third axis perpendicular to the plane. The joint distribution forms a surface arising from that plane—"mountains" or "ridges" indicate areas where the frequency of instances is high. Two factors are critical to the topography of the surface; the relation between values on different dimensions, and variations in the frequency (density) of the values at various locations.

a. Relations among Dimensions. Category boundaries may be formed where there is a certain correlation among the values on different dimensions, but that correlation holds only across a limited range of values. Two dimensions may be correlated, but only across a delimited range of values, or there may be different correlations across different ranges of values. For example, the relation between intelligence and attentiveness might be positive in the range from low to normal intelligence but negative in the range from normal intelligence to genius (where people are "dreamy"). To construct a boundary where the relation between dimensions changes

---

[1] In defining a category as a region that covers a range of fine grain values, we ignore the degenerate case, generally involving artifacts, where the instances are veritably identical; e.g., the design features of items that are produced by machine such as 32-ounce cans of V-8™, paper diapers of a particular brand and size, nickels or dimes, etc. For these, irrelevant attributes can vary, but relevant ones take only a single value and different instances cannot be distinguished.

direction, that change must be detected from samples of instances in the regions where each relation holds. The precision of the boundary will vary with the degree of difference between the two relations.

A category also may be formed when the values on different dimensions are uncorrelated within a limited range of values, but extension of the range may reveal a relation; e.g., the sizes of flowers and the thickness of their stems might be uncorrelated within certain ranges, but a correlation may emerge when the full range is considered (e.g., big flowers have thick stems). In such a case, category boundaries may arise at the point at which there is an increase (a jump) in stimulus values. The precision of the boundary will vary with the size of the jump.

b. Mapping onto a Defining Dimension.   Another (and classic) case where the relation among dimensions may lead to category formation is when fine grain values on certain dimensions map onto a single value on a dimension which defines category membership. Category boundaries on the fine grain dimensions are formed where there is a change in value on the defining dimension; for instance, berries having a particular range of shapes and colors are poisonous. A value on the defining dimension creates a shadow category (i.e., a bounded region) on the fine grain dimensions. In the canonical case, the defining dimension takes a single value such that all members have equal status with respect to the category; for instance, being dead (alive), being male (female). Alternatively, the defining dimension may itself be categorized; for instance, sickness might be the defining value, with degree of fever and pallor as the fine grain dimensions. Yet sickness covers a cluster of discriminable values (different degrees of sickness); hence the category will have a graded structure.

c. Variations in Density.   The extent of correlation among dimensions restricts but does not define the pattern of density (the joint distribution). That is, a given relation among dimensions may arise from very different frequency distributions. As we noted in discussing the case of a single dimension above, variations in the frequency (density) of values may give rise to categories. A region that has a peak (area of high density) and troughs (areas of sparsity) may define (or help to define) a category with boundaries in the troughs. For example, rods might cluster by both length and diameter; clumps around 4 inches (10 cm) long and $\frac{1}{2}$ inch (1 cm) in diameter, around 12 inches (30 cm) long and $1\frac{1}{2}$ inches (3 cm) in diameter.

Density variations may be used in establishing boundaries (i.e., in determining extreme category values) by minimizing the number of misclassifications in the sample of instances observed. In this case, the boundary will be more uncertain the smaller the number of instances near the boundary. Alternatively, the sample may be used to impute or estimate the shape of the distribution, and that information may be used in establishing boundaries. When the distribution of instances in a category is most dense near the center of the category (e.g., when instances are normally distributed in a category), there will be few instances near the boundaries. However, information about the boundaries can be derived by extrapolation from the pattern of density, which is clearest near the center of the category. The boundary may be defined more precisely when two normal distributions form two adjacent categories than when a category is juxtaposed to a region with a relatively flat distribution (since the tail of the distribution is also flat, this precludes a fine distinction).

2. The Pattern of Values

Joint distributions of stimulus values give rise not only to category boundaries, but also to a pattern of values within a category. That is, the set of dimensions that characterizes a category may have either correlated or independent values. Given any particular relation, the values may be dispersed in various ways. The observed patterns of values in a category can be captured by a measure of central tendency (a prototype) and a measure of the dispersion of values (prototype inexactness). Our earlier work dealt only with prototypes along a single dimension (spatial categories were treated as made up of two single dimensions). In these cases, there is only one "direction" in the category along which dispersion can occur.

In multidimensional categories, the inexactness of the prototype extends in every possible direction. The inexactness in different directions may vary, but a few basic pieces of information permit the evaluation of uncertainty along any (of the infinite number of) directions; namely, the dispersion along each of the natural dimensions, and the correlations between values on different dimensions. Because the prototype is used to represent the dispersion of stimuli in the category, its inexactness in any direction reflects the dispersion of instances in that direction. When the values on the two dimensions are correlated, the dispersion of values will tend to be elliptical (e.g., if the distribution is bivariate normal) and inclined at an angle. The direction of greatest prototype inexactness will be along the regression line, and the direction of smallest inexactness will be perpendicular to the regression line.

Prototype inexactness reflects two different factors. One is the actual dispersion in the pattern of values across the category; this would ideally be used in the adjustment of fine grain values if the subject had information concerning the precise pattern of values in the category. The other is sampling inexactness. There are two sources of inexactness in inferring the pattern of values from observed data. One consists of a limited sample of instances available during the formation of the category and essentially disappears with additional instances. The other consists of coding errors (i.e., measurement error). This component is always present. Because both the actual pattern and the sampling inexactness contribute to the representation of the inexactness of the actual pattern of values, the inexactness associated with a prototype, that inexactness will be greater than just the dispersion of instances.

Sampling inexactness also affects establishment of the relation between dimensions. To determine the actual relation among dimensions is the problem discussed in measurement theory of determining a latent (i.e., true) relation from observed values which are measured with error. Again, error reflects both limited sample size and coding errors. The inexactness arising from coding errors adds "noise" in estimating the true relation that does not completely go away even with large sample sizes. Hence the observed correlation between values on two dimensions will be less than the true (latent) relation between those values.

3. The Shapes of Multivariate Categories

The shape of the bounded region that forms a category will affect how that category is used in estimation. Both the relation between dimensions and the differential density of instances affect the shapes of multivariate categories. If stimulus values on different dimensions are independent, the pattern of instances typically would be widely dispersed and symmetric about the center of the category, whereas, if stimulus values on different dimensions are correlated, then the joint distribution would be an inclined ellipse.

Differential density affects category shape, even when the relation between values on different dimensions is constant (Huttenlocher and Hedges, in preparation). Consider, for example, two different category shapes that may arise with two uncorrelated dimensions, where each dimension has a dispersion of values that is symmetric around the center. If the instances on each dimension are uniformly distributed, the multivariate category formed from these univariate distributions will form a rectangular mesa. However, if the instances on each dimension are normally distributed, the category will form a symmetric bell-shaped mound with a circular base. The circular shaped category arising from two normally distributed uncorrelated dimensions has certain interesting properties, as shown in Fig. 5A. Notably, the allowable range of values on one dimension is wider when the value on other dimension is near the middle. Figure 5A shows that a particular value on one dimension may lie inside or outside the category, depending on its value on the other dimension.

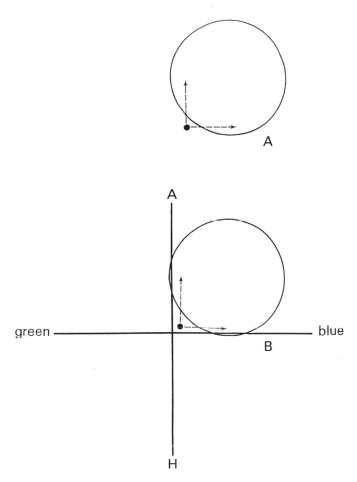

Fig. 5. Circular shaped bivariate category illustrating that the allowable range of values on one dimension is greater near the center of the other dimension. A, without superimposed dimension; B, with superimposed dimensions.

What has been said about category shape implies that it is not possible to predict whether a stimulus will be a member of a multivariate category (such as a "blue A") from its membership in the constituent univariate categories (blue and A). Consider a two-dimensional category. The two dimensions might or might not be correlated. The relation between dimensions affects multivariate category shape. Futher, the distribution of values in a univariate category may be obtained in a variety of contexts and need not be the same as the distribution of values along that dimension in the context of the multivariate category. The distribution of values also affects multivariate category shape. Finally, even if the distribution of values is the same as that in the multivariate category (and the relation between dimensions has been fixed), membership in a multivariate category may require joint consideration of the constituent univariate categories. Figure 5B shows two uncorrelated dimensions, each of which forms two univariate categories; one consists of shapes ranging from A through H, and the other of colors ranging from green through blue (univariate category breaks lie at the origin). If the distribution for each univariate category is normal, a conjoint category such as "blue As" will be circular. Hence a stimulus might be "blue" and an "A," yet not be a "blue A." If either the blue or the A were more prototypical, the value *would* be a "blue A." Hampton (1991) did a study which shows that boundaries do differ for univariate and multivariate categories of this sort.

In short, a deterministic view of "conceptual combination" is necessarily unsatisfactory for inductively based multivariate categories. Yet the traditional view in logic is that membership in a multivariate category such as "blue As" should include just the intersect of those things that are blue and those that are As (a view that has already been criticized in the literature; e.g., Smith and Osherson, 1984).

C. CATEGORY LIKELIHOOD

More than one level of conceptual structure may be relevant to the use of category information in estimating particulars. Just as the pattern of values within a category may provide important contextual information for estimation of an uncertain fine grain value, so too can the pattern of categories be important in estimation of an uncertain category value. The hierarchy may extend to larger and larger aggregates and its use in estimation may be essentially recursive. Indeed the roles of "category" and "fine grain" in the model can be extended so as to treat any two levels of detail that are mutually constraining.

The distributional facts about categories can be used to improve estimation of the category, and thus, in turn, the estimation of particular stimulus values within a category. That is, relative to other categories, different categories within a superordinate category may have different frequencies of occurrence. The base rate for categories is an important property of those categories with respect to one another because they would affect the probability that a stimulus is in a particular category. For content categories, as opposed to spatial or temporal categories, the likelihood that stimuli are from particular categories can vary widely, depending on the context. That is, if the larger conceptual structure is recovered, it will affect the base rates for different categories. Indeed, the context, or frame of occurrence (e.g., that an event occurred in Paris, at school, etc.), can have large effects on category assignment and hence on estimation. That is, while the category might have been quite uncertain in the absence of a constraining context, the larger conceptual structure may reduce or eliminate ambiguity concerning the category.

A category can be more or less prototypical relative to other categories with respect to centrality of location. The position of a category and the distance among categories can also affect estimation. Given equal base rates and dispersion within categories, an instance is more likely to have arisen from a category whose values are more similar (a nearby category) than one whose values are more different (a distant category). A rational (Bayesian) analysis would make use of both base rates and distance between categories (cf. Anderson, 1991; Medin & Edelson, 1988).

D. ESTIMATION

We are concerned with the role of categories in the estimation of particular stimulus values when the information in memory is less exact than what a person seeks. The occasion for reconstructing fine grain stimulus values arises when information about some past episode is relevant to a current question or problem. Our estimation model evaluates the possibility that fine grain information is inexact but unbiased. In recollection, a value is sampled from this distribution, and category information is used to adjust this inexact value. The nature of the adjustment will depend on the topography of the category. Above we discussed some features of category structure and of multilevel organization, and here we consider the implications for adjustment processes.

1. Category Assignment

The use of category information in adjusting fine grain stimulus values will occur only if a category is recovered at retrieval. In our earlier work, we dealt with only category uncertainty, namely uncertainty as to the location of category boundaries. That is, we simply assumed recovery of a category and focused on explicating the ways category information—boundaries and prototype—might be used in adjusting fine grain values. With respect to boundary uncertainty, we pointed out that the location of a boundary might not be known precisely even if that boundary is sharp, with no possibility of intermediate fine grain values. Alternatively, there might be an ambiguous area between categorized regions; that is, the boundaries between categories may be vague, with ambiguous or indeterminate cases. We modeled both such situations as arising from an average of a distribu-

272   **Janellen Huttenlocher and Larry V. Hedges**

tion of possible boundary values, weighted acccording to the probability of occurrence of each. Differences between sharp and vague boundaries should be discernible from variance of reports. If items in the region of the boundary are treated as lying in one or another adjacent category, they will be adjusted inward in opposite directions. In contrast, if there is an intermediate region in which items are not categorized, values will not be adjusted; variance therefore should be greater in the first than in the second case.

In extending the model, it is clearly important to consider cases where the category itself is uncertain. We noted above that a general superordinate category may be recovered in cases where there is uncertainty concerning a more specific category that might, potentially, be used in adjusting fine grain stimulus values. Thus the information recovered concerning an episode may be uncertain at more than one level—at the fine grain and category levels. Consider a person who recovers information about an episode involving an accident in which a tall woman emerged from a damaged vehicle. One piece of information involves the specifics of the particular vehicle. Larger conceptual structures may provide information that can be used to reduce uncertainty about the category (car vs. truck). There may be differences in base rates or a priori probability; vehicles are more frequently cars than trucks. Further, the other characteristics recovered (e.g., that the driver was a woman) may lead to an even greater probability that the vehicle was a car rather than a truck.

In short, not only may a fine grain stimulus value be adjusted in accordance with the category, but the category may be adjusted in accordance with the fine grain value. This could be done optimally by using Bayes theorem, taking account of the conditional probability of each fine grain value given the category, and the probability of each category based on the distribution of category uncertainty. Thus the uncertainty of the category would affect estimation. Subjects would choose a category with a probability equal to the category uncertainty adjusted for base rate. The probability distribution of reports would then be a mixture of the reports that would be obtained as different categories are selected. An alternative would be to reduce the weight given to category information (shrinkage toward category prototypes) in proportion to category uncertainty.

2. *Estimating Fine Grain Values Given the Category*

Below we consider, as a theoretical issue, the way information about inductively based categories might be used in adjusting fine grain stimulus values. Earlier we discussed the use of boundaries and prototypes in one dimension. Here we are concerned with the extension of these adjustment procedures to multidimensional inductively based categories. Although the extension is straightforward, category shape, an issue that does not arise in one-dimensional categories, has important effects on the direction and magnitude of category effects on estimation.

a. Adjustment from Boundaries. According to the model, the inexact recollection of a fine grain stimulus value consists of a multivariate normal distribution around the actual stimulus value. For an actual value near a boundary, a large proportion of the distribution of uncertainty would fall outside that boundary. However, if the category is recovered, those values are constrained to lie inside the category. Truncation of the distribution of memory inexactness in multidimensional categories is more complicated than that in one dimension, but is not different in principle. That is, for multidimensional categories, the location of boundaries on constituent dimensions and hence the extent of truncation on those dimensions varies with the shape of the boundary in the multidimensional space.

Consider a multidimensional category with a curved boundary. Truncation of memory inexactness at the category boundary leads to different effects along different dimensions, depending on where the stimulus is located in the category. Although the detailed mathematics of truncation along curved surfaces is complicated, qualitative insight (and a good quantitative approximation) can be obtained by approximating the category boundary by a tangent line (or plane) at the point nearest the stimulus location. Truncation produces bias in the direction perpendicular to the tangent, and the direction of this bias is always toward the interior of the category. The effects of truncation can be described in terms of independent dimensions, one perpendicular to the tangent (where all bias occurs) and one (or more) parallel to the tangent, where no bias occurs. These dimensions typically are not the natural dimensions of the category, but rather linear combinations of those dimensions which may have little psychological meaning. (They are useful primarily as a tool for understanding the relation between the shape of the category boundary and bias due to truncation.)

Figure 4B shows truncation of the distribution of inexactness around the actual stimulus value and a curved boundary. [The category is displayed as a two-dimensional shape to allow us to show the direction of truncation; note, however, that it also has height reflecting the frequency (density) of values at different locations.] When the category is two-dimensional and circular, truncation at any location produces bias toward the center of the circle. The bias due to truncation is perpendicular to the tangent. The magnitude of the bias is greatest near the boundary. If the shape of the category is elliptical rather than circular (e.g., when the dimensions are correlated or unequally variable), inward bias will not always be toward the center of the category, as can be seen in Fig. 4B. In general, the pattern of bias will differ depending on the shape of the boundary.

b. Adjustment from Prototypes.   In previous work we dealt with the use of prototypes in estimation for one-dimensional categories (in the temporal domain, and in the spatial domain where dimensions could be examined one at a time). We showed that the use of prototypes to adjust fine grain values can improve accuracy of estimation. The rationale for the adjustment is that the fine grain value is compared to the pattern of actual values and adjusted in the direction of the center of that pattern (that is, toward the prototype). The amount of the adjustment depends on the size of the dispersion of the pattern of actual values (which we might call the inexactness of the prototype) relative to the inexactness of the remembered value. The greater the inexactness of the remembered value relative to that of the prototype, the greater the shrinkage toward the prototype.

In multidimensional categories, values are adjusted by shrinking them toward the center of the multidimensional distribution of values in the category. The direction of shrinkage will not typically be along one of the natural dimensions of the category when the dimensions are correlated. The *direction* of shrinkage of any particular value will be along a line joining the remembered fine grain value and the (two-dimensional) category prototype. The *amount* of shrinkage along this line will depend on the relative inexactness of the remembered values on the two natural dimensions, the dispersion of stimulus values on those dimensions, and the correlation between stimulus values on the two dimensions. Thus it is always possible to conceive of shrinkage toward a prototype as occurring along a synthetic "dimension" whose direction is from the fine grain value toward the prototype. Hence adjustment of fine grain values via a category prototype (shrinkage toward a prototype) is, in principle, no more complicated in multidimensional categories than in unidimensional ones.

Because the amount of shrinkage toward the prototype depends on the pattern of values, and because the pattern of values (through sparsity at boundaries) determines the shape of the category, that shape gives some insight into the pattern of shrinkage that would be expected. If the category is symmetrically shaped, and the inexactness of values on each dimension is reasonably similar, the amount of shrinkage toward the prototype should be the same regardless of the direction in which the shrinkage occurs. If the category is elongated because the dimensions have unequal dispersion or are correlated, there should be more shrinkage toward the prototype along the narrowest direction (i.e., across the category) than along the longest direction (i.e., along the length of the category).

c. Adjustment Based on Correlation. To elucidate the role of correlation in estimation, consider the process of adjustment of each natural dimension separately across the range of a category. There are degenerate cases that represent unusual or extreme situations. An example arises when the actual stimulus values are perfectly correlated, and there is no inexactness of fine grain values in memory on one dimension. If the actual correlation is perfect, the inexactness of the representation of any one dimension does not matter since its value can be predicted perfectly from the others. Extending this argument, greater weight should be given to information from the dimensions for which values are most exact.

In a category with two correlated dimensions, the value on one dimension yields a predicted value on the other. Thus there are two sources of information about the value of the stimulus on a target dimension: the value derived entirely from that dimension itself, and the value derived entirely from the value on the other dimension (via the relation between the two dimensions). To use both values will give a better estimate of the value on the large dimension than the inexactly remembered value on that dimension alone. Each of these two sources of information has an associated inexactness. The inexactness of the information derived from the second dimension (and hence the optimal weight given to it) depends on the strength of the correlation between dimensions, on the inexactness of values on the two dimensions, and on the inexactness of the correlation.

E. ESTIMATION IN OTHER CASES

In extending our model to inductively based categories, we have focused on stimuli which have objectively measurable values on a set of continuous dimensions. Categories based on such stimuli consist of bounded regions containing particular patterns of values that can be captured by a mean and standard deviation. The estimation processes we have posited, involving boundary adjustment and weighting with a prototype, are justifiable and well defined in these cases. It should be noted that the model may apply to stimuli for which some, but not all, characteristics can be captured by values on a set of such dimensions. For example, consider animals for which size and thickness of fur can be evaluated, and for which certain ranges of size and thickness of fur are characteristic of particular animal categories. When memory for the particular size and furriness of an individual animal in a particular category of animals is inexact, a remembered value may be adjusted using the boundaries and pattern of values on these dimensions for that animal category.

The model clearly is applicable to dimensions which, while actually discontinuous, can be treated as continuous. Thus counts of discrete entities are discontinuous (the entities lose their identity if divided; e.g., a person-part is not a person), yet objectively measurable, and practically continuous when the number is large (e.g., 5,372). Hence, the normal approximation to the binomial distribution can be quite good, particularly when most values are near the center of the category. The inexactness of fine grain values in memory can be similarly approximated.

Since the model concerns bias in reconstruction of the past that arises from category effects on inexact but unbiased fine grain representations, it is only applicable if fine grain stimulus values can be determined in a way that is unaffected by category information. Suppose objective measurement of stimulus values along a set of dimensions is not available, so it is not possible to evaluate the distances between stimuli. However, subjects may have an intuitive sense of stimulus values and the distances between them; for instance, for dimensions of usefulness, ferocity, aesthetic value, and so on. The intuitive sense of distances along such dimensions may permit reliable judgments of the distances between different pairs of stimuli. Then multidimensional scaling could be used to construct a pattern of locations from the order of the interstimulus distances. The model could not be assessed since those judgments of distance would be affected by categorization. Yet there might be cases where uncategorized stimulus values could be recovered. For example, it might be possible to develop tasks which impose alternative category structures on a set of stimuli (e.g., by varying their frequency of presentation). The data from several tasks which alter judged interstimulus distances and hence the pattern of locations in the multidimensional scaling solution might be used to estimate uncategorized stimulus values, since categorization affects judgments of distances within and across category boundaries in a predictable way.

Suppose stimulus values are only ordered; for instance, the hardness of objects is established by ordering pairs (a harder substance produces a scratch on a softer one), but there is no way to evaluate the distance between them. Categorization does not affect order and, in that sense, judgments will not be affected by categorization. However, there are other problems. A scale that captures only order is defined, at any particular time, by the set of instances that presently form the scale. That is, since an item in an ordered scale is defined by its relation to other items, a new value can only be added by placing it relative to existing values, thus redefining the scale.

Consider the applicability of the model if the present set of stimulus values includes all possible values (the present set might include only a subset of possible values, as discussed later on). While the median or modal value can provide a well defined prototype, the use of a prototype value in estimation requires a measure of inexactness for both fine grain and prototype values. Indices of inexactness such as the range or the standard deviation involve differences between scale values and have no meaning for ordered scales. However, in establishing the inexactness of values on an ordered scale, one could posit that an error of 1 ordinal position in a given direction will be more likely than an error of 2 ordinal positions in that direction, and so on. That is, a pattern of errors which is unimodal might resemble the pattern found where there is underlying objective measurement. Then the sense of inexactness is one of the likelihood of different values, and use of category information to adjust inexact fine grain values will be rational as in other cases. Consider an item near a boundary; since most of the values will lie toward the center of the category, shrinkage toward the center is reasonable.

The boundaries of categories covering a subset of items along an ordered dimension are simply the extreme values for the category. These boundary values can be used in estimation, leading to adjustments of uncertain fine grained values toward interior positions in the category. As for the continuous dimensions, the process would involve drawing a new value if the value sampled lies outside the category. The pattern of values within the category also can be used in estimation. That pattern would consist of a bar graph depicting frequencies of occurrence of each value. The optimal adjustment is to "shrink" the distribution of inexactness of particular values, in relation to the probabilities in the pattern of values, using Bayes theorem. If the distribution of instances in the category as well as the uncertainty of the particular values are symmetric and unimodal, this shrinkage will resemble the linear combination of prototype with the particular value in cases of objective measurement.

For ordered scales where the present set of values is only a sample, the model does not seem applicable. No unambiguous definition can be given for a boundary. Contrary to continuous measured domains where distance between values is well defined, allowing discovery of gaps that may reflect nonrepresentative samples, when a dimension is only ordered, discovery of gaps is not possible. Many intermediate items may be added between one presently adjacent pair of items, and none between another adjacent pair, radically altering the pattern of values. Hence a simple summary cannot characterize the distribution—either a middle value, or the dispersion of values. This is in contrast with the case where the underlying sense of distance for a dimension supports an assumption about the shape of the distribution (e.g., that values can be treated as essentially normally distributed such that the center and spread of the distribution are well estimated from a few values).

Finally, ordered scales may be established even for conceptually continuous dimensions, such as the months of the year. Features of the ordered scales may incorporate information concerning the underlying continuity.

For example, discrete units can be constructed to meet at a point, thus partitioning the dimension so there can be no intermediate value; for instance, the months of the year, the states (e.g., Maine, Texas). Alternatively, the present set may not partition the underlying dimension. The possibility of new items is known because of the continuity of the dimension. Also, it is known that the distances between adjacent pairs may be unequal. Consider the exits on a road (e.g., on Lake Shore Drive in Chicago, North Avenue, Fullerton, Belmont). Further, the units have a determinate size which may or may not be equal (the months vary in length; the states vary in size).

The usefulness of category information may be defined either in terms of the ordered scale or the underlying dimension. With respect to the continuous dimension, the median ordered value need not correspond to the center, because scale values may not be equally placed. Hence the use of the median as a prototype has unknown consequences for estimation. For example, the scale values may be of distinct (and unequal) sizes, such as using an ordered scale for the states of the United States, running north–south or east–west, could be very inaccurate with respect to the geographical middle of the country. However, truncation at category boundaries will still improve accuracy of estimation. If there is a known mapping between the continuous domain and the ordinal scale values, each scale value could be made to correspond to a domain value. If it is only known that the mapping is linear (i.e., that scale values are equally spaced), or even linear to a working approximation, such as that freeway exits in cities are relatively uniformly spaced [e.g., half a mile (0.8 km) apart] and that suburban exits are also relatively uniformly spaced [e.g., every 2 miles (3.2 km)], ordered scale values might be treated as if they were continuous values and use of a prototype may be justified.

IV. Conclusions

We have presented a set of speculative arguments concerning category effects in reconstructing the past. These were based on an extension of our earlier model of category effects in estimation to the case of inductively based multidimensional categories. We dealt in some detail with certain characteristics of such categories. The role of category prototypes and boundaries in multidimensional categories was shown to be analogous to, if more complex than, their roles in unidimensional categories. For example, both boundaries and uncertainty have directions in the multidimensional case but not in the univariate case we had dealt with earlier. Several features of multidimensional categories do not arise in unidimensional categories. For example, multidimensional categories may be based on a relation between the defining dimensions, which cannot occur in only one dimension. The geometry (shape) of categories in two or more dimensions is qualitatively more complex than in one dimension. Consideration of category shape can explain otherwise puzzling findings in classification experiments. Since the joint distribution of instances cannot, in general, be predicted from the marginal distributions on constituent dimensions, geometrical considerations have implications for conceptual combination of categorized dimensions to produce multidimensional categories. Estimation of fine grain structures for mutidimensional stimuli that are represented inexactly is analogous to, but more complex than, estimation along a single dimension. Direction of truncation and shrinkage toward a prototype is determined by category shape.

Acknowledgments

Preparation of this chapter was supported by grants from the Air Force Office of Scientific Research, Program in Cognition (AFOSR 88-0215), and from the National Institute of Mental Health (Grant RO1MH45402). The authors thank Nora Newcombe for her helpful comments on the manuscript.

References

Anderson, J. R. (1991). The adaptive nature of human categorization. *Psychological Review*, *98*, 409–429.
Bartlett, F. C. (1932). *Remembering: A study in experimental and social psychology*. Cambridge, England: Cambridge University Press.
Belli, R. F. (1988). Color blend retrievals: Compromise memories or deliberate compromise responses? *Memory and Cognition, 16*, 314–326.
Brewer, W. F., & Nakamura, G. V. (1984). The nature and functions of schemas. In R. S. Wyer & T. K. Srull (Eds.), *Handbook of social cognition* (Vol. 1, pp. 119–160). Hillsdale, NJ: Erlbaum.
Friedman, W. J. (1987). A follow-up to ''Scale effects in memory for the time of events'': The earthquake study. *Memory and Cognition, 15*, 518–520.
Friedman, W. J., & Wilkins, A. J. (1985). Scale effects in memory for the time of events. *Memory and Cognition, 13*, 168–175.
Goodman, N. (1972). Seven strictures on similarity. In N. Goodman (Ed.), *Problems and projects* (pp. 437–447). Indianapolis: Bobbs Merrill.
Hampton, J. (1991, July). Conceptual Combination. Paper presented at International Conference on Memory, Lancaster, England.
Hirtle, S. C., & Jonides, J. (1985). Evidence of hierarchies in cognitive maps. *Memory and Cognition, 13*, 208–217.
Homa, D., & Cultice, J. (1984). Role of feedback, category size, and stimulus distortion in the acquisition and utilization of ill-defined categories. *Journal of Experimental Psychology: Learning, Memory, and Cognition, 10*, 83–94.

Homa, D., & Vosburgh, R. (1976). Category breadth and abstraction of prototypical information. *Journal of Experimental Psychology: Human Learning and Memory, 2,* 322–330.

Huttenlocher, J., & Hedges, L. V. (in preparation). *Conceptual combination: Multivariate from univariate categories.*

Huttenlocher, J., Hedges, L. V., & Duncan, S. (1991). Categories and particulars: Prototype effects in estimating spatial location. *Psychological Review, 98,* 352–376.

Huttenlocher, J., Hedges, L. V., & Prohaska, V. (1988). Hierarchical organization in ordered domains: Estimating the dates of events. *Psychological Review, 95,* 471–484.

Huttenlocher, J., Hedges, L. V., & Prohaska, V. (in press). Memory for day of the week: A five plus two day cycle. *Journal of Experimental Psychology: General.*

Loftus, E. F., Miller, D. G., & Burns, H. J. (1978). Semantic integration of verbal information into a visual memory. *Journal of Experimental Psychology: Human Learning and Memory, 13,* 585–589.

MacNamara, T. P., Hardy, J. K., & Hirtle, S. C. (1989). Subjective hierarchies in spatial memory. *Journal of Experimental Psychology: Learning, Memory, and Cognition, 15,* 211–227.

Medin, D. L., & Edelson, S. M. (1988). Problem structure and the use of base-rate information from experience. *Journal of Experimental Psychology: General, 117,* 68–85.

Murphy, G. L., & Medin, D. L. (1985). The role of theories in conceptual coherence. *Psychological Review, 92,* 289–316.

Smith, E. E., & Osherson, D. N. (1984). Conceptual combination with prototype concepts. *Cognitive Science, 8,* 337–361.

INDEX

CONTENTS OF RECENT VOLUMES

ISBN 0-12-543328-X

9 780125 433280   90065